# Scriptures at Your Fingertips for Teens

Over
250 Topics
and
2000 Verses

Compiled by
Merry Graham and
Tiffany Michelle Graham

HOWARD BOOKS
A DIVISION OF SIMON & SCHUSTER
New York   London   Toronto   Sydney

DEC   2008

Our purpose at Howard Books is to:
• *Increase faith in the hearts of growing Christians*
• *Inspire holiness in the lives of believers*
• *Instill hope in the hearts of struggling people everywhere*
Because He's coming again!

Published by Howard Books, a division of Simon & Schuster, Inc.
1230 Avenue of the Americas, New York, NY 10020
www.howardpublishing.com

HOWARD
BOOKS

*Scriptures at Your Fingertips for Teens* © 2008 Merry Graham

Library of Congress Cataloging-in-Publication Data

Scriptures at your fingertips for teens: over 250 topics and 2000 verses / compiled by Merry Graham and Tiffany Graham.
p. cm.
1. Bible—Indexes. 2. Bible—Quotations. 3. Christian teenagers—Religious life. I. Graham, Merry. II. Graham, Tiffany.
BS432.S39 2008
220.5'2—dc22
2008011087

ISBN-13: 978-1-4165-7910-6
ISBN-10:    1-4165-7910-9

10  8  6  4  2  1  3  5  7  9

HOWARD and colophon are registered trademarks of Simon & Schuster, Inc.

Manufactured in the United States of America

For information regarding special discounts for bulk purchases, please contact:
Simon & Schuster Special Sales at 1-800-456-6798 or business@simonandschuster.com.

Cover design by Masterpeace Studiology
Interior design by Davina Mock-Maniscalco

Scripture permissions will be found on page 276.

# CONTENTS

# CONTENTS

# CONTENTS

# CONTENTS

# CONTENTS

# GREETINGS

I hope you know what a treasure you're holding in your hands! I was very excited to work on this project with my mom after being touched by her previous book, *Scriptures at Your Fingertips*. I was amazed at how I could hear God's voice speaking to me through the topics and how I was led to the perfect verses at the exact moment I needed them. I hope you'll find truth, wisdom, comfort, encouragement, and advice in these pages. Most of all, I pray you will hear the Lord speaking directly to you and sense His presence leading you to the pages He wants you to see.

You'll find verses from both the Old and New Testaments, so remember to consider *who* is speaking in the verse, *to whom* the writer is speaking, and *what was occurring* at that time period. The Bible version used is abbreviated at the beginning of each verse and may vary slightly from other editions of that version (online editions or updated editions). A list of abbreviations can be found on page 276.

It was hard cutting down the number of entries and length of each verse, but the good news is this is just the beginning! All of these verses are straight from the Bible, so if you're hungry for more or are looking for additional insight on a verse or topic, grab your Bible, dive right in, and read the whole chapter for yourself. These scriptures may be ages old, but they still hold just as much life and power today as always.

Much Love,
Tiffany

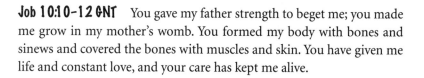

**Job 10:10-12 GNT**   You gave my father strength to beget me; you made me grow in my mother's womb. You formed my body with bones and sinews and covered the bones with muscles and skin. You have given me life and constant love, and your care has kept me alive.

**Job 12:9-10 HCSB**   The life of every living thing is in His hand, as well as the breath of all mankind.

**Psalm 32:3-5 BBE**   When I kept my mouth shut, my bones were wasted, because of my crying all through the day. For the weight of your hand was on me day and night; my body became dry like the earth in summer. I made my wrongdoing clear to you, and did not keep back my sin. I said, I will put it all before the Lord; and you took away my wrongdoing and my sin.

**Proverbs 24:11-12 NCV**   Save those who are being led to their death; rescue those who are about to be killed. If you say, "We don't know anything about this," God, who knows what's in your mind, will notice. He is watching you, and he will know. He will reward each person for what he has done.

**Proverbs 31:8-9 HCSB**   Speak up for those who have no voice, for the justice of all who are dispossessed. Speak up, judge righteously, and defend the cause of the oppressed and needy.

**Isaiah 49:15 GNT**   So the Lord answers, "Can a woman forget her own baby and not love the child she bore? Even if a mother should forget her child, I will never forget you."

**Jeremiah 1:5 NLT**   I knew you before I formed you in your mother's womb. Before you were born I set you apart and appointed you as my prophet to the nations.

**Psalm 11:5 NCV**   The LORD tests those who do right, but he hates the wicked and those who love to hurt others.

**Psalm 79:8-9 NLT**   Oh, do not hold us guilty for the sins of our ancestors! Let your tenderhearted mercies quickly meet our needs. . . . Help us, O God of our salvation! Help us for the honor of your name. Oh, save us and forgive our sins for the sake of your name.

**Psalm 86:5-6 NIV**   You are forgiving and good, O Lord, abounding in love to all who call to you. Hear my prayer, O LORD; listen to my cry for mercy.

**Jeremiah 22:3 NLT**   This is what the LORD says: Be fair-minded and just. Do what is right! Help those who have been robbed; rescue them from their oppressors. Quit your evil deeds! Do not mistreat foreigners, orphans, and widows. Stop murdering the innocent.

**Acts 8:21-23 NKJV**   Your heart is not right in the sight of God. Repent therefore of this your wickedness, and pray God if perhaps the thought of your heart may be forgiven you. For I see that you are poisoned by bitterness and bound by iniquity.

**Ephesians 5:5 WEB**   No sexually immoral person, nor unclean person, nor covetous man, who is an idolater, has any inheritance in the kingdom of Christ and God.

**1 Thessalonians 5:15 NIV**   Make sure that nobody pays back wrong for wrong, but always try to be kind to each other and to everyone else.

**James 1:19-21 NCV**   Do not become angry easily, because anger will not help you live the right kind of life God wants. So put out of your life every evil thing and every kind of wrong. Then in gentleness accept God's teaching.

**James 5:16 NIV**   Confess your sins to each other and pray for each other so that you may be healed.

**Psalm 17:6-9 WEB**   I have called on you, for you will answer me, God: Turn your ear to me. Hear my speech. Show your marvelous lovingkindness, you who save those who take refuge by your right hand from their enemies. Keep me as the apple of your eye; hide me under the shadow of your wings, from the wicked who oppress me.

**Psalm 22:24 NLT**   He has not ignored the suffering of the needy. He has not turned and walked away. He has listened to their cries for help.

**Psalm 40:1-3 NCV**   I waited patiently for the LORD. He turned to me and heard my cry. He lifted me out of the pit of destruction, out of the sticky mud. He stood me on a rock and made my feet steady. He put a new song in my mouth, a song of praise to our God. Many people will see this and worship him. Then they will trust the LORD.

**Isaiah 43:18-19 NIV**   Forget the former things; do not dwell on the past. See, I am doing a new thing! Now it springs up; do you not perceive it?

**Jeremiah 17:14-15 NASB**   Heal me, O LORD, and I will be healed; save me and I will be saved, for You are my praise. Look, they keep saying to me, "Where is the word of the LORD? Let it come now!"

**Matthew 11:28 NIV**   Come to me, all you who are weary and burdened, and I will give you rest.

**Mark 11:25 WEB**   Whenever you stand praying, forgive, if you have anything against anyone; so that your Father, who is in heaven, may also forgive you your transgressions.

**Romans 12:19 NCV**   My friends, do not try to punish others when they wrong you, but wait for God to punish them with his anger. It is written: "I will punish those who do wrong; I will repay them," says the Lord.

**Romans 12:21 NLT**   Don't let evil conquer you, but conquer evil by doing good.

# ACTIONS

**Psalm 34:1 NRSV**   I will bless the Lord at all times; his praise shall continually be in my mouth.

**Psalm 38:18 NLT**   I confess my sins; I am deeply sorry for what I have done.

**Luke 6:37-38 MSG**   Don't pick on people, jump on their failures, criticize their faults—unless, of course, you want the same treatment. Don't condemn those who are down; that hardness can boomerang. Be easy on people; you'll find life a lot easier. Give away your life; you'll find life given back, but not merely given back—given back with bonus and blessing. Giving, not getting, is the way. Generosity begets generosity.

**Acts 20:35 NIV**   In everything I did, I showed you that by this kind of hard work we must help the weak, remembering the words the Lord Jesus himself said: "It is more blessed to give than to receive."

**Titus 1:16 NRSV**   They profess to know God, but they deny him by their actions. They are detestable, disobedient, unfit for any good work.

**Philemon 1:6-7 NLT**   I am praying that you will put into action the generosity that comes from your faith as you understand and experience all the good things we have in Christ. Your love has given me much joy and comfort, my brother, for your kindness has often refreshed the hearts of God's people.

**James 2:17-18 NIV**   In the same way, faith by itself, if it is not accompanied by action, is dead. But someone will say, "You have faith; I have deeds." Show me your faith without deeds, and I will show you my faith by what I do.

**1 John 3:18 GNT**   My children, our love should not be just words and talk; it must be true love, which shows itself in action.

# ADDICTIONS

**Psalm 16:11 NKJV**  You will show me the path of life; in Your presence is fullness of joy; at Your right hand are pleasures forevermore.

**Psalm 18:36 NCV**  You give me a better way to live, so I live as you want me to.

**Isaiah 41:10 NCV**  Don't worry, because I am with you. Don't be afraid, because I am your God. I will make you strong and will help you; I will support you with my right hand that saves you.

**Matthew 5:6 MSG**  You're blessed when you've worked up a good appetite for God. He's food and drink in the best meal you'll ever eat.

**Romans 6:12-14 NLT**  Do not let sin control the way you live; do not give in to sinful desires. Do not let any part of your body become an instrument of evil to serve sin. Instead, give yourselves completely to God, for you were dead, but now you have new life. So use your whole body as an instrument to do what is right for the glory of God. Sin is no longer your master, for you no longer live under the requirements of the law. Instead, you live under the freedom of God's grace.

**Galatians 5:19-21 MSG**  It is obvious what kind of life develops out of trying to get your own way all the time: repetitive, loveless, cheap sex; a stinking accumulation of mental and emotional garbage; frenzied and joyless grabs for happiness; trinket gods; magic-show religion; paranoid loneliness; cutthroat competition; all-consuming-yet-never-satisfied wants; a brutal temper; an impotence to love or be loved; divided homes and divided lives; small-minded and lopsided pursuits; the vicious habit of depersonalizing everyone into a rival; uncontrolled and uncontrollable addictions; ugly parodies of community. I could go on.

**Ephesians 5:8-10 NCV**  In the past you were full of darkness, but now you are full of light in the Lord. So live like children who belong to the light. Light brings every kind of goodness, right living, and truth. Try to learn what pleases the Lord.

# ADOPTION

**Psalm 40:5 NIV**   Many, O LORD my God, are the wonders you have done. The things you planned for us no one can recount to you; were I to speak and tell of them, they would be too many to declare.

**Matthew 18:4–5 WEB**   Whoever therefore will humble himself as this little child, the same is the greatest in the Kingdom of Heaven. Whoever will receive one such little child in my name receives me.

**John 14:18 NKJV**   I will not leave you orphans; I will come to you.

**Romans 8:14–17 NCV**   The true children of God are those who let God's Spirit lead them. The Spirit we received does not make us slaves again to fear; it makes us children of God. With that Spirit we cry out, "Father." And the Spirit himself joins with our spirits to say we are God's children. If we are God's children, we will receive blessings from God together with Christ. But we must suffer as Christ suffered so that we will have glory as Christ has glory.

**2 Corinthians 6:18 NCV**   I will be your father, and you will be my sons and daughters, says the Lord Almighty.

**Ephesians 1:4–6 WEB**   Even as he chose us in him before the foundation of the world, that we would be holy and without blemish before him in love; having predestined us for adoption as sons through Jesus Christ to himself, according to the good pleasure of his desire, to the praise of the glory of his grace, by which he freely bestowed favor on us in the Beloved.

**Philippians 1:6 NRSV**   I am confident of this, that the one who began a good work among you will bring it to completion by the day of Jesus Christ.

**James 1:27 NKJV**   Pure and undefiled religion before God and the Father is this: to visit orphans and widows in their trouble, and to keep oneself unspotted from the world.

# ADULTERY

**Proverbs 5:18-20 HCSB** Let your fountain be blessed, and take pleasure in the wife of your youth. A loving doe, a graceful fawn—let her breasts always satisfy you; be lost in her love forever. Why, my son, would you be infatuated with a forbidden woman or embrace the breast of a stranger?

**Proverbs 6:27-29 NLT** Can a man scoop a flame into his lap and not have his clothes catch on fire? Can he walk on hot coals and not blister his feet? So it is with the man who sleeps with another man's wife. He who embraces her will not go unpunished.

**Proverbs 6:32 NKJV** Whoever commits adultery with a woman lacks understanding; he who does so destroys his own soul.

**Proverbs 28:13 GNT** You will never succeed in life if you try to hide your sins. Confess them and give them up; then God will show mercy to you.

**Matthew 5:27-28 MSG** You know the next commandment pretty well, too: "Don't go to bed with another's spouse." But don't think you've preserved your virtue simply by staying out of bed. Your heart can be corrupted by lust even quicker than your body. Those leering looks you think nobody notices—they also corrupt.

**1 Corinthians 6:9-10 NCV** Do not be fooled. Those who sin sexually, worship idols, take part in adultery, those who are male prostitutes, or men who have sexual relations with other men . . . these people will not inherit God's kingdom.

**Hebrews 13:4 TNIV** Marriage should be honored by all, and the marriage bed kept pure, for God will judge the adulterer and all the sexually immoral.

**1 John 1:9 NCV** If we confess our sins, he will forgive our sins, because we can trust God to do what is right. He will cleanse us from all the wrongs we have done.

**Proverbs 13:13-14 GNT**  If you refuse good advice, you are asking for trouble; follow it and you are safe. The teachings of the wise are a fountain of life; they will help you escape when your life is in danger.

**Proverbs 13:20 NASB**  He who walks with wise men will be wise, but the companion of fools will suffer harm.

**Proverbs 27:10 GNT**  Do not forget your friends or your father's friends. If you are in trouble, don't ask a relative for help; a nearby neighbor can help you more than relatives who are far away.

**Ephesians 4:3 NIV**  Make every effort to keep the unity of the Spirit through the bond of peace.

**Titus 3:1-2 NIV**  Remind the people to be subject to rulers and authorities, to be obedient, to be ready to do whatever is good, to slander no one, to be peaceable and considerate, and to show true humility toward all men.

**Hebrews 13:17 NIV**  Obey your leaders and submit to their authority. They keep watch over you as men who must give an account. Obey them so that their work will be a joy, not a burden, for that would be of no advantage to you.

**1 Peter 3:8 NIV**  Live in harmony with one another; be sympathetic, love as brothers, be compassionate and humble.

**1 Peter 5:5-6 WEB**  You younger ones, be subject to the elder. Yes, all of you gird yourselves with humility, to subject yourselves to one another; for "God resists the proud, but gives grace to the humble." Humble yourselves therefore under the mighty hand of God, that he may exalt you in due time.

**1 John 3:11 NASB**  This is the message which you have heard from the beginning, that we should love one another.

**Leviticus 19:31 BBE** Do not go after those who make use of spirits, or wonder-workers; do not go in their ways or become unclean through them: I am the Lord your God.

**2 Samuel 2:1 HCSB** Some time later, David inquired of the LORD: "Should I go to one of the towns of Judah?" The LORD answered him, "Go." Then David asked, "Where should I go?" "To Hebron," the LORD replied.

**Proverbs 1:7-9 NCV** Knowledge begins with respect for the LORD, but fools hate wisdom and discipline. My child, listen to your father's teaching and do not forget your mother's advice. Their teaching will be like flowers in your hair or a necklace around your neck.

**Proverbs 12:15 NRSV** Fools think their own way is right, but the wise listen to advice.

**Proverbs 12:26 NRSV** The righteous gives good advice to friends, but the way of the wicked leads astray.

**Proverbs 16:23 NIV** A wise man's heart guides his mouth, and his lips promote instruction.

**Proverbs 18:13 NLT** What a shame, what folly, to give advice before listening to the facts!

**Proverbs 20:18 NRSV** Plans are established by taking advice.

**Proverbs 27:9 NASB** Oil and perfume make the heart glad, so a man's counsel is sweet to his friend.

**Ecclesiastes 4:13 HCSB** Better is a poor but wise youth than an old but foolish king who no longer pays attention to warnings.

**Psalm 18:29-32 NKJV**   By You I can run against a troop, by my God I can leap over a wall. As for God, His way is perfect; the word of the LORD is proven; He is a shield to all who trust in Him. For who is God, except the LORD? And who is a rock, except our God? It is God who arms me with strength, and makes my way perfect.

**Psalm 34:4 NIV**   I sought the LORD, and he answered me; he delivered me from all my fears.

**Psalm 36:7 GNT**   How precious, O God, is your constant love! We find protection under the shadow of your wings.

**Psalm 56:10-11 NCV**   I praise God for his word to me; I praise the LORD for his word. I trust in God. I will not be afraid. What can people do to me?

**Psalm 91:9-15 NIV**   If you make the Most High your dwelling—even the LORD, who is my refuge—then no harm will befall you, no disaster will come near your tent. For he will command his angels concerning you to guard you in all your ways; they will lift you up in their hands, so that you will not strike your foot against a stone. You will tread upon the lion and the cobra; you will trample the great lion and the serpent. "Because he loves me," says the LORD, "I will rescue him; I will protect him, for he acknowledges my name. He will call upon me, and I will answer him; I will be with him in trouble, I will deliver him and honor him."

**Proverbs 3:21-26 NCV**   My child, hold on to wisdom and good sense. Don't let them out of your sight. They will give you life and beauty like a necklace around your neck. Then you will go your way in safety, and you will not get hurt. When you lie down, you won't be afraid; when you lie down, you will sleep in peace. You won't be afraid of sudden trouble; you won't fear the ruin that comes to the wicked, because the Lord will keep you safe. He will keep you from being trapped.

**Isaiah 41:13 HCSB**   For I, the LORD your God, hold your right hand and say to you: Do not fear, I will help you.

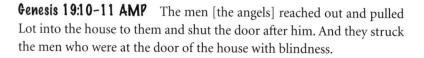

**Genesis 19:10–11 AMP**    The men [the angels] reached out and pulled Lot into the house to them and shut the door after him. And they struck the men who were at the door of the house with blindness.

**Judges 6:12 NASB**    The angel of the Lord appeared to him and said to him, "The Lord is with you, O valiant warrior."

**2 Samuel 14:20 NCV**    My master, you are wise like an angel of God who knows everything that happens on earth.

**Daniel 6:22 MSG**    My God sent his angel, who closed the mouths of the lions so that they would not hurt me.

**Matthew 4:11 HCSB**    Then the Devil left Him, and immediately angels came and began to serve Him.

**Matthew 26:53 NKJV**    Do you think that I cannot now pray to My Father, and He will provide Me with more than twelve legions of angels?

**Matthew 28:2–3 TNIV**    There was a violent earthquake, for an angel of the Lord came down from heaven and, going to the tomb, rolled back the stone and sat on it. His appearance was like lightning, and his clothes were white as snow.

**Luke 15:10 NLT**    There is joy in the presence of God's angels when even one sinner repents.

**Acts 12:11 NLT**    Peter finally realized what had happened. "It's really true!" he said to himself. "The Lord has sent his angel and saved me from Herod and from what the Jews were hoping to do to me!"

**Acts 12:23 TNIV**    Immediately, because Herod did not give praise to God, an angel of the Lord struck him down, and he was eaten by worms and died.

**Proverbs 15:1 NASB**   A gentle answer turns away wrath, but a harsh word stirs up anger.

**Matthew 5:22 NIV**   I tell you that anyone who is angry with his brother will be subject to judgment.

**Matthew 21:12–13 MSG**   Jesus went straight to the Temple and threw out everyone who had set up shop, buying and selling. He kicked over the tables of loan sharks and the stalls of dove merchants. He quoted this text: My house was designated a house of prayer; you have made it a hangout for thieves.

**Mark 3:5 NCV**   Jesus was angry as he looked at the people, and he felt very sad because they were stubborn.

**1 Corinthians 13:5 BBE**   Love's ways are ever fair, it takes no thought for itself; it is not quickly made angry, it takes no account of evil.

**Ephesians 4:26–27 NKJV**   "Be angry and do not sin": do not let the sun go down on your wrath, nor give place to the devil.

**Ephesians 4:31–32 NRSV**   Put away from you all bitterness and wrath and anger and wrangling and slander, together with all malice, and be kind to one another, tenderhearted, forgiving one another, as God in Christ has forgiven you.

**James 1:19–21 GNT**   Everyone must be quick to listen, but slow to speak and slow to become angry. Human anger does not achieve God's righteous purpose. So get rid of every filthy habit and all wicked conduct. Submit to God and accept the word that he plants in your hearts, which is able to save you.

**Psalm 16:11 GNT**   You will show me the path that leads to life; your presence fills me with joy and brings me pleasure forever.

**Proverbs 12:25 NKJV**   Anxiety in the heart of man causes depression, but a good word makes it glad.

**Isaiah 26:3-4 GNT**   You, Lord, give perfect peace to those who keep their purpose firm and put their trust in you. Trust in the Lord forever; he will always protect us.

**Isaiah 41:10 NKJV**   Fear not, for I am with you; be not dismayed, for I am your God. I will strengthen you, yes, I will help you, I will uphold you with My righteous right hand.

**Romans 8:26 ESV**   The Spirit helps us in our weakness. For we do not know what to pray for as we ought, but the Spirit himself intercedes for us with groanings too deep for words.

**Philippians 4:6-7 WEB**   In nothing be anxious, but in everything, by prayer and petition with thanksgiving, let your requests be made known to God. The peace of God, which surpasses all understanding, will guard your hearts and minds in Christ Jesus.

**Philippians 4:8-9 NKJV**   Whatever things are true, whatever things are noble, whatever things are just, whatever things are pure, whatever things are lovely, whatever things are of good report, if there is any virtue and if there is anything praiseworthy—meditate on these things. The things which you learned and received and heard and saw in me, these do, and the God of peace will be with you.

**Philippians 4:19 NKJV**   My God shall supply all your need according to his riches in glory by Christ Jesus.

**1 Peter 5:7-8 NRSV**   Cast all your anxiety on him, because he cares for you. Discipline yourselves, keep alert. Like a roaring lion your adversary the devil prowls around, looking for someone to devour.

**Genesis 1:27 WEB**   God created man in his own image. In God's image he created him; male and female he created them.

**1 Samuel 16:7 TNIV**   The LORD said to Samuel, "Do not consider his appearance or his height, for I have rejected him. The LORD does not look at the things human beings look at. People look at the outward appearance, but the LORD looks at the heart."

**Proverbs 3:26 NKJV**   The LORD will be your confidence.

**Proverbs 15:13 HCSB**   A joyful heart makes a face cheerful, but a sad heart produces a broken spirit.

**Galatians 2:20 NIV**   I have been crucified with Christ and I no longer live, but Christ lives in me. The life I live in the body, I live by faith in the Son of God, who loved me and gave himself for me.

**Ephesians 2:10 WEB**   We are his workmanship, created in Christ Jesus for good works, which God prepared before that we would walk in them.

**Ephesians 5:6 ESV**   Let no one deceive you with empty words.

**Philippians 1:6 BBE**   I am certain of this very thing, that he by whom the good work was started in you will make it complete till the day of Jesus Christ.

**1 Peter 1:13-16 NRSV**   Prepare your minds for action; discipline yourselves; set all your hope on the grace that Jesus Christ will bring you when he is revealed. Like obedient children, do not be conformed to the desires that you formerly had in ignorance. Instead, as he who called you is holy, be holy yourselves in all your conduct; for it is written, "You shall be holy, for I am holy."

**Proverbs 15:1-2 BBE**  By a soft answer wrath is turned away, but a bitter word is a cause of angry feelings. Knowledge is dropping from the tongue of the wise; but from the mouth of the foolish comes a stream of foolish words.

**Proverbs 26:17 GNT**  Getting involved in an argument that is none of your business is like going down the street and grabbing a dog by the ears.

**1 Corinthians 1:10 WEB**  I beg you, brothers, through the name of our Lord, Jesus Christ, that you all speak the same thing and that there be no divisions among you, but that you be perfected together in the same mind and in the same judgment.

**Philippians 2:14-16 GNT**  Do everything without complaining or arguing, so that you may be innocent and pure as God's perfect children, who live in a world of corrupt and sinful people. You must shine among them like stars lighting up the sky, as you offer them the message of life. If you do so, I shall have reason to be proud of you on the Day of Christ, because it will show that all my effort and work have not been wasted.

**Colossians 3:12-16 ESV**  Put on then, as God's chosen ones, holy and beloved, compassionate hearts, kindness, humility, meekness, and patience, bearing with one another and, if one has a complaint against another, forgiving each other; as the Lord has forgiven you, so you also must forgive. And above all these put on love, which binds everything together in perfect harmony. And let the peace of Christ rule in your hearts, to which indeed you were called in one body. And be thankful. Let the word of Christ dwell in you richly, teaching and admonishing one another in all wisdom.

**Titus 3:9-11 NIV**  Avoid foolish controversies and genealogies and arguments and quarrels about the law, because these are unprofitable and useless. Warn a divisive person once, and then warn him a second time. After that, have nothing to do with him. You may be sure that such a man is warped and sinful; he is self-condemned.

**Genesis 1:16-18 GNT**   God made the two larger lights, the sun to rule over the day and the moon to rule over the night; he also made the stars. He placed the lights in the sky to shine on the earth, to rule over the day and the night, and to separate light from darkness. And God was pleased with what he saw.

**Exodus 20:3-4 NRSV**   You shall have no other gods before me. You shall not make for yourself an idol, whether in the form of anything that is in heaven above, or that is on the earth beneath, or that is in the water under the earth.

**Deuteronomy 4:19 NIV**   And when you look up to the sky and see the sun, the moon and the stars—all the heavenly array—do not be enticed into bowing down to them and worshiping things the Lord your God has apportioned to all the nations under heaven.

**Isaiah 47:12-15 GNT**   Keep all your magic spells and charms; you have used them since you were young. Perhaps they will be of some help to you; perhaps you can frighten your enemies. You are powerless in spite of the advice you get. Let your astrologers come forward and save you— those people who study the stars, who map out the zones of the heavens and tell you from month to month what is going to happen to you. "They will be like bits of straw, and a fire will burn them up! They will not even be able to save themselves—the flames will be too hot for them, not a cozy fire to warm themselves by. That is all the good they will do you—those astrologers you've consulted all your life. They all will leave you and go their own way, and none will be left to save you."

**Zephaniah 1:5 MSG**   I'll get rid of the people who sneak up to their rooftops at night to worship the star gods and goddesses; also those who continue to worship God but cover their bases by worshiping other king-gods as well.

**Isaiah 40:29-31 GNT**  He strengthens those who are weak and tired. Even those who are young grow weak; young people can fall exhausted. But those who trust in the Lord for help will find their strength renewed. They will rise on wings like eagles; they will run and not get weary; they will walk and not grow weak.

**Romans 6:13-14 TNIV**  Offer yourselves to God as those who have been brought from death to life; and offer every part of yourself to him as an instrument of righteousness. For sin shall no longer be your master, because you are not under the law, but under grace.

**Romans 12:8 NCV**  Anyone who has the gift of being a leader should try hard when he leads.

**Philippians 2:1-5 CEV**  Christ encourages you, and his love comforts you. God's Spirit unites you, and you are concerned for others. Now make me completely happy! Live in harmony by showing love for each other. Be united in what you think, as if you were only one person. Don't be jealous or proud, but be humble and consider others more important than yourselves. Care about them as much as you care about yourselves and think the same way that Christ Jesus thought.

**Philippians 2:12-13 NLT**  Work hard to show the results of your salvation, obeying God with deep reverence and fear. For God is working in you, giving you the desire and the power to do what pleases him.

**1 Timothy 4:8 NIV**  Physical training is of some value, but godliness has value for all things, holding promise for both the present life and the life to come.

**1 John 5:21 AMP**  Keep yourselves from idols (false gods)—[from anything and everything that would occupy the place in your heart due to God, from any sort of substitute for Him that would take first place in your life]. Amen (so let it be).

# ATTITUDE

**Proverbs 15:15 MSG**   A miserable heart means a miserable life; a cheerful heart fills the day with song.

**Proverbs 17:22 NKJV**   A merry heart does good, like medicine, But a broken spirit dries the bones.

**Jeremiah 12:2-3 NASB**   You are near to their lips but far from their mind. But You know me, O Lord; You see me; and You examine my heart's attitude toward You.

**Romans 15:5-6 TNIV**   May the God who gives endurance and encouragement give you the same attitude of mind toward each other that Christ Jesus had, so that with one mind and one voice you may glorify the God and Father of our Lord Jesus Christ.

**Ephesians 4:22-24 NIV**   You were taught, with regard to your former way of life, to put off your old self, which is being corrupted by its deceitful desires; to be made new in the attitude of your minds; and to put on the new self, created to be like God in true righteousness and holiness.

**Philippians 2:4-5 NCV**   Do not be interested only in your own life, but be interested in the lives of others. In your lives you must think and act like Christ Jesus.

**Colossians 4:2-3 NASB**   Devote yourselves to prayer, keeping alert in it with an attitude of thanksgiving.

**Hebrews 4:12 TNIV**   The word of God is alive and active. Sharper than any double-edged sword, it penetrates even to dividing soul and spirit, joints and marrow; it judges the thoughts and attitudes of the heart.

**1 Peter 4:1-2 NLT**   Since Christ suffered physical pain, you must arm yourselves with the same attitude he had, and be ready to suffer, too. For if you are willing to suffer for Christ, you have decided to stop sinning. And you won't spend the rest of your life chasing after evil desires, but you will be anxious to do the will of God.

**Psalm 22:27-29 GNT**   All nations will remember the Lord. From every part of the world they will turn to him; all races will worship him. The Lord is king, and he rules the nations. All proud people will bow down to him.

**Matthew 28:18-22 TNIV**   Jesus came to them and said, "All authority in heaven and on earth has been given to me. Therefore go and make disciples of all nations, baptizing them in the name of the Father and of the Son and of the Holy Spirit, and teaching them to obey everything I have commanded you. And surely I am with you always, to the very end of the age."

**Romans 13:1-5 TNIV**   Let everyone be subject to the governing authorities, for there is no authority except that which God has established. The authorities that exist have been established by God. Consequently, whoever rebels against the authority is rebelling against what God has instituted, and those who do so will bring judgment on themselves. For rulers hold no terror for those who do right, but for those who do wrong. Do you want to be free from fear of the one in authority? Then do what is right and you will be commended. For the one in authority is God's servant for your good. But if you do wrong, be afraid, for rulers do not bear the sword for no reason. They are God's servants, agents of wrath to bring punishment on the wrongdoer. Therefore, it is necessary to submit to the authorities, not only because of possible punishment but also as a matter of conscience.

**Colossians 3:20 HCSB**   Obey your parents in everything, for this is pleasing in the Lord.

**Hebrews 13:17 NASB**   Obey your leaders and submit to them, for they keep watch over your souls as those who will give an account. Let them do this with joy and not with grief, for this would be unprofitable for you.

**BAPTISM**

**Mark 1:4–8 CEV**   So John the Baptist showed up in the desert and told everyone, "Turn back to God and be baptized! Then your sins will be forgiven." . . . John also told the people, "Someone more powerful is going to come. And I am not good enough even to stoop down and untie his sandals. I baptize you with water, but he will baptize you with the Holy Spirit!"

**John 3:5 CEV**   Jesus answered: "I tell you for certain that before you can get into God's kingdom, you must be born not only by water, but by the Spirit."

**Acts 2:38 GNT**   Peter said to them, "Each one of you must turn away from your sins and be baptized in the name of Jesus Christ, so that your sins will be forgiven; and you will receive God's gift, the Holy Spirit."

**Acts 8:36–37 NKJV**   The eunuch said, "See, here is water. What hinders me from being baptized?" Then Philip said, "If you believe with all your heart, you may." And he answered and said, "I believe that Jesus Christ is the Son of God."

**Galatians 3:26–27 TNIV**   In Christ Jesus you are all children of God through faith, for all of you who were baptized into Christ have clothed yourselves with Christ.

**Colossians 2:12–14 NCV**   When you were baptized, you were buried with Christ, and you were raised up with him through your faith in God's power that was shown when he raised Christ from the dead. When you were spiritually dead because of your sins and because you were not free from the power of your sinful self, God made you alive with Christ, and he forgave all our sins. He canceled the debt, which listed all the rules we failed to follow. He took away that record with its rules and nailed it to the cross.

**1 Peter 3:21 CEV**   Baptism is more than just washing your body. It means turning to God with a clear conscience, because Jesus Christ was raised from death.

**Matthew 10:16 NCV**   Be as clever as snakes and as innocent as doves.

**Luke 12:15 NCV**   Be careful and guard against all kinds of greed.

**Romans 12:2 NASB**   Be transformed by the renewing of your mind.

**Romans 12:12 ESV**   Be constant in prayer.

**1 Corinthians 14:20 ESV**   Be infants in evil, but in your thinking be mature.

**1 Corinthians 15:58 ESV**   Be steadfast, immovable, always abounding in the work of the Lord.

**Ephesians 4:26 NKJV**   Be angry, and do not sin.

**Ephesians 5:18 NKJV**   Be filled with the Spirit.

**Philippians 4:6 NKJV**   Be anxious for nothing.

**1 Thessalonians 5:6 NASB**   Be alert and sober.

**1 Timothy 4:12 NKJV**   Be an example to the believers in word, in conduct, in love, in spirit, in faith, in purity.

**1 Timothy 4:16 CEV**   Be careful about the way you live and about what you teach.

**2 Timothy 2:24 TNIV**   Be kind to everyone, able to teach, not resentful

**2 Timothy 2:25 CEV**   Be humble when you correct people who oppose you.

**Hebrews 13:5 TNIV**   Be content with what you have.

# BEAUTY

**Psalm 27:4 NRSV**   One thing I asked of the Lord, that will I seek after: to live in the house of the Lord all the days of my life, to behold the beauty of the Lord.

**Psalm 96:5-6 NRSV**   The Lord made the heavens. Honor and majesty are before him; strength and beauty are in his sanctuary.

**Proverbs 11:22 HCSB**   A beautiful woman who rejects good sense is like a gold ring in a pig's snout.

**Proverbs 31:30 GNT**   Charm is deceptive and beauty disappears, but a woman who honors the Lord should be praised.

**Ecclesiastes 3:11 MSG**   God made everything beautiful in itself and in its time.

**Matthew 23:27-28 NIV**   Woe to you, teachers of the law and Pharisees, you hypocrites! You are like whitewashed tombs, which look beautiful on the outside but on the inside are full of dead men's bones and everything unclean. In the same way, on the outside you appear to people as righteous but on the inside you are full of hypocrisy and wickedness.

**Romans 10:15 WEB**   How beautiful are the feet of those who preach the gospel of peace, who bring glad tidings of good things!

**1 Peter 1:24-25 NLT**   People are like grass that dies away; their beauty fades as quickly as the beauty of wildflowers. The grass withers, and the flowers fall away. But the word of the Lord will last forever. And that word is the Good News that was preached to you.

**1 Peter 3:3-4 WEB**   Let your beauty be not just the outward adorning of braiding the hair, and of wearing jewels of gold, or of putting on fine clothing; but in the hidden person of the heart, in the incorruptible adornment of a gentle and quiet spirit, which is in the sight of God very precious.

**Matthew 9:28-30 NKJV**   When He had come into the house, the blind men came to Him. And Jesus said to them, "Do you believe that I am able to do this?" They said to Him, "Yes, Lord." Then He touched their eyes, saying, "According to your faith let it be to you." And their eyes were opened.

**Mark 9:23-24 NRSV**   Jesus said to him, "If you are able! All things can be done for the one who believes." Immediately the father of the child cried out, "I believe; help my unbelief!"

**Mark 11:23-24 NASB**   Whoever says to this mountain, "Be taken up and cast into the sea," and does not doubt in his heart, but believes that what he says is going to happen, it will be granted him. Therefore I say to you, all things for which you pray and ask, believe that you have received them, and they will be granted you.

**Romans 10:9-10 NIV**   If you confess with your mouth, "Jesus is Lord," and believe in your heart that God raised him from the dead, you will be saved. For it is with your heart that you believe and are justified, and it is with your mouth that you confess and are saved.

**Romans 10:11 NKJV**   The Scripture says, "Whoever believes on Him will not be put to shame."

**Romans 15:13 NASB**   Now may the God of hope fill you with all joy and peace in believing, so that you will abound in hope by the power of the Holy Spirit.

**Ephesians 1:17-19 NIV**   I keep asking that the God of our Lord Jesus Christ, the glorious Father, may give you the Spirit of wisdom and revelation, so that you may know him better. I pray also that the eyes of your heart may be enlightened in order that you may know the hope to which he has called you, the riches of his glorious inheritance in the saints, and his incomparably great power for us who believe.

# BETRAYAL

**Isaiah 26:3 NCV**   You, LORD, give true peace to those who depend on you, because they trust you.

**Isaiah 63:9-10 CEV**   The LORD was truly merciful, so he rescued his people. He took them in his arms and carried them all those years. Then the LORD's people turned against him and made his Holy Spirit sad.

**Matthew 5:44-45 NCV**   Love your enemies. Pray for those who hurt you. If you do this, you will be true children of your Father in heaven.

**Matthew 10:21-22 HCSB**   Brother will betray brother to death, and a father his child. Children will even rise up against their parents and have them put to death. You will be hated by everybody because of My name. And the one who endures to the end will be delivered.

**Matthew 15:18-19 NCV**   But what people say with their mouths comes from the way they think; these are the things that make people unclean. Out of the mind come evil thoughts, murder, adultery, sexual sins, stealing, lying, and speaking evil of others.

**Matthew 18:21-22 NIV**   "Lord, how many time shall I forgive my brother when he sins against me? Up to seven times?" Jesus answered, "I tell you, not seven times, but seventy-seven times."

**Mark 14:21 CEV**   The Son of Man will die, just as the Scriptures say. But it is going to be terrible for the one who betrays me. That man would be better off if he had never been born.

**2 Timothy 3:1-5 HCSB**   But know this: difficult times will come in the last days. For people will be lovers of self, lovers of money, boastful, proud, blasphemers, disobedient to parents, ungrateful, unholy, unloving, irreconcilable, slanderers, without self-control, brutal, without love for what is good, traitors, reckless, conceited, lovers of pleasure rather than lovers of God, holding to the form of religion but denying its power. Avoid these people!

**Joshua 1:8 NIV** Do not let this Book of the Law depart from your mouth; meditate on it day and night, so that you may be careful to do everything written in it. Then you will be prosperous and successful.

**Psalm 119:9-12 BBE** How may a young man make his way clean? By guiding it after your word. I have made search for you with all my heart: O let me not go wandering far from your teaching. I have kept your sayings secretly in my heart, so that I might do no sin against you. Praise be to you, O Lord: give me knowledge of your rules.

**Psalm 119:14-18 BBE** I have taken as much delight in the way of your unchanging word, as in all wealth. I will give thought to your orders, and have respect for your ways. I will have delight in your rules; I will not let your word go out of my mind. Give me, your servant, the reward of life, so that I may keep your word; let my eyes be open to see the wonders of your law.

**Luke 11:28 NCV** Jesus said, "No, blessed are those who hear the teaching of God and obey it."

**John 5:39-40 ESV** You search the Scriptures because you think that in them you have eternal life; and it is they that bear witness about me, yet you refuse to come to me that you may have life.

**Galatians 3:10 MSG** Anyone who tries to live by his own effort, independent of God, is doomed to failure. Scripture backs this up: "Utterly cursed is every person who fails to carry out every detail written in the Book of the law."

**Ephesians 6:17 NRSV** Take the helmet of salvation, and the sword of the Spirit, which is the word of God.

**Colossians 3:16 NCV** Let the teaching of Christ live in you richly. Use all wisdom to teach and instruct each other by singing psalms, hymns, and spiritual songs with thankfulness in your hearts to God.

**1 Timothy 1:8-9 CEV**   We know that the Law is good, if it is used in the right way. We also understand that it wasn't given to control people who please God, but to control lawbreakers, criminals, godless people, and sinners.

**2 Timothy 2:15 TNIV**   Do your best to present yourself to God as one approved, a worker who does not need to be ashamed and who correctly handles the word of truth.

**2 Timothy 3:16-17 HCSB**   All Scripture is inspired by God and is profitable for teaching, for rebuking, for correcting, for training in righteousness, so that the man of God may be complete, equipped for every good work.

**Hebrews 4:12 CEV**   What God has said isn't only alive and active! It is sharper than any double-edged sword. His word can cut through our spirits and souls and through our joints and marrow, until it discovers the desires and thoughts of our hearts.

**James 1:21-24 TNIV**   Get rid of all moral filth and the evil that is so prevalent and humbly accept the word planted in you, which can save you. Do not merely listen to the word, and so deceive yourselves. Do what it says. Those who listen to the word but do not do what it says are like people who look at their faces in a mirror and, after looking at themselves, go away and immediately forget what they look like.

**Revelation 1:3 NCV**   Blessed is the one who reads the words of God's message, and blessed are the people who hear this message and do what is written in it. The time is near when all of this will happen.

**Revelation 22:18-19 NLT**   I solemnly declare to everyone who hears the words of prophecy written in this book: If anyone adds anything to what is written here, God will add to that person the plagues described in this book. And if anyone removes any of the words from this book of prophecy, God will remove that person's share in the tree of life and in the holy city that are described in this book.

**Leviticus 19:18 NCV**   Forget about the wrong things people do to you, and do not try to get even. Love your neighbor as you love yourself. I am the Lord.

**Mark 11:25 BBE**   Whenever you make a prayer, let there be forgiveness in your hearts, if you have anything against anyone; so that you may have forgiveness for your sins from your Father who is in heaven.

**Ephesians 4:30-32 NKJV**   Do not grieve the Holy Spirit of God, by whom you were sealed for the day of redemption. Let all bitterness, wrath, anger, clamor, and evil speaking be put away from you, with all malice. And be kind to one another, tenderhearted, forgiving one another, just as God in Christ forgave you.

**Philippians 3:13 GNT**   Of course, my friends, I really do not think that I have already won it; the one thing I do, however, is to forget what is behind me and do my best to reach what is ahead.

**Colossians 3:12-13 NKJV**   As the elect of God, holy and beloved, put on tender mercies, kindness, humility, meekness, longsuffering; bearing with one another, and forgiving one another, if anyone has a complaint against another; even as Christ forgave you, so you also must do.

**Hebrews 12:14-15 TNIV**   Make every effort to live in peace with everyone and to be holy; without holiness no one will see the Lord. See to it that no one falls short of the grace of God and that no bitter root grows up to cause trouble and defile many.

**James 3:14-16 HCSB**   If you have bitter envy and selfish ambition in your heart, don't brag and lie in defiance of the truth. Such wisdom does not come down from above, but is earthly, sensual, demonic. For where envy and selfish ambition exist, there is disorder and every kind of evil.

# BLASPHEMY

**1 Samuel 3:11–13 TNIV** The LORD said to Samuel, "... I told [Eli] that I would judge his family forever because of the sin he knew about; his sons blasphemed God, and he failed to restrain them."

**Matthew 9:3 NCV** Some of the teachers of the law said to themselves, "This man speaks as if he were God. That is blasphemy!"

**Mark 3:28–29 TNIV** Truly I tell you, people will be forgiven all their sins and all the blasphemies they utter. But whoever blasphemes against the Holy Spirit will never be forgiven, but is guilty of an eternal sin.

**John 10:32–37 GNT** Jesus said to them, "I have done many good deeds in your presence which the Father gave me to do; for which one of these do you want to stone me?" They answered, "We do not want to stone you because of any good deeds, but because of your blasphemy! You are only a man, but you are trying to make yourself God!" Jesus answered, "It is written in your own Law that God said, 'You are gods.' We know that what the scripture says is true forever; and God called those people gods, the people to whom his message was given. As for me, the Father chose me and sent me into the world. How, then, can you say that I blaspheme because I said that I am the Son of God?"

**2 Peter 2:11 CEV** Although angels are more powerful than these evil beings, even the angels don't dare to accuse them to the Lord.

**Jude 1:9–10 GNT** Not even the chief angel Michael did this. In his quarrel with the Devil, when they argued about who would have the body of Moses, Michael did not dare condemn the Devil with insulting words, but said, "The Lord rebuke you!" But these people attack with insults anything they do not understand; and those things that they know by instinct, like wild animals, are the very things that destroy them.

**Genesis 1:28 BBE**  God gave them his blessing and said to them, Be fertile and have increase, and make the earth full and be masters of it; be rulers over the fish of the sea and over the birds of the air and over every living thing moving on the earth.

**Numbers 6:24–26 NKJV**  The LORD bless you and keep you; the LORD make His face shine upon you, and be gracious to you; the LORD lift up His countenance upon you, and give you peace.

**Psalm 5:12 BBE**  For you, Lord, will send a blessing on the upright man; your grace will be round him, and you will be his strength.

**Psalm 34:8 NASB**  O taste and see that the LORD is good; how blessed is the man who takes refuge in Him!

**Psalm 40:4 MSG**  Blessed are you who give yourselves over to GOD, turn your backs on the world's "sure thing," ignore what the world worships.

**Psalm 112:2–3 TNIV**  The generation of the upright will be blessed. Wealth and riches are in their houses, and their righteousness endures forever.

**Psalm 119:1–2 NKJV**  Blessed are the undefiled in the way, who walk in the law of the Lord! Blessed are those who keep His testimonies, who seek Him with the whole heart!

**Psalm 144:15 ESV**  Blessed are the people whose God is the LORD!

**John 8:50–51 MSG**  God intends something gloriously grand here and is making the decisions that will bring it about. I say this with absolute confidence. If you practice what I'm telling you, you'll never have to look death in the face.

**John 20:29 NIV**  Jesus told him, "Because you have seen me, you have believed; blessed are those who have not seen and yet have believed."

**Joshua 1:9 MSG**   Haven't I commanded you? Strength! Courage! Don't be timid; don't get discouraged. God, your God, is with you every step you take.

**Luke 11:8–10 NCV**   I tell you, if friendship is not enough to make him get up to give you the bread, your boldness will make him get up and give you whatever you need. So I tell you, ask, and God will give to you. Search, and you will find. Knock, and the door will open for you. Yes, everyone who asks will receive. The one who searches will find. And everyone who knocks will have the door opened.

**Acts 4:13 WEB**   Now when they saw the boldness of Peter and John, and had perceived that they were unlearned and ignorant men, they marveled. They recognized that they had been with Jesus.

**Acts 4:31 TNIV**   After they prayed, the place where they were meeting was shaken. And they were all filled with the Holy Spirit and spoke the word of God boldly.

**2 Corinthians 3:12 NIV**   Since we have such a hope, we are very bold.

**Ephesians 3:12 GNT**   In union with Christ and through our faith in him we have the boldness to go into God's presence with all confidence.

**Ephesians 6:19–20 NKJV**   That I may open my mouth boldly to make known the mystery of the gospel, for which I am an ambassador in chains; that in it I may speak boldly, as I ought to speak.

**Philippians 1:20 NRSV**   It is my eager expectation and hope that I will not be put to shame in any way, but that by my speaking with all boldness, Christ will be exalted now as always in my body, whether by life or by death.

**John 3:3-7 NCV** Jesus answered, "I tell you the truth, unless you are born again, you cannot be in God's kingdom." Nicodemus said, "But if a person is already old, how can he be born again? He cannot enter his mother's womb again. So how can a person be born a second time?" But Jesus answered, "I tell you the truth, unless you are born from water and the Spirit, you cannot enter God's kingdom. Human life comes from human parents, but spiritual life comes from the Spirit. Don't be surprised when I tell you, 'You must all be born again.'"

**John 3:16-17 NASB** God so loved the world, that He gave His only begotten Son, that whoever believes in Him shall not perish, but have eternal life. "For God did not send the Son into the world to judge the world, but that the world might be saved through Him."

**John 14:6 NASB** Jesus said to him, "I am the way, and the truth, and the life; no one comes to the Father but though Me."

**Acts 3:19-20 TNIV** Repent, then, and turn to God, so that your sins may be wiped out, that times of refreshing may come from the Lord, and that he may send the Messiah, who has been appointed for you—even Jesus.

**Ephesians 2:4-10 NRSV** God, who is rich in mercy, out of the great love with which he loved us even when we were dead through our trespasses, made us alive together with Christ . . . and raised us up with him and seated us with him in the heavenly places in Christ Jesus, so that in the ages to come he might show the immeasurable riches of his grace in kindness toward us. . . . For we are what he has made us, created in Christ Jesus for good works, which God prepared beforehand to be our way of life.

**1 Peter 1:3 ESV** Blessed be the God and Father of our Lord Jesus Christ! According to his great mercy, he has caused us to be born again to a living hope through the resurrection of Jesus Christ from the dead.

**1 Peter 1:23 TNIV** You have been born again, not of perishable seed, but of imperishable, through the living and enduring word of God.

# BUSINESS

**Deuteronomy 25:13-14 CEV**   Don't try to cheat people by having two sets of weights or measures, one to get more when you are buying, and the other to give less when you are selling.

**Psalm 112:5-6 NCV**   Those who are fair in their business will never be defeated. Good people will always be remembered.

**Ezekiel 28:5 CEV**   You're a clever businessman and are extremely wealthy, but your wealth has led to arrogance!

**Matthew 6:33 NLT**   Seek the Kingdom of God above all else, and live righteously, and he will give you everything you need.

**Romans 12:11-14 TNIV**   Never be lacking in zeal, but keep your spiritual fervor, serving the Lord. Be joyful in hope, patient in affliction, faithful in prayer. Share with the Lord's people who are in need. Practice hospitality. Bless those who persecute you; bless and do not curse.

**2 Corinthians 5:9-10 TNIV**   We make it our goal to please him, whether we are at home in the body or away from it. For we must all appear before the judgment seat of Christ, that everyone may receive what is due them for the things done while in the body, whether good or bad.

**Galatians 6:9-10 ESV**   Let us not grow weary of doing good, for in due season we will reap, if we do not give up. So then, as we have opportunity, let us do good to everyone, and especially to those who are of the household of faith.

**Philippians 2:3-6 NCV**   When you do things, do not let selfishness or pride be your guide. Instead, be humble and give more honor to others than to yourselves. Do not be interested only in your own life, but be interested in the lives of others. In your lives you must think and act like Christ Jesus.

**Job 10:12 GNT**   You have given me life and constant love, and your care has kept me alive.

**Psalm 31:7 CEV**   I celebrate and shout because you are kind. You saw all my suffering, and you cared for me.

**Psalm 41:1-2 NKJV**   Blessed is he who considers the poor; the LORD will deliver him in time of trouble. The LORD will preserve him and keep him alive, and he will be blessed on the earth.

**Matthew 25:44-45 GNT**   Then they will answer him, "When, Lord, did we ever see you hungry or thirsty or a stranger or naked or sick or in prison, and we would not help you?" The King will reply, "I tell you, whenever you refused to help one of these least important ones, you refused to help me."

**1 Corinthians 12:24-26 WEB**   God composed the body together, giving more abundant honor to the inferior part, that there should be no division in the body, but that the members should have the same care for one another. When one member suffers, all the members suffer with it. Or when one member is honored, all the members rejoice with it.

**Ephesians 4:11 NCV**   Christ gave gifts to people—he made some to be apostles, some to be prophets, some to go and tell the Good News, and some to have the work of caring for and teaching God's people.

**Hebrews 6:10-12 NLT**   God is not unjust. He will not forget how hard you have worked for him and how you have shown your love to him by caring for other believers, as you still do. Our great desire is that you will keep on loving others as long as life lasts, in order to make certain that what you hope for will come true. Then you will not become spiritually dull and indifferent. Instead, you will follow the example of those who are going to inherit God's promises because of their faith and endurance.

**Deuteronomy 16:18-19 CEV**   Those of you that become judges must be completely fair when you make legal decisions, even if someone important is involved. Don't take bribes to give unfair decisions. Bribes keep people who are wise from seeing the truth and turn honest people into liars.

**Proverbs 11:3 NCV**   Good people will be guided by honesty; dishonesty will destroy those who are not trustworthy.

**Philippians 2:14-16 MSG**   Do everything readily and cheerfully— no bickering, no second-guessing allowed! Go out into the world uncorrupted, a breath of fresh air in this squalid and polluted society. Provide people with a glimpse of good living and of the living God. Carry the light-giving Message into the night so I'll have good cause to be proud of you on the day that Christ returns. You'll be living proof that I didn't go to all this work for nothing.

**Colossians 3:15-17 MSG**   Let the peace of Christ keep you in tune with each other, in step with each other . . . cultivate thankfulness. Let the Word of Christ—the Message—have the run of the house. Give it plenty of room in your lives. Instruct and direct one another using good common sense. And sing, sing your hearts out to God! Let every detail in your lives—words, actions, whatever—be done in the name of the Master, Jesus, thanking God the Father every step of the way.

**Titus 3:1-2 NKJV**   Remind them to be subject to rulers and authorities, to obey, to be ready for every good work, to speak evil of no one, to be peaceable.

**1 John 2:4-6 GNT**   If we say that we know him, but do not obey his commands, we are liars and there is no truth in us. But if we obey his word, we are the ones whose love for God has really been made perfect. This is how we can be sure that we are in union with God: if we say that we remain in union with God, we should live just as Jesus Christ did.

**Deuteronomy 30:19-20 CEV** I am offering you this choice. Will you choose for the LORD to make you prosperous and give you a long life? Or will he put you under a curse and kill you? Choose life! Be completely faithful to the LORD your God, love him, and do whatever he tells you. The LORD is the only one who can give life.

**Psalm 119:103-104 GNT** How sweet is the taste of your instructions—sweeter even than honey! I gain wisdom from your laws, and so I hate all bad conduct.

**Proverbs 28:13 CEV** If you don't confess your sins, you will be a failure. But God will be merciful if you confess your sins and give them up.

**John 15:15-16 HCSB** I have called you friends, because I have made known to you everything I have heard from My Father. You did not choose Me, but I chose you. I appointed you that you should go out and produce fruit and that your fruit should remain, so that whatever you ask the Father in My name, He will give you.

**Galatians 5:13-14 NIV** You, my brothers, were called to be free. But do not use your freedom to indulge the sinful nature; rather, serve one another in love. The entire law is summed up in a single command: "Love your neighbor as yourself."

**Colossians 1:9-11 NCV** We have continued praying for you, asking God that you will know fully what he wants. We pray that you will also have great wisdom and understanding in spiritual things so that you will live the kind of life that honors and pleases the Lord in every way. You will produce fruit in every good work and grow in the knowledge of God. God will strengthen you with his own great power so that you will not give up when troubles come, but you will be patient.

**2 Timothy 2:15 GNT** Do your best to win full approval in God's sight, as a worker who is not ashamed of his work, one who correctly teaches the message of God's truth.

# CHRISTIAN

**John 13:34-35 NIV**   A new command I give you: Love one another. As I have loved you, so you must love one another. By this all men will know that you are my disciples, if you love one another.

**2 Corinthians 3:16-17 NRSV**   When one turns to the Lord, the veil is removed. Now the Lord is the Spirit, and where the Spirit of the Lord is, there is freedom.

**2 Corinthians 5:17 NASB**   If anyone is in Christ, he is a new creature; the old things passed away; behold, new things have come.

**Galatians 3:3 NLT**   How foolish can you be? After starting your Christian lives in the Spirit, why are you now trying to become perfect by your own human effort?

**Colossians 2:6-7 NASB**   As you have received Christ Jesus the Lord, so walk in Him, having been firmly rooted and now being built up in Him and established in your faith, just as you were instructed, and overflowing with gratitude.

**2 Timothy 2:19 ESV**   God's firm foundation stands, bearing this seal: "The Lord knows those who are his," and, "Let everyone who names the name of the Lord depart from iniquity."

**2 Peter 1:5-8 NCV**   Do your best to add these things to your lives: to your faith, add goodness; and to your goodness, add knowledge; and to your knowledge, add self-control; and to your self-control, add patience; and to your patience, add service for God; and to your service for God, add kindness for your brothers and sisters in Christ; and to this kindness, add love. If all these things are in you and are growing, they will help you to be useful and productive in your knowledge of our Lord Jesus Christ.

**1 John 1:7 NKJV**   If we walk in the light as He is in the light, we have fellowship with one another, and the blood of Jesus Christ His Son cleanses us from all sin.

**Psalm 122:1 NKJV**   I was glad when they said to me, "Let us go into the house of the LORD."

**Matthew 18:20 NRSV**   Where two or three are gathered in my name, I am there among them.

**Acts 2:42-47 ESV**   They devoted themselves to the apostles' teaching and the fellowship, to the breaking of bread and the prayers. And awe came upon every soul, and many wonders and signs were being done through the apostles. And all who believed were together and had all things in common. And they were selling their possessions and belongings and distributing the proceeds to all, as any had need. And day by day, attending the temple together and breaking bread in their homes, they received their food with glad and generous hearts, praising God and having favor with all the people. And the Lord added to their number day by day those who were being saved.

**Ephesians 1:22-23 TNIV**   God placed all things under his feet and appointed him to be head over everything for the church, which is his body, the fullness of him who fills everything in every way.

**Ephesians 5:23-24 GNT**   A husband has authority over his wife just as Christ has authority over the church; and Christ is himself the Savior of the church, his body. And so wives must submit themselves completely to their husbands just as the church submits itself to Christ.

**2 Timothy 2:19 NCV**   God's strong foundation continues to stand. These words are written on the seal: "The Lord knows those who belong to him," and "Everyone who wants to belong to the Lord must stop doing wrong."

**Hebrews 13:7 NASB**   Remember those who led you, who spoke the word of God to you; and considering the result of their conduct, imitate their faith.

**Proverbs 31:25 TNIV**   She is clothed with strength and dignity; she can laugh at the days to come.

**Matthew 7:15-16 NASB**   Beware of the false prophets, who come to you in sheep's clothing, but inwardly are ravenous wolves. You will know them by their fruits.

**Matthew 5:8 NCV**   They are blessed whose thoughts are pure, for they will see God.

**1 Corinthians 6:19-20 NKJV**   Do you not know that your body is the temple of the Holy Spirit who is in you, whom you have from God, and you are not your own? For you were bought at a price; therefore glorify God in your body and in your spirit, which are God's.

**Colossians 3:12 MSG**   Chosen by God for this new life of love, dress in the wardrobe God picked out for you: compassion, kindness, humility, quiet strength, discipline.

**1 Timothy 2:9-10 ESV**   Women should adorn themselves in respectable apparel, with modesty and self-control, not with braided hair and gold or pearls or costly attire, but with what is proper for women who profess godliness—with good works.

**James 2:1-4 NIV**   Don't show favoritism. Suppose a man comes into your meeting wearing a gold ring and fine clothes, and a poor man in shabby clothes also comes in. If you show special attention to the man wearing fine clothes and say, "Here's a good seat for you," but say to the poor man, "You stand there" or "Sit on the floor by my feet," have you not discriminated among yourselves and become judges with evil thoughts?

**1 Peter 3:3-4 NLT**   Don't be concerned about the outward beauty that depends on fancy hairstyles, expensive jewelry, or beautiful clothes. You should be known for the beauty that comes from within, the unfading beauty of a gentle and quiet spirit, which is so precious to God.

**Psalm 27:4-5 NIV**   One thing I ask of the LORD, this is what I seek: that I may dwell in the house of the LORD all the days of my life, to gaze upon the beauty of the LORD and to seek him in his temple. For in the day of trouble he will keep me safe in his dwelling; he will hide me in the shelter of his tabernacle and set me high upon a rock.

**Psalm 62:5-6 NIV**   Find rest, O my soul, in God alone; my hope comes from him. He alone is my rock and my salvation; he is my fortress, I will not be shaken.

**Psalm 71:21 NCV**   You will make me greater than ever, and you will comfort me again.

**Psalm 94:19 NKJV**   In the multitude of my anxieties within me, Your comforts delight my soul.

**Isaiah 40:28-31 NCV**   The LORD is the God who lives forever, who created all the world. He does not become tired or need to rest. No one can understand how great his wisdom is. He gives strength to those who are tired and more power to those who are weak. Even children become tired and need to rest, and young people trip and fall. But the people who trust the LORD will become strong again. They will rise up as an eagle in the sky; they will run and not need rest; they will walk and not become tired.

**Jeremiah 8:18 NCV**   God, you are my comfort when I am very sad and when I am afraid.

**Lamentations 3:22-24 NRSV**   The steadfast love of the Lord never ceases, his mercies never come to an end; they are new every morning; great is your faithfulness. "The Lord is my portion," says my soul, "therefore I will hope in him."

**2 Corinthians 1:3-4 NCV**   God is the Father who is full of mercy and all comfort. He comforts us every time we have trouble, so when others have trouble, we can comfort them with the same comfort God gives us.

# COMPASSION

**Psalm 145:9 NIV**   The Lord is good to all; he has compassion on all he has made.

**Proverbs 19:17 NCV**   Being kind to the poor is like lending to the Lord; he will reward you for what you have done.

**Isaiah 30:18 TNIV**   The Lord longs to be gracious to you; therefore he will rise up to show you compassion. For the Lord is a God of justice. Blessed are all who wait for him!

**Zechariah 7:9-10 NIV**   This is what the Lord Almighty says: "Administer true justice; show mercy and compassion to one another."

**Matthew 20:34 NASB**   Moved with compassion, Jesus touched their eyes; and immediately they regained their sight and followed Him.

**2 Corinthians 1:6 NLT**   Even when we are weighed down with troubles, it is for your benefit and salvation! For when God comforts us, it is so that we, in turn, can be an encouragement to you.

**Colossians 3:12-13 HCSB**   Therefore, God's chosen ones, holy and loved, put on heartfelt compassion, kindness, humility, gentleness, and patience, accepting one another and forgiving one another.

**1 Thessalonians 5:11 NCV**   So encourage each other and give each other strength, just as you are doing now.

**1 Thessalonians 5:14 ESV**   We urge you, brothers, admonish the idle, encourage the fainthearted, help the weak, be patient with them all.

**Hebrews 13:3 NCV**   Remember those who are in prison as if you were in prison with them. Remember those who are suffering as if you were suffering with them.

**1 Peter 3:8-9 NRSV**   Finally, all of you, have unity of spirit, sympathy, love for one another, a tender heart, and a humble mind. Do not repay evil for evil or abuse for abuse; but, on the contrary, repay with a blessing.

# COMPETITION

**Luke 18:14 CEV**   If you put yourself above others, you will be put down. But if you humble yourself, you will be honored.

**Acts 20:24 CEV**   I don't care what happens to me, as long as I finish the work that the Lord Jesus gave me to do. And that work is to tell the good news about God's great kindness.

**1 Corinthians 9:24–27 GNT**   Surely you know that many runners take part in a race, but only one of them wins the prize. Run, then, in such a way as to win the prize. Every athlete in training submits to strict discipline, in order to be crowned with a wreath that will not last; but we do it for one that will last forever. That is why I run straight for the finish line; that is why I am like a boxer who does not waste his punches. I harden my body with blows and bring it under complete control, to keep myself from being disqualified after having called others to the contest.

**Galatians 5:7–8 NCV**   You were running a good race. Who stopped you from following the true way? This change did not come from the One who chose you.

**Galatians 5:19–20 MSG**   It is obvious what kind of life develops out of trying to get your own way all the time: repetitive, loveless, cheap sex; a stinking accumulation of mental and emotional garbage; frenzied and joyless grabs for happiness; trinket gods; magic-show religion; paranoid loneliness; cutthroat competition.

**Philippians 4:13 GNT**   I have the strength to face all conditions by the power that Christ gives me.

**Hebrews 12:3 CEV**   So keep your mind on Jesus, who put up with many insults from sinners. Then you won't get discouraged and give up.

**James 1:12 ESV**   Blessed is the man who remains steadfast under trial, for when he has stood the test he will receive the crown of life, which God has promised to those who love him.

**Proverbs 15:23 NLT**   Everyone enjoys a fitting reply; it is wonderful to say the right thing at the right time!

**John 6:43 NIV**   "Stop grumbling among yourselves," Jesus answered.

**Philippians 2:14-15 ESV**   Do all things without grumbling or questioning, that you may be blameless and innocent, children of God without blemish in the midst of a crooked and twisted generation, among whom you shine as lights in the world.

**Colossians 3:12-13 ESV**   Put on then, as God's chosen ones, holy and beloved, compassionate hearts, kindness, humility, meekness, and patience, bearing with one another and, if one has a complaint against another, forgiving each other; as the Lord has forgiven you, so you also must forgive.

**Colossians 4:6 GNT**   Your speech should always be pleasant and interesting, and you should know how to give the right answer to everyone.

**1 Thessalonians 5:16-18 NCV**   Always be joyful. Pray continually, and give thanks whatever happens. That is what God wants for you in Christ Jesus.

**2 Timothy 2:16-17 ESV**   Avoid irreverent babble, for it will lead people into more and more ungodliness, and their talk will spread like gangrene.

**James 1:26 WEB**   If anyone among you thinks himself to be religious, while he doesn't bridle his tongue, but deceives his heart, this man's religion is worthless.

**1 Peter 4:8-10 ESV**   Keep loving one another earnestly, since love covers a multitude of sins. Show hospitality to one another without grumbling. As each has received a gift, use it to serve one another.

**Ezekiel 11:12 TNIV**   You will know that I am the LORD, for you have not followed my decrees or kept my laws but have conformed to the standards of the nations around you.

**Mark 8:36-38 CEV**   What will you gain, if you own the whole world but destroy yourself? What could you give to get back your soul? Don't be ashamed of me and my message among these unfaithful and sinful people! If you are, the Son of Man will be ashamed of you when he comes in the glory of his Father with the holy angels.

**Luke 11:23 NIV**   He who is not with me is against me, and he who does not gather with me, scatters.

**Romans 12:1-2 NCV**   Since God has shown us great mercy, I beg you to offer your lives as a living sacrifice to him. Your offering must be only for God and pleasing to him, which is the spiritual way for you to worship. Do not be shaped by this world; instead be changed within by a new way of thinking. Then you will be able to decide what God wants for you; you will know what is good and pleasing to him and what is perfect.

**1 Thessalonians 2:4 NLT**   We speak as messengers approved by God to be entrusted with the Good News. Our purpose is to please God, not people. He alone examines the motives of our hearts.

**Hebrews 10:23 TNIV**   Let us hold unswervingly to the hope we profess, for he who promised is faithful.

**James 1:14-15 NKJV**   Each one is tempted when he is drawn away by his own desires and enticed. Then, when desire has conceived, it gives birth to sin; and sin, when it is full-grown, brings forth death.

**Revelation 3:15-16 NKJV**   I know your works, that you are neither cold nor hot. I could wish you were cold or hot. So then, because you are lukewarm, and neither cold nor hot, I will vomit you out of My mouth.

**Psalm 36:1-3 NLT**   Sin whispers to the wicked, deep within their hearts. They have no fear of God at all. In their blind conceit, they cannot see how wicked they really are. Everything they say is crooked and deceitful. They refuse to act wisely or do good.

**Psalm 73:6-8 NIV**   Pride is their necklace; they clothe themselves with violence. From their callous hearts comes iniquity; the evil conceits of their minds know no limits. They scoff, and speak with malice; in their arrogance they threaten oppression.

**Psalm 123:3-4 CEV**   Please have mercy, LORD! We have been insulted more than we can stand, and we can't take more abuse from those proud, conceited people.

**Psalm 131:1-2 CEV**   I am not conceited, LORD, and I don't waste my time on impossible schemes. But I have learned to feel safe and satisfied, just like a young child on its mother's lap.

**Jeremiah 9:23-24 TNIV**   Let not the wise boast of their wisdom or the strong boast of their strength or the rich boast of their riches, but let those who boast boast about this: that they understand and know me, that I am the LORD, who exercises kindness, justice and righteousness on earth, for in these I delight.

**Romans 12:16 NIV**   Live in harmony with one another. Do not be proud, but be willing to associate with people of low position. Do not be conceited.

**Galatians 5:25-26 TNIV**   Since we live by the Spirit, let us keep in step with the Spirit. Let us not become conceited, provoking and envying each other.

**Psalm 32:3-6 TNIV**   When I kept silent, my bones wasted away through my groaning all day long. For day and night your hand was heavy on me; my strength was sapped as in the heat of summer. Then I acknowledged my sin to you and did not cover up my iniquity. I said, "I will confess my transgressions to the LORD." And you forgave the guilt of my sin. Therefore let all the faithful pray to you while you may be found.

**Psalm 66:18 NLT**   If I had not confessed the sin in my heart, the Lord would not have listened.

**Matthew 7:21-23 NCV**   Not all those who say "You are the Lord" will enter the kingdom of heaven. The only people who will enter the kingdom of heaven are those who do what my Father in heaven wants. On the last day many people will say to me, "Lord, Lord, we spoke for you, and through you we forced out demons and did many miracles." Then I will tell them clearly, "Get away from me, you who do evil. I never knew you."

**Romans 10:9-10 HCSB**   If you confess with your mouth, "Jesus is Lord," and believe in your heart that God raised Him from the dead, you will be saved. With the heart one believes, resulting in righteousness, and with the mouth one confesses, resulting in salvation.

**James 5:16 WEB**   Confess your offenses one to another, and pray one for another, that you may be healed. The effective, earnest prayer of a righteous man is powerfully effective.

**1 John 1:9 GNT**   If we confess our sins to God, he will keep his promise and do what is right: he will forgive us our sins and purify us from all our wrongdoing.

**1 John 4:15-16 NCV**   Whoever confesses that Jesus is the Son of God has God living inside, and that person lives in God. And so we know the love that God has for us, and we trust that love. God is love. Those who live in love live in God.

**Joshua 1:5 NCV**   No one will be able to defeat you all your life. Just as I was with Moses, so I will be with you. I will not leave you or forget you.

**Psalm 71:5 NASB**   You are my hope; O Lord God, You are my confidence from my youth.

**Psalm 146:3-5 NLT**   Don't put your confidence in powerful people; there is no help for you there. When their breathing stops, they return to the earth, and all their plans die with them. But joyful are those who have the God of Israel as their helper, whose hope is in the Lord their God.

**Proverbs 3:26 NKJV**   The Lord will be your confidence, and will keep your foot from being caught.

**Jeremiah 17:7 AMP**   Blessed is the man who believes in, trusts in, and relies on the Lord, and whose hope and confidence the Lord is.

**John 15:7 AMP**   If you live in Me [abide vitally united to Me] and My words remain in you and continue to live in your hearts, ask whatever you will, and it shall be done for you.

**Romans 12:3 NCV**   Do not think you are better than you are. You must decide what you really are by the amount of faith God has given you.

**Philippians 3:3 NKJV**   We are the circumcision, who worship God in the Spirit, rejoice in Christ Jesus, and have no confidence in the flesh.

**Hebrews 10:35 ESV**   Do not throw away your confidence, which has a great reward.

**1 John 5:14-15 CEV**   We are certain that God will hear our prayers when we ask for what pleases him. And if we know that God listens when we pray, we are sure that our prayers have already been answered.

# CONFORMITY

**Ezekiel 11:12 CEV**   You will realize that while you were following the laws of nearby nations, you were disobeying my laws and teachings. And I am the LORD!

**Romans 8:29 TNIV**   Those God foreknew he also predestined to be conformed to the image of his Son.

**Romans 12:1-2 NCV**   I beg you to offer your lives as a living sacrifice to him. Your offering must be only for God and pleasing to him, which is the spiritual way for you to worship. Do not be shaped by this world; instead be changed within by a new way of thinking. Then you will be able to decide what God wants for you; you will know what is good and pleasing to him and what is perfect.

**2 Corinthians 6:14-16 CEV**   Stay away from people who are not followers of the Lord! Can someone who is good get along with someone who is evil? Are light and darkness the same? Is Christ a friend of Satan? Can people who follow the Lord have anything in common with those who don't? Do idols belong in the temple of God? We are the temple of the living God, as God himself says, "I will live with these people and walk among them. I will be their God, and they will be my people."

**Philippians 2:13 HCSB**   For it is God who is working in you, enabling you both to will and to act for His good purpose.

**Philippians 4:13 CEV**   Christ gives me the strength to face anything.

**1 Peter 1:13-17 NCV**   Prepare your minds for service and have self-control. All your hope should be for the gift of grace that will be yours when Jesus Christ is shown to you. Now that you are obedient children of God do not live as you did in the past. You did not understand, so you did the evil things you wanted. But be holy in all you do, just as God, the One who called you, is holy. It is written in the Scriptures: "You must be holy, because I am holy." You pray to God and call him Father, and he judges each person's work equally. So while you are here on earth, you should live with respect for God.

# CONFUSION

**Proverbs 3:5-6 CEV**   With all your heart you must trust the LORD and not your own judgment. Always let him lead you, and he will clear the road for you to follow.

**Isaiah 30:21 NCV**   If you go the wrong way—to the right or to the left—you will hear a voice behind you saying, "This is the right way. You should go this way."

**Romans 8:6 NCV**   If people's thinking is controlled by the sinful self, there is death. But if their thinking is controlled by the Spirit, there is life and peace.

**1 Corinthians 14:33 NKJV**   God is not the author of confusion but of peace, as in all the churches of the saints.

**Ephesians 4:17-21 CEV**   As a follower of the Lord, I order you to stop living like stupid, godless people. Their minds are in the dark, and they are stubborn and ignorant and have missed out on the life that comes from God. They no longer have any feelings about what is right, and they are so greedy that they do all kinds of indecent things. But that isn't what you were taught about Jesus Christ. He is the truth, and you heard about him and learned about him.

**Philippians 4:6-7 NCV**   Do not worry about anything, but pray and ask God for everything you need, always giving thanks. And God's peace, which is so great we cannot understand it, will keep your hearts and minds in Christ Jesus.

**James 3:16-17 NKJV**   Where envy and self-seeking exist, confusion and every evil thing are there. But the wisdom that is from above is first pure, then peaceable, gentle, willing to yield, full of mercy and good fruits, without partiality and without hypocrisy.

**1 Peter 5:7 CEV**   God cares for you, so turn all your worries over to him.

**2 Samuel 24:10 NLT**   After he had taken the census, David's conscience began to bother him. And he said to the LORD, "I have sinned greatly and shouldn't have taken the census. Please forgive me, LORD, for doing this foolish thing."

**Proverbs 28:13-14 TNIV**   Those who conceal their sins do not prosper, but those who confess and renounce them find mercy. Blessed are those who always tremble before God, but those who harden their hearts fall into trouble.

**Acts 24:16 TNIV**   I strive always to keep my conscience clear before God and all people.

**1 Corinthians 4:3-4 NIV**   I care very little if I am judged by you or by any human court; indeed, I do not even judge myself. My conscience is clear, but that does not make me innocent. It is the Lord who judges me.

**Hebrews 9:14 NCV**   How much more is done by the blood of Christ. He offered himself through the eternal Spirit as a perfect sacrifice to God. His blood will make our consciences pure from useless acts so we may serve the living God.

**Hebrews 10:22-24 TNIV**   Let us draw near to God with a sincere heart in full assurance of faith, having our hearts sprinkled to cleanse us from a guilty conscience and having our bodies washed with pure water. Let us hold unswervingly to the hope we profess, for he who promised is faithful. And let us consider how we may spur one another on toward love and good deeds.

**Hebrews 13:18 NIV**   Pray for us. We are sure that we have a clear conscience and desire to live honorably in every way.

**1 John 3:21 GNT**   If our conscience does not condemn us, we have courage in God's presence.

# CONSEQUENCES

**Matthew 5:9 WEB**   Blessed are the peacemakers, for they shall be called sons of God.

**Mark 8:38 CEV**   Don't be ashamed of me and my message among these unfaithful and sinful people! If you are, the Son of Man will be ashamed of you when he comes in the glory of his Father with the holy angels.

**Mark 16:16 NCV**   Anyone who believes and is baptized will be saved, but anyone who does not believe will be punished.

**Luke 6:35 NLT**   Love your enemies! Do good to them! Lend to them without expecting to be repaid. Then your reward from heaven will be very great, and you will truly be acting as children of the Most High, for he is kind to those who are unthankful and wicked.

**John 3:16 NKJV**   God so loved the world that He gave His only begotten Son, that whoever believes in Him should not perish but have everlasting life.

**Acts 3:19-20 NCV**   You must change your hearts and lives! Come back to God, and he will forgive your sins. Then the Lord will send the time of rest. And he will send Jesus, the One he chose to be the Christ.

**Romans 5:12 NCV**   Sin came into the world because of what one man did, and with sin came death. This is why everyone must die—because everyone sinned.

**2 Corinthians 3:16-17 NRSV**   When one turns to the Lord, the veil is removed. Now the Lord is the Spirit, and where the Spirit of the Lord is, there is freedom.

**Hebrews 11:6 WEB**   Without faith it is impossible to be well pleasing to him, for he who comes to God must believe that he exists, and that he is a rewarder of those who seek him.

**Psalm 90:14 GNT**   Fill us each morning with your constant love, so that we may sing and be glad all our life.

**Proverbs 14:30 NKJV**   A sound heart is life to the body, but envy is rottenness to the bones.

**Proverbs 15:16 NCV**   It is better to be poor and respect the LORD than to be wealthy and have much trouble.

**Habakkuk 3:17-19 TNIV**   Though the fig tree does not bud and there are no grapes on the vines, though the olive crop fails and the fields produce no food, though there are no sheep in the pen and no cattle in the stalls, yet I will rejoice in the LORD, I will be joyful in God my Savior. The Sovereign LORD is my strength; he makes my feet like the feet of a deer, he enables me to tread on the heights.

**Matthew 6:33 TNIV**   Seek first his kingdom and his righteousness, and all these things will be given to you as well.

**Luke 12:15 NCV**   Be careful and guard against all kinds of greed. Life is not measured by how much one owns.

**Philippians 4:12 NIV**   I know what it is to be in need, and I know what it is to have plenty. I have learned the secret of being content in any and every situation, whether well fed or hungry, whether living in plenty or in want.

**1 Timothy 6:6-8 MSG**   A devout life does bring wealth, but it's the rich simplicity of being yourself before God. Since we entered the world penniless and will leave it penniless, if we have bread on the table and shoes on our feet, that's enough.

**Hebrews 13:5 CEV**   Don't fall in love with money. Be satisfied with what you have. The Lord has promised that he will not leave us or desert us.

**Job 6:24-25 NIV**   Teach me, and I will be quiet; show me where I have been wrong. How painful are honest words! But what do your arguments prove?

**Psalm 141:5 NCV**   If a good person punished me, that would be kind. If he corrected me, that would be like perfumed oil on my head. I shouldn't refuse it. But I pray against those who do evil.

**Proverbs 3:11-12 NCV**   Do not reject the LORD's discipline, and don't get angry when he corrects you. The LORD corrects those he loves, just as parents correct the child they delight in.

**Proverbs 6:20-23 NCV**   My son, keep your father's commands, and don't forget your mother's teaching. Keep their words in mind forever as though you had them tied around your neck. They will guide you when you walk. They will guard you when you sleep. They will speak to you when you are awake. These commands are like a lamp; this teaching is like a light. And the correction that comes from them will help you have life.

**Proverbs 10:17 GNT**   People who listen when they are corrected will live, but those who will not admit that they are wrong are in danger.

**Proverbs 12:1 NKJV**   Whoever loves instruction loves knowledge, but he who hates correction is stupid.

**Proverbs 13:24 MSG**   A refusal to correct is a refusal to love; love your children by disciplining them.

**Proverbs 19:18 NCV**   Correct your children while there is still hope; do not let them destroy themselves.

**Proverbs 29:15-17 WEB**   The rod of correction gives wisdom, but a child left to himself causes shame to his mother. When the wicked increase, sin increases; but the righteous will see their downfall. Correct your son, and he will give you peace; yes, he will bring delight to your soul.

# COUNSELING

**Job 12:13 WEB**   With God is wisdom and might. He has counsel and understanding.

**Psalm 32:8 WEB**   I will instruct you and teach you in the way which you shall go. I will counsel you with my eye on you.

**Psalm 107:10-11 HCSB**   Others sat in darkness and gloom—prisoners in cruel chains—because they rebelled against God's commands and despised the counsel of the Most High.

**Proverbs 1:5 NKJV**   A wise man will hear and increase learning, And a man of understanding will attain wise counsel.

**Proverbs 1:33 NCV**   Those who listen to me will live in safety and be at peace, without fear of injury.

**Proverbs 13:10 MSG**   Arrogant know-it-alls stir up discord, but wise men and women listen to each other's counsel.

**Proverbs 15:7 NLT**   The lips of the wise give good advice; the heart of a fool has none to give.

**Proverbs 15:22 WEB**   Where there is no counsel, plans fail; but in a multitude of counselors they are established.

**Proverbs 19:20-21 NKJV**   Listen to counsel and receive instruction, That you may be wise in your latter days. There are many plans in a man's heart, Nevertheless the Lord's counsel—that will stand.

**Galatians 6:1-2 WEB**   Brothers, even if a man is caught in some fault, you who are spiritual must restore such a one in a spirit of gentleness; looking to yourself so that you also aren't tempted. Bear one another's burdens, and so fulfill the law of Christ.

**James 5:16 NCV**   Confess your sins to each other and pray for each other so God can heal you. When a believing person prays, great things happen.

# COURAGE

**Deuteronomy 31:6 TNIV**   Be strong and courageous. Do not be afraid or terrified because of them, for the LORD your God goes with you; he will never leave you nor forsake you.

**Joshua 1:7 NLT**   Be strong and very courageous. Be careful to obey all the instructions Moses gave you. Do not deviate from them, turning either to the right or to the left. Then you will be successful in everything you do.

**2 Samuel 10:12 NCV**   Be strong. We must fight bravely for our people and the cities of our God. The LORD will do what he thinks is right.

**2 Chronicles 20:17 NASB**   Do not fear or be dismayed; tomorrow go out to face them, for the LORD is with you.

**2 Chronicles 32:7-8 TNIV**   Be strong and courageous. Do not be afraid or discouraged because of the king of Assyria and the vast army with him, for there is a greater power with us than with him. . . . With us is the LORD our God to help us and to fight our battles.

**Psalm 27:14 NASB**   Wait for the LORD; be strong and let your heart take courage; yes, wait for the LORD.

**1 Corinthians 16:13-14 TNIV**   Be on your guard; stand firm in the faith; be courageous; be strong. Do everything in love.

**Philippians 1:19-20 NCV**   Because you are praying for me and the Spirit of Jesus Christ is helping me, I know this trouble will bring my freedom. I expect and hope that I will not fail Christ in anything but that I will have the courage now, as always, to show the greatness of Christ in my life here on earth, whether I live or die.

**Hebrews 13:20-21 NIV**   May the God of peace, who through the blood of the eternal covenant brought back from the dead our Lord Jesus, that great Shepherd of the sheep, equip you with everything good for doing his will, and may he work in us what is pleasing to him, through Jesus Christ, to whom be glory for ever and ever. Amen.

**Nehemiah 9:6 CEV**   You alone are the LORD, Creator of the heavens and all the stars, Creator of the earth and those who live on it, Creator of the ocean and all its creatures. You are the source of life, praised by the stars that fill the heavens.

**Psalm 19:1 CEV**   The heavens keep telling the wonders of God, and the skies declare what he has done.

**Psalm 33:6-9 NCV**   The sky was made at the LORD's command. By the breath from his mouth, he made all the stars. He gathered the water of the sea into a heap. He made the great ocean stay in its place. All the earth should worship the LORD; the whole world should fear him. He spoke, and it happened. He commanded, and it appeared.

**Psalm 46:8 NCV**   Come and see what the LORD has done, the amazing things he has done on the earth.

**Psalm 64:9 AMP**   All men shall [reverently] fear and be in awe; and they will declare the work of God, for they will wisely consider and acknowledge that it is His doing.

**Psalm 65:9-10 NASB**   You visit the earth and cause it to overflow; You greatly enrich it; the stream of God is full of water; You prepare their grain, for thus You prepare the earth. You water its furrows abundantly, You settle its ridges, You soften it with showers, You bless its growth.

**Psalm 147:4 AMP**   He determines and counts the number of the stars; He calls them all by their names.

**Hebrews 11:3 ESV**   By faith we understand that the universe was created by the word of God, so that what is seen was not made out of things that are visible.

**Revelation 4:11 WEB**   Worthy are you, our Lord and our God, to receive the glory, the honor, and the power, for you created all things, and because of your desire they existed, and were created.

**Psalm 7:1-2 AMP**  O Lord my God, in You I take refuge and put my trust; save me from all those who pursue and persecute me, and deliver me, Lest my foe tear my life [from my body] like a lion, dragging me away while there is none to deliver.

**Psalm 19:14 WEB**  Let the words of my mouth and the meditation of my heart be acceptable in your sight, O Yahweh, my rock and my redeemer.

**Proverbs 15:31-32 NLT**  If you listen to constructive criticism, you will be at home among the wise. If you reject criticism, you only harm yourself; but if you listen to correction, you grow in understanding.

**Proverbs 19:11 NCV**  The wise are patient; they will be honored if they ignore insults.

**Matthew 5:11 ESV**  Blessed are you when others revile you and persecute you and utter all kinds of evil against you falsely on my account.

**Matthew 7:3-5 CEV**  You can see the speck in your friend's eye, but you don't notice the log in your own eye. How can you say, "My friend, let me take the speck out of your eye," when you don't see the log in your own eye? You're nothing but show-offs! First, take the log out of your own eye. Then you can see how to take the speck out of your friend's eye.

**2 Corinthians 8:20 NCV**  We are being careful so that no one will criticize us for the way we are handling this large gift.

**James 3:9-11 NCV**  We use our tongues to praise our Lord and Father, but then we curse people, whom God made like himself. Praises and curses come from the same mouth! My brothers and sisters, this should not happen. Do good and bad water flow from the same spring?

**Isaiah 53:4-5 ESV**   Surely he has borne our griefs and carried our sorrows; yet we esteemed him stricken, smitten by God, and afflicted. But he was wounded for our transgressions; he was crushed for our iniquities; upon him was the chastisement that brought us peace, and with his stripes we are healed.

**Matthew 10:38 ESV**   Whoever does not take his cross and follow me is not worthy of me.

**Mark 14:35-36 WEB**   He went forward a little, and fell on the ground, and prayed that, if it were possible, the hour might pass away from him. He said, "Abba, Father, all things are possible to you. Please remove this cup from me. However, not what I want, but what you want."

**Luke 14:27 NASB**   Whoever does not carry his own cross and come after Me cannot be My disciple.

**Romans 6:6 CEV**   We know that the persons we used to be were nailed to the cross with Jesus. This was done, so that our sinful bodies would no longer be the slaves of sin.

**1 Corinthians 1:18 NCV**   The teaching about the cross is foolishness to those who are being lost, but to us who are being saved it is the power of God.

**Galatians 2:20 NCV**   I was put to death on the cross with Christ, and I do not live anymore—it is Christ who lives in me. I still live in my body, but I live by faith in the Son of God who loved me and gave himself to save me.

**Galatians 6:14 TNIV**   May I never boast except in the cross of our Lord Jesus Christ, through which the world has been crucified to me, and I to the world.

**1 Peter 2:24 NCV**   Christ carried our sins in his body on the cross so we would stop living for sin and start living for what is right.

**Genesis 21:17-18 TNIV**   God heard the boy crying, and the angel of God called to Hagar from heaven and said to her, "What is the matter, Hagar? Do not be afraid; God has heard the boy crying as he lies there. Lift the boy up and take him by the hand, for I will make him into a great nation."

**Exodus 3:7-8 HCSB**   I have observed the misery of My people in Egypt, and have heard them crying out because of their oppressors, and I know about their sufferings. I have come down to rescue them.

**Psalm 34:17-18 MSG**   Is anyone crying for help? GOD is listening, ready to rescue you. If your heart is broken, you'll find GOD right there; if you're kicked in the gut, he'll help you catch your breath.

**Psalm 69:2-3 AMP**   I sink in deep mire, where there is no foothold; I have come into deep waters, where the floods overwhelm me. I am weary with my crying; my throat is parched; my eyes fail with waiting [hopefully] for my God.

**Psalm 88:9 HCSB**   My eyes are worn out from crying. LORD, I cry out to You all day long; I spread out my hands to You.

**Psalm 116:7-9 ESV**   Return, O my soul, to your rest; for the LORD has dealt bountifully with you. For you have delivered my soul from death, my eyes from tears, my feet from stumbling; I will walk before the LORD in the land of the living.

**John 16:22 CEV**   You are now very sad. But later I will see you, and you will be so happy that no one will be able to change the way you feel.

**Revelation 21:3-4 ESV**   Behold, the dwelling place of God is with man. He will dwell with them, and they will be his people, and God himself will be with them as their God. He will wipe away every tear from their eyes, and death shall be no more, neither shall there be mourning, nor crying, nor pain anymore, for the former things have passed away.

**Exodus 20:7 CEV**   Do not misuse my name. I am the LORD your God, and I will punish anyone who misuses my name.

**Psalm 141:3 ESV**   Set a guard, O LORD, over my mouth; keep watch over the door of my lips!

**Proverbs 13:3 NIV**   He who guards his lips guards his life, but he who speaks rashly will come to ruin.

**Proverbs 21:23 MSG**   Watch your words and hold your tongue; you'll save yourself a lot of grief.

**Ephesians 4:29 NLT**   Don't use foul or abusive language. Let everything you say be good and helpful, so that your words will be an encouragement to those who hear them.

**Colossians 3:8 BBE**   It is right for you to put away all these things; wrath, passion, bad feeling, curses, unclean talk.

**James 1:26 ESV**   If anyone thinks he is religious and does not bridle his tongue but deceives his heart, this person's religion is worthless.

**James 3:8-10 WEB**   Nobody can tame the tongue. It is a restless evil, full of deadly poison. With it we bless our God and Father, and with it we curse men, who are made in the image of God. Out of the same mouth comes forth blessing and cursing. My brothers, these things ought not to be so.

**1 Peter 2:21-23 BBE**   This is God's purpose for you: because Jesus himself underwent punishment for you, giving you an example, so that you might go in his footsteps: Who did no evil, and there was no deceit in his mouth: To sharp words he gave no sharp answer; when he was undergoing pain, no angry word came from his lips; but he put himself into the hands of the judge of righteousness.

**Leviticus 19:28 NCV**   You must not cut your body to show sadness for someone who died or put tattoo marks on yourselves. I am the LORD.

**Proverbs 3:5–8 TNIV**   Trust in the LORD with all your heart and lean not on your own understanding; in all your ways submit to him, and he will make your paths straight. Do not be wise in your own eyes; fear the LORD and shun evil. This will bring health to your body and nourishment to your bones.

**Isaiah 49:13 NLT**   The LORD has comforted his people and will have compassion on them in their suffering.

**Romans 12:1 MSG**   Take your everyday, ordinary life—your sleeping, eating, going-to-work, and walking-around life—and place it before God as an offering. Embracing what God does for you is the best thing you can do for him.

**Romans 15:13 ESV**   May the God of hope fill you with all joy and peace in believing, so that by the power of the Holy Spirit you may abound in hope.

**2 Timothy 2:22 CEV**   Run from temptations that capture young people. Always do the right thing. Be faithful, loving, and easy to get along with. Worship with people whose hearts are pure.

**Hebrews 10:22–23 NCV**   Let us come near to God with a sincere heart and a sure faith, because we have been made free from a guilty conscience, and our bodies have been washed with pure water. Let us hold firmly to the hope that we have confessed, because we can trust God to do what he promised.

**James 5:16 NCV**   Confess your sins to each other and pray for each other so God can heal you. When a believing person prays, great things happen.

**Exodus 15:20-21 NCV** Aaron's sister Miriam, a prophetess, took a tambourine in her hand. All the women followed her, playing tambourines and dancing. Miriam told them: "Sing to the Lord, because he is worthy of great honor; he has thrown the horse and its rider into the sea."

**1 Samuel 18:6 NCV** After David had killed the Philistine, he and the men returned home. Women came out from all the towns of Israel to meet King Saul. They sang songs of joy, danced, and played tambourines and stringed instruments.

**2 Samuel 6:14-15 HCSB** David was dancing with all his might before the Lord wearing a linen ephod. He and the whole house of Israel were bringing up the ark of the Lord with shouts and the sound of the ram's horn.

**Psalm 30:11-12 NCV** You changed my sorrow into dancing. You took away my clothes of sadness, and clothed me in happiness. I will sing to you and not be silent. Lord, my God, I will praise you forever.

**Psalm 149:3 WEB** Let them praise his name in the dance! Let them sing praises to him with tambourine and harp!

**Jeremiah 31:11-13 NLT** The Lord has redeemed Israel from those too strong for them. They will come home and sing songs of joy on the heights of Jerusalem. They will be radiant because of the Lord's good gifts. . . . The young women will dance for joy, and the men—old and young—will join in the celebration.

**1 Corinthians 6:20 NASB** You have been bought with a price: therefore glorify God in your body.

**2 Timothy 2:22 NKJV** Flee also youthful lusts; but pursue righteousness, faith, love, peace with those who call on the Lord out of a pure heart.

# DARKNESS

**Psalm 18:28-30 NIV**   You, O LORD, keep my lamp burning; my God turns my darkness into light. With your help I can advance against a troop; with my God I can scale a wall. As for God, his way is perfect; the word of the LORD is flawless. He is a shield for all who take refuge in him.

**Isaiah 50:10 TNIV**   Who among you fears the LORD and obeys the word of his servant? Let those who walk in the dark, who have no light, trust in the name of the LORD and rely on their God.

**John 3:19-20 NLT**   God's light came into the world, but people loved the darkness more than the light, for their actions were evil. All who do evil hate the light and refuse to go near it for fear their sins will be exposed.

**Romans 13:12-14 ESV**   Let us cast off the works of darkness and put on the armor of light. Let us walk properly as in the daytime, not in orgies and drunkenness, not in sexual immorality and sensuality, not in quarreling and jealousy. But put on the Lord Jesus Christ, and make no provision for the flesh, to gratify its desires.

**1 Corinthians 4:5 CEV**   Don't judge anyone until the Lord returns. He will show what is hidden in the dark and what is in everyone's heart.

**1 Thessalonians 5:3-6 NCV**   While people are saying, "We have peace and we are safe," they will be destroyed quickly. It is like pains that come quickly to a woman having a baby. Those people will not escape. But you, brothers and sisters, are not living in darkness, and so that day will not surprise you like a thief. You are all people who belong to the light and to the day. We do not belong to the night or to darkness. So we should not be like other people who are sleeping, but we should be alert and have self-control.

**1 Peter 2:9 NRSV**   You are a chosen race, a royal priesthood, a holy nation, God's own people, in order that you may proclaim the mighty acts of him who called you out of darkness into his marvelous light.

**Exodus 20:12 ESV**   Honor your father and your mother, that your days may be long in the land that the LORD your God is giving you.

**1 Chronicles 28:9 NCV**   The LORD knows what is in everyone's mind. He understands everything you think. If you go to him for help, you will get an answer.

**Psalm 119:9–11 TNIV**   How can those who are young keep their way pure? By living according to your word. I seek you with all my heart; do not let me stray from your commands. I have hidden your word in my heart that I might not sin against you.

**Psalm 147:3 ESV**   He heals the brokenhearted and binds up their wounds.

**Proverbs 20:11 MSG**   Young people eventually reveal by their actions if their motives are on the up and up.

**Song of Songs 8:4 MSG**   Don't excite love, don't stir it up, until the time is ripe—and you're ready.

**Matthew 5:8 HCSB**   Blessed are the pure in heart, because they will see God.

**1 Corinthians 13:4 NASB**   Love is patient, love is kind and is not jealous; love does not brag and is not arrogant.

**2 Corinthians 6:14 ESV**   Do not be unequally yoked with unbelievers. For what partnership has righteousness with lawlessness? Or what fellowship has light with darkness?

**Ephesians 4:1 TNIV**   I urge you to live a life worthy of the calling you have received.

# DEATH

**Genesis 9:6 AMP**   Whoever sheds man's blood, by man shall his blood be shed; for in the image of God He made man.

**2 Samuel 14:14 NLT**   All of us must die eventually. Our lives are like water spilled out on the ground, which cannot be gathered up again. But God does not just sweep life away; instead, he devises ways to bring us back when we have been separated from him.

**Psalm 33:18-19 NIV**   The eyes of the LORD are on those who fear him, on those whose hope is in his unfailing love, to deliver them from death.

**Psalm 49:10-12 NCV**   See, even wise people die. Fools and stupid people also die and leave their wealth to others. Their graves will always be their homes. They will live there from now on, even though they named places after themselves. Even rich people do not live forever; like the animals, people die.

**Psalm 49:14-15 NCV**   Like sheep, they must die, and death will be their shepherd. Honest people will rule over them in the morning, and their bodies will rot in a grave far from home. But God will save my life and will take me from the grave.

**Psalm 116:15 NASB**   Precious in the sight of the LORD is the death of His godly ones.

**Proverbs 14:32 CEV**   In times of trouble the wicked are destroyed, but even at death the innocent have faith.

**Ecclesiastes 8:8 MSG**   No one can control the wind or lock it in a box. No one has any say-so regarding the day of death.

**John 8:7 NIV**   If any one of you is without sin, let him be the first to throw a stone at her.

**John 10:27-29 GNT**  My sheep listen to my voice; I know them, and they follow me. I give them eternal life, and they shall never die. No one can snatch them away from me. What my Father has given me is greater than everything, and no one can snatch them away from the Father's care.

**John 11:25 NKJV**  Jesus said to her, "I am the resurrection and the life. He who believes in Me, though he may die, he shall live."

**Romans 5:8 NASB**  God demonstrates His own love toward us, in that while we were yet sinners, Christ died for us.

**Romans 6:23 ESV**  The wages of sin is death, but the free gift of God is eternal life in Christ Jesus our Lord.

**Romans 14:8-9 NLT**  If we live, it's to honor the Lord. And if we die, it's to honor the Lord. So whether we live or die, we belong to the Lord. Christ died and rose again for this very purpose—to be Lord both of the living and of the dead.

**1 Corinthians 15:55-57 NASB**  O death, where is your victory? O death, where is your sting? The sting of death is sin, and the power of sin is the law; but thanks be to God, who gives us the victory through our Lord Jesus Christ.

**2 Timothy 1:10 CEV**  Now Christ Jesus has come to show us the kindness of God. Christ our Savior defeated death and brought us the good news. It shines like a light and offers life that never ends.

**Revelation 21:4 AMP**  God will wipe away every tear from their eyes; and death shall be no more, neither shall there be anguish (sorrow and mourning) nor grief nor pain any more, for the old conditions and the former order of things have passed away.

# DEBT

**Exodus 22:25 CEV**   Don't charge interest when you lend money to any of my people who are in need.

**Deuteronomy 24:10-13 TNIV**   When you make a loan of any kind to a neighbor, do not go into the neighbor's house to get what is offered to you as a pledge. Stay outside and let the neighbor to whom you are making the loan bring the pledge out to you. If the neighbor is poor, do not go to sleep with that pledge in your possession. . . . Then you will be thanked, and it will be regarded as a righteous act in the sight of the LORD your God.

**Leviticus 25:16-17 ESV**   If the years are many, you shall increase the price, and if the years are few, you shall reduce the price, for it is the number of the crops that he is selling to you. You shall not wrong one another, but you shall fear your God, for I am the LORD your God.

**Proverbs 6:1-4 HCSB**   My son, if you have put up security for your neighbor or entered into an agreement with a stranger, you have been trapped by the words of your lips—ensnared by the words of your mouth. Do this, then, my son, and free yourself, for you have put yourself in your neighbor's power: Go, humble yourself, and plead with your neighbor. Don't give sleep to your eyes or slumber to your eyelids.

**Matthew 18:23-27 ESV**   The kingdom of heaven may be compared to a king who wished to settle accounts with his servants. When he began to settle, one was brought to him who owed him ten thousand talents. And since he could not pay, his master ordered him to be sold, with his wife and children and all that he had, and payment to be made. So the servant fell on his knees, imploring him, "Have patience with me, and I will pay you everything." And out of pity for him, the master of that servant released him and forgave him the debt.

**Romans 13:7-8 CEV**   Pay all that you owe, whether it is taxes and fees or respect and honor. Let love be your only debt! If you love others, you have done all that the Law demands.

**Leviticus 19:11 MSG**   Don't steal. Don't lie. Don't deceive anyone.

**Psalm 36:1–4 NLT**   Sin whispers to the wicked, deep within their hearts. They have no fear of God at all. In their blind conceit, they cannot see how wicked they really are. Everything they say is crooked and deceitful. They refuse to act wisely or do good. They lie awake at night, hatching sinful plots. Their actions are never good. They make no attempt to turn from evil.

**Psalm 55:23 NASB**   You, O God, will bring them down to the pit of destruction; men of bloodshed and deceit will not live out half their days. But I will trust in You.

**Jeremiah 17:9–10 NKJV**   The heart is deceitful above all things, and desperately wicked; who can know it? I, the Lord, search the heart, I test the mind, even to give every man according to his ways, according to the fruit of his doings.

**Romans 1:21–23 NCV**   They knew God, but they did not give glory to God or thank him. Their thinking became useless. Their foolish minds were filled with darkness. They said they were wise, but they became fools. They traded the glory of God who lives forever for the worship of idols made to look like earthly people, birds, animals, and snakes.

**Colossians 2:4–7 HCSB**   I am saying this so that no one will deceive you with persuasive arguments. For I may be absent in body, but I am with you in spirit, rejoicing to see your good order and the strength of your faith in Christ. Therefore as you have received Christ Jesus the Lord, walk in Him, rooted and built up in Him and established in the faith, just as you were taught, and overflowing with thankfulness.

**1 Peter 3:10–11 ESV**   Whoever desires to love life and see good days, let him keep his tongue from evil and his lips from speaking deceit; let him turn away from evil and do good; let him seek peace and pursue it.

**Psalm 119:133-138 NCV**   Guide my steps as you promised; don't let any sin control me. Save me from harmful people so I can obey your orders. Show your kindness to me, your servant. Teach me your demands. Tears stream from my eyes, because people do not obey your teachings. Lord, you do what is right, and your laws are fair. The rules you commanded are right and completely trustworthy.

**Proverbs 14:12 ESV**   There is a way that seems right to a man, but it's end is the way to death.

**Proverbs 21:2 NASB**   Every man's way is right in his own eyes, But the LORD weighs the hearts.

**Isaiah 53:6 NRSV**   All we like sheep have gone astray; we have all turned to our own way, and the Lord has laid on him the iniquity of us all.

**Matthew 6:33 WEB**   Seek first God's Kingdom, and his righteousness; and all these things shall be added to you.

**Philippians 1:9-11 NCV**   This is my prayer for you: that your love will grow more and more; that you will have knowledge and understanding with your love; that you will see the difference between good and bad and will choose the good; that you will be pure and without wrong for the coming of Christ; that you will do many good things with the help of Christ to bring glory and praise to God.

**Philippians 2:13 NCV**   God is working in you to help you want to do and be able to do what pleases him.

**2 Timothy 3:14-17 WEB**   Remain in the things which you have learned and have been assured of, knowing from whom you have learned them. From infancy, you have known the sacred writings which are able to make you wise to salvation through faith, which is in Christ Jesus. Every writing inspired by God is profitable for teaching, for reproof, for correction, and for instruction which is in righteousness, that the man of God may be complete, thoroughly equipped for every good work.

**Ezra 8:22-23 HCSB** "The hand of our God is gracious to all who seek Him, but His great anger is against all who abandon Him." So we fasted and pleaded with our God about this, and He granted our request.

**Psalm 50:15 ESV** Call upon me in the day of trouble; I will deliver you, and you shall glorify me.

**Isaiah 49:9 CEV** You will set prisoners free from dark dungeons to see the light of day.

**Matthew 8:16 CEV** That evening many people with demons in them were brought to Jesus. And with only a word he forced out the evil spirits and healed everyone who was sick.

**Matthew 10:7-8 HCSB** As you go, announce this: "The kingdom of heaven has come near." Heal the sick, raise the dead, cleanse those with skin diseases, drive out demons. You have received free of charge; give free of charge.

**Mark 16:17 NASB** These signs will accompany those who have believed: in My name they will cast out demons, they will speak with new tongues.

**Luke 10:17 HCSB** The Seventy returned with joy, saying, "Lord, even the demons submit to us in Your name."

**Acts 8:7 TNIV** With shrieks, evil spirits came out of many, and many who were paralyzed or lame were healed.

**Acts 10:38 ESV** God anointed Jesus of Nazareth with the Holy Spirit and with power. He went about doing good and healing all who were oppressed by the devil, for God was with him.

**Titus 2:14 NASB** Who gave Himself for us to redeem us from every lawless deed, and to purify for Himself a people for His own possession, zealous for good deeds.

**Matthew 8:16 NCV**  People brought to Jesus many who had demons. Jesus spoke and the demons left them, and he healed all the sick.

**Matthew 17:18 HCSB**  Jesus rebuked the demon, and it came out of him, and from that moment the boy was healed.

**Mark 9:19-20 CEV**  Jesus said, "You people don't have any faith! How much longer must I be with you? Why do I have to put up with you? Bring the boy to me." They brought the boy, and as soon as the demon saw Jesus, it made the boy shake all over. He fell down and began rolling on the ground and foaming at the mouth.

**Mark 9:21-24 TNIV**  Jesus asked the boy's father, "How long has he been like this?" "From childhood," he answered. "It has often thrown him into fire or water to kill him. But if you can do anything, take pity on us and help us." "'If you can'?" said Jesus. "Everything is possible for one who believes." Immediately the boy's fathers exclaimed, "I do believe; help me overcome my unbelief!"

**Mark 9:25-29 HCSB**  When Jesus saw that a crowd was rapidly coming together, He rebuked the unclean spirit, saying to it, "You mute and deaf spirit, I command you: come out of him and never enter him again!" Then it came out, shrieking and convulsing him violently. The boy became like a corpse, so that many said, "He's dead." But Jesus, taking him by the hand, raised him, and he stood up. After He went into a house, His disciples asked Him privately, "Why couldn't we drive it out?" And He told them, "This kind can come out by nothing but prayer and fasting."

**1 Corinthians 10:20-22 ESV**  I do not want you to be participants with demons. You cannot drink the cup of the Lord and the cup of demons. You cannot partake of the table of the Lord and the table of demons. Shall we provoke the Lord to jealousy? Are we stronger than he?

**James 2:19 TNIV**  You believe that there is one God. Good! Even the demons believe that—and shudder.

**Psalm 42:5 GNT**   Why am I so sad? Why am I so troubled? I will put my hope in God, and once again I will praise him, my savior and my God.

**Psalm 79:9 NKJV**   Help us, O God of our salvation, For the glory of Your name; and deliver us, and provide atonement for our sins, for Your name's sake!

**Psalm 143:3-8 NRSV**   The enemy has pursued me, crushing my life to the ground, making me sit in darkness like those long dead. Therefore my spirit faints within me; my heart within me is appalled. I remember the days of old, I think about all your deeds, I meditate on the works of your hands. I stretch out my hands to you; my soul thirsts for you like a parched land. Answer me quickly, O Lord; my spirit fails. Do not hide your face from me, or I shall be like those who go down to the Pit. Let me hear of your steadfast love in the morning, for in you I put my trust. Teach me the way I should go, for to you I lift up my soul.

**Isaiah 40:27-31 NIV**   Do you not know? Have you not heard? The Lord is the everlasting God, the Creator of the ends of the earth. He will not grow tired or weary, and his understanding no one can fathom. He gives strength to the weary and increases the power of the weak. Even youths grow tired and weary, and young men stumble and fall; but those who hope in the Lord will renew their strength. They will soar on wings like eagles; they will run and not grow weary, they will walk and not be faint.

**Isaiah 61:3 NLT**   To all who mourn in Israel, he will give beauty for ashes, joy instead of mourning, praise instead of despair. For the Lord has planted them like strong and graceful oaks for his own glory.

**1 Peter 5:6-9 NKJV**   Humble yourselves under the mighty hand of God, that He may exalt you in due time, casting all your care upon Him, for He cares for you. Be sober, be vigilant; because your adversary the devil walks about like a roaring lion, seeking whom he may devour. Resist him, steadfast in the faith, knowing that the same sufferings are experienced by your brotherhood in the world.

**Proverbs 3:15 CEV**   Wisdom is more valuable than precious jewels; nothing you want compares with her.

**Proverbs 11:23 NKJV**   The desire of the righteous is only good, but the expectation of the wicked is wrath.

**Isaiah 26:8 NASB**   We have waited for You eagerly; Your name, even Your memory, is the desire of our souls.

**Romans 7:18-19 TNIV**   I know that good itself does not dwell in me, that is, in my sinful nature. For I have the desire to do what is good, but I cannot carry it out. For I do not do the good I want to do, but the evil I do not want to do—this I keep on doing.

**Romans 9:16 GNT**   So then, everything depends, not on what we humans want or do, but only on God's mercy.

**Galatians 5:16-18 NASB**   Walk by the Spirit, and you will not carry out the desire of the flesh. For the flesh sets its desire against the Spirit, and the Spirit against the flesh; for these are in opposition to one another, so that you may not do the things that you please. But if you are led by the Spirit, you are not under the Law.

**2 Timothy 2:22 BBE**   Keep yourself from those desires of the flesh which are strong when the body is young, and go after righteousness, faith, love, peace, with those whose prayers go up to the Lord from a clean heart.

**Hebrews 13:18 NIV**   Pray for us. We are sure that we have a clear conscience and desire to live honorably in every way.

**James 1:13-15 CEV**   Don't blame God when you are tempted! God cannot be tempted by evil, and he doesn't use evil to tempt others. We are tempted by our own desires that drag us off and trap us. Our desires make us sin, and when sin is finished with us, it leaves us dead.

**Deuteronomy 4:9 NCV**   Be careful! Watch out and don't forget the things you have seen. Don't forget them as long as you live, but teach them to your children and grandchildren.

**Proverbs 4:23 TNIV**   Above all else, guard your heart, for everything you do flows from it.

**Isaiah 56:1–2 CEV**   The LORD said: Be honest and fair! Soon I will come to save you; my saving power will be seen everywhere on earth. I will bless everyone who respects the Sabbath and refuses to do wrong.

**Mark 1:35 NIV**   Very early in the morning, while it was still dark, Jesus got up, left the house and went off to a solitary place, where he prayed.

**Romans 12:10–13 NKJV**   Be kindly affectionate to one another with brotherly love, in honor giving preference to one another; not lagging in diligence, fervent in spirit, serving the Lord; rejoicing in hope, patient in tribulation, continuing steadfastly in prayer, distributing to the needs of the saints, given to hospitality.

**1 Corinthians 15:58 CEV**   Stand firm and don't be shaken. Always keep busy working for the Lord. You know that everything you do for him is worthwhile.

**2 Corinthians 8:7 NKJV**   But as you abound in everything—in faith, in speech, in knowledge, in all diligence, and in your love for us—see that you abound in this grace also.

**Galatians 6:9 TNIV**   Let us not become weary in doing good, for at the proper time we will reap a harvest if we do not give up.

**Hebrews 6:11–12 TNIV**   We want each of you to show this same diligence to the very end, in order to make your hope sure. We do not want you to become lazy, but to imitate those who through faith and patience inherit what has been promised.

**Psalm 22:5 GNT**   They called to you and escaped from danger; they trusted you and were not disappointed.

**Isaiah 28:16-17 CEV**   I'm laying a firm foundation for the city of Zion. It's a valuable cornerstone proven to be trustworthy; no one who trusts it will ever be disappointed. Justice and fairness will be the measuring lines that help me build.

**Isaiah 40:31 NCV**   The people who trust the LORD will become strong again. They will rise up as an eagle in the sky; they will run and not need rest; they will walk and not become tired.

**Isaiah 49:23 CEV**   Then you will know that I am the LORD. You won't be disappointed if you trust in me.

**Isaiah 54:4 CEV**   Don't be afraid or ashamed and don't be discouraged. You won't be disappointed. Forget how sinful you were when you were young.

**Luke 1:45 ESV**   Blessed is she who believed that there would be a fulfillment of what was spoken to her from the Lord.

**Romans 10:11-12 NCV**   As the Scripture says, "Anyone who trusts in him will never be disappointed." That Scripture says "anyone" because there is no difference between those who are Jews and those who are not. The same Lord is the Lord of all and gives many blessings to all who trust in him.

**2 Corinthians 4:8-9 CEV**   We often suffer, but we are never crushed. Even when we don't know what to do, we never give up. In times of trouble, God is with us, and when we are knocked down, we get up again.

**2 Corinthians 12:10 TNIV**   For Christ's sake, I delight in weaknesses, in insults, in hardships, in persecutions, in difficulties. For when I am weak, then I am strong.

# DISCERNMENT

**Psalm 119:65-69 WEB**  Do good to your servant, according to your word, Yahweh. Teach me good judgment and knowledge, for I believe in your commandments. Before I was afflicted, I went astray; but now I observe your word. You are good, and do good. Teach me your statutes. The proud have smeared a lie upon me. With my whole heart, I will keep your precepts.

**Psalm 119:169 NLT**  O Lord, listen to my cry; give me the discerning mind you promised.

**Isaiah 11:2 WEB**  The Spirit of Yahweh shall rest on Him, the spirit of wisdom and understanding, the spirit of counsel and might, the spirit of knowledge.

**John 14:16-17 NIV**  I will ask the Father, and he will give you another Counselor to be with you forever—the Spirit of truth. The world cannot accept him, because it neither sees him nor knows him. But you know him, for he lives with you and will be in you.

**1 Corinthians 2:15-16 WEB**  He who is spiritual discerns all things, and he himself is judged by no one. For who has known the mind of the Lord, that he should instruct him? But we have Christ's mind.

**Philippians 1:9-11 NCV**  This is my prayer for you: that your love will grow more and more; that you will have knowledge and understanding with your love; that you will see the difference between good and bad and will choose the good; that you will be pure and without wrong for the coming of Christ; that you will do many good things with the help of Christ to bring glory and praise to God.

**Colossians 1:9-10 NKJV**  For this reason we also, since the day we heard it, do not cease to pray for you, and to ask that you may be filled with the knowledge of His will in all wisdom and spiritual understanding; that you may walk worthy of the Lord, fully pleasing Him.

**Matthew 10:1 ESV**   He called to him his twelve disciples and gave them authority over unclean spirits, to cast them out, and to heal every disease and every affliction.

**Matthew 16:24 NLT**   Jesus said to the disciples, "If any of you wants to be my follower, you must put aside your selfish ambition, shoulder your cross, and follow me."

**Mark 16:17-18 TNIV**   These signs will accompany those who believe: In my name they will drive out demons; they will speak in new tongues; they will pick up snakes with their hands; and when they drink deadly poison, it will not hurt them at all; they will place their hands on sick people, and they will get well.

**John 17:16-19 CEV**   They don't belong to this world, and neither do I. Your word is the truth. So let this truth make them completely yours. I am sending them into the world, just as you sent me. I have given myself completely for their sake, so that they may belong completely to the truth.

**Ephesians 5:1-2 ESV**   Be imitators of God, as beloved children. And walk in love, as Christ loved us and gave himself up for us, a fragrant offering and sacrifice to God.

**James 1:26 NLT**   If you claim to be religious but don't control your tongue, you are just fooling yourself, and your religion is worthless.

**1 Peter 2:4-5 ESV**   As you come to him, a living stone rejected by men but in the sight of God chosen and precious, you yourselves like living stones are being built up as a spiritual house, to be a holy priesthood, to offer spiritual sacrifices acceptable to God through Jesus Christ.

**1 Peter 2:16-17 ESV**   Live as people who are free, not using your freedom as a cover-up for evil, but living as servants of God. Honor everyone. Love the brotherhood. Fear God.

**Job 5:17-18 MSG**   What a blessing when God steps in and corrects you! Mind you, don't despise the discipline of Almighty God! True, he wounds, but he also dresses the wound; the same hand that hurts you, heals you.

**Proverbs 1:7 NLT**   Fear of the LORD is the foundation of true knowledge, but fools despise wisdom and discipline.

**Proverbs 15:32 NCV**   Those who refuse correction hate themselves, but those who accept correction gain understanding.

**Proverbs 22:15 MSG**   Young people are prone to foolishness and fads; the cure comes through tough-minded discipline.

**Proverbs 23:13-14 NLT**   Don't fail to discipline your children. They won't die if you spank them. Physical discipline may well save them from death.

**Romans 8:28 NASB**   We know that God causes all things to work together for good to those who love God, to those who are called according to His purpose.

**1 Corinthians 11:32 TNIV**   Nevertheless, when we are judged in this way by the Lord, we are being disciplined so that we will not be finally condemned with the world.

**Hebrews 12:10-13 TNIV**   Our parents disciplined us for a little while as they thought best; but God disciplines us for our good, that we may share in his holiness. No discipline seems pleasant at the time, but painful. Later on, however, it produces a harvest of righteousness and peace for those who have been trained by it. Therefore, strengthen your feeble arms and weak knees. "Make level paths for your feet," so that the lame may not be disabled, but rather healed.

**Joshua 1:9 HCSB**   Haven't I commanded you: be strong and courageous? Do not be afraid or discouraged, for the LORD your God is with you wherever you go.

**Psalm 34:17-20 GNT**   The righteous call to the Lord, and he listens; he rescues them from all their troubles. The Lord is near to those who are discouraged; he saves those who have lost all hope. Good people suffer many troubles, but the Lord saves them from them all; the Lord preserves them completely; not one of their bones is broken.

**Psalm 37:7 NIV**   Be still before the LORD and wait patiently for him; do not fret when men succeed in their ways, when they carry out their wicked schemes.

**Psalm 143:8 CEV**   Each morning let me learn more about your love because I trust you. I come to you in prayer, asking for your guidance.

**Psalm 147:2-5 HCSB**   The LORD rebuilds Jerusalem; He gathers Israel's exiled people. He heals the brokenhearted and binds up their wounds. He counts the number of the stars; He gives names to all of them. Our Lord is great, vast in power; His understanding is infinite.

**Isaiah 41:10 NIV**   Do not fear, for I am with you; do not be dismayed, for I am your God. I will strengthen you and help you; I will uphold you with my righteous right hand.

**Lamentations 3:21-26 GNT**   Hope returns when I remember this one thing: The Lord's unfailing love and mercy still continue, fresh as the morning, as sure as the sunrise. The Lord is all I have, and so in him I put my hope. The Lord is good to everyone who trusts in him, so it is best for us to wait in patience—to wait for him to save us.

**Hebrews 6:18-19 GNT**   We who have found safety with him are greatly encouraged to hold firmly to the hope placed before us. We have this hope as an anchor for our lives. It is safe and sure.

**Genesis 1:27 AMP**   God created man in His own image, in the image and likeness of God He created him; male and female He created them.

**Acts 10:28 NCV**   You people understand that it is against our Jewish law for Jewish people to associate with or visit anyone who is not Jewish. But God has shown me that I should not call any person "unholy" or "unclean."

**Romans 2:11 GNT**   God judges everyone by the same standard.

**Romans 12:10-14 ESV**   Love one another with brotherly affection. Outdo one another in showing honor. Do not be slothful in zeal, be fervent in spirit, serve the Lord. Rejoice in hope, be patient in tribulation, be constant in prayer. Contribute to the needs of the saints and seek to show hospitality. Bless those who persecute you; bless and do not curse them.

**Romans 12:16-17 ESV**   Live in harmony with one another. Do not be haughty, but associate with the lowly. Never be wise in your own sight. Repay no one evil for evil, but give thought to do what is honorable in the sight of all.

**Galatians 3:27-28 ESV**   For as many of you as were baptized into Christ have put on Christ. There is neither Jew nor Greek, there is neither slave nor free, there is no male and female, for you are all one in Christ Jesus.

**Ephesians 2:14 CEV**   Christ has made peace between Jews and Gentiles, and he has united us by breaking down the wall of hatred that separated us.

**James 2:1 NCV**   My dear brothers and sisters, as believers in our glorious Lord Jesus Christ, never think some people are more important than others.

**Genesis 26:24 NIV**   Do not be afraid, for I am with you.

**Exodus 20:3 HCSB**   Do not have other gods besides Me.

**Romans 6:12 NCV**   Do not let sin control your life here on earth.

**Romans 12:2 NASB**   Do not be conformed to this world, but be transformed by the renewing of your mind.

**Romans 12:16 GNT**   Do not be proud, but accept humble duties.

**1 Corinthians 15:33 TNIV**   Do not be misled: "Bad company corrupts good character."

**2 Corinthians 6:14 TNIV**   Do not be yoked together with unbelievers.

**Ephesians 4:26 ESV**   Do not let the sun go down on your anger.

**Ephesians 4:27 NCV**   Do not give the devil a way to defeat you.

**Ephesians 4:30 NLT**   Do not bring sorrow to God's Holy Spirit by the way you live.

**Ephesians 5:17 NKJV**   Do not be unwise, but understand what the will of the Lord is.

**Ephesians 5:18 NKJV**   Do not be drunk with wine.

**Hebrews 10:35 NASB**   Do not throw away your confidence, which has a great reward.

**1 Peter 3:3-4 ESV**   Do not let your adorning be external—the braiding of hair and the putting on of gold jewelry, or the clothing you wear—but let your adorning be the hidden person of the heart with the imperishable beauty of a gentle and quiet spirit, which in God's sight is very precious.

# DOUBT

**Psalm 32:8 NCV**   The LORD says, "I will make you wise and show you where to go. I will guide you and watch over you."

**Isaiah 40:28-29 ESV**   Have you not known? Have you not heard? The LORD is the everlasting God, the Creator of the ends of the earth. He does not faint or grow weary; his understanding is unsearchable. He gives power to the faint, and to him who has no might he increases strength.

**Matthew 14:30-32 NASB**   Seeing the wind, he became frightened, and beginning to sink, he cried out, "Lord, save me!" Immediately Jesus stretched out His hand and took hold of him, and said to him, "You of little faith, why did you doubt?" When they got into the boat, the wind stopped.

**Mark 11:23 NASB**   Truly I say to you, whoever says to this mountain, "Be taken up and cast into the sea," and does not doubt in his heart, but believes that what he says is going to happen, it will be granted him.

**Romans 10:16-17 GNT**   Not all have accepted the Good News. Isaiah himself said, "Lord, who believed our message?" So then, faith comes from hearing the message, and the message comes through preaching Christ.

**Hebrews 11:1-3 TNIV**   Now faith is being sure of what we hope for and certain of what we do not see. This is what the ancients were commended for. By faith we understand that the universe was formed at God's command, so that what is seen was not made out of what was visible.

**James 1:6 NASB**   He must ask in faith without any doubting, for the one who doubts is like the surf of the sea, driven and tossed by the wind.

# DRINKING

**Proverbs 13:20 NCV**   Spend time with the wise and you will become wise, but the friends of fools will suffer.

**Proverbs 23:17-21 CEV**   Don't be jealous of sinners, but always honor the LORD. Then you will truly have hope for the future. Listen to me, my children! Be wise and have enough sense to follow the right path. Don't be a heavy drinker or stuff yourself with food. It will make you feel drowsy, and you will end up poor with only rags to wear.

**Matthew 26:41 WEB**   Watch and pray, that you don't enter into temptation. The spirit indeed is willing, but the flesh is weak.

**Romans 13:12-14 ESV**   Let us walk properly as in the daytime, not in orgies and drunkenness, not in sexual immorality and sensuality, not in quarreling and jealousy. But put on the Lord Jesus Christ, and make no provision for the flesh, to gratify its desires.

**1 Corinthians 5:6-7 NLT**   How terrible that you should boast about your spirituality, and yet you let this sort of thing go on. Don't you realize that if even one person is allowed to go on sinning, soon all will be affected? Remove this wicked person from among you so that you can stay pure.

**1 Thessalonians 5:6-8 NCV**   We should not be like other people who are sleeping, but we should be alert and have self-control. Those who sleep, sleep at night. Those who get drunk, get drunk at night. But we belong to the day, so we should control ourselves. We should wear faith and love to protect us, and the hope of salvation should be our helmet.

**James 4:4 NCV**   You are not loyal to God! You should know that loving the world is the same as hating God. Anyone who wants to be a friend of the world becomes God's enemy.

**1 Peter 2:12 CEV**   Always let others see you behaving properly, even though they may still accuse you of doing wrong. Then on the day of judgment, they will honor God by telling the good things they saw you do.

**Psalm 62:8 CEV**  Trust God, my friends, and always tell him each one of your concerns. God is our place of safety.

**Luke 17:3 CEV**  Be careful what you do. Correct any followers of mine who sin, and forgive the ones who say they are sorry.

**Romans 13:1-3 MSG**  Live responsibly as a citizen. If you're irresponsible to the state, then you're irresponsible with God, and God will hold you responsible. Duly constituted authorities are only a threat if you're trying to get by with something. Decent citizens should have nothing to fear.

**Romans 13:4-5 MSG**  If you're breaking the rules right and left, watch out. The police aren't there just to be admired in their uniforms. God also has an interest in keeping order, and he uses them to do it. That's why you must live responsibly—not just to avoid punishment but also because it's the right way to live.

**1 Corinthians 15:33-34 NCV**  Do not be fooled: "Bad friends will ruin good habits." Come back to your right way of thinking and stop sinning.

**1 Peter 2:11-12 NCV**  Dear friends, you are like foreigners and strangers in this world. I beg you to avoid the evil things your bodies want to do that fight against your soul. People who do not believe are living all around you and might say that you are doing wrong. Live such good lives that they will see the good things you do and will give glory to God on the day when Christ comes again.

**1 John 2:15-17 TNIV**  Do not love the world or anything in the world. If you love the world, love for the Father is not in you. For everything in the world—the cravings of sinful people, the lust of their eyes and their boasting about what they have and do—comes not from the Father but from the world. The world and its desires pass away, but whoever does the will of God lives forever.

# DRUG ABUSE

**Psalm 107:28-32 NCV**   In their misery they cried out to the Lord, and he saved them from their troubles. He stilled the storm and calmed the waves. They were happy that it was quiet, and God guided them to the port they wanted. Let them give thanks to the Lord for his love and for the miracles he does for people.

**Proverbs 22:3 GNT**   Sensible people will see trouble coming and avoid it, but an unthinking person will walk right into it and regret it later.

**Matthew 11:28-29 NCV**   Come to me, all of you who are tired and have heavy loads, and I will give you rest. Accept my teachings and learn from me, because I am gentle and humble in spirit, and you will find rest for your lives.

**Romans 13:1-2 GNT**   Everyone must obey state authorities, because no authority exists without God's permission, and the existing authorities have been put there by God. Whoever opposes the existing authority opposes what God has ordered; and anyone who does so will bring judgment on himself.

**1 Corinthians 6:19-20 BBE**   Are you not conscious that your body is a house for the Holy Spirit which is in you, and which has been given to you by God? and you are not the owners of yourselves; for a payment has been made for you: let God be honoured in your body.

**1 Peter 1:14-15 MSG**   Don't lazily slip back into those old grooves of evil, doing just what you feel like doing. You didn't know any better then; you do now. As obedient children, let yourselves be pulled into a way of life shaped by God's life, a life energetic and blazing with holiness.

**1 Peter 5:8-9 NRSV**   Discipline yourselves, keep alert. Like a roaring lion your adversary the devil prowls around, looking for someone to devour. Resist him, steadfast in your faith, for you know that your brothers and sisters in all the world are undergoing the same kinds of suffering.

**Psalm 103:2-6 MSG**   O my soul, bless GOD, don't forget a single blessing! He forgives your sins—every one. He heals your diseases—every one. He redeems you from hell—saves your life! He crowns you with love and mercy—a paradise crown. He wraps you in goodness—beauty eternal. He renews your youth—you're always young in his presence. GOD makes everything come out right; he puts victims back on their feet.

**Psalm 107:17-21 MSG**   Some of you were sick because you'd lived a bad life, your bodies feeling the effects of your sin; you couldn't stand the sight of food, so miserable you thought you'd be better off dead. Then you called out to GOD in your desperate condition; he got you out in the nick of time. He spoke the word that healed you, that pulled you back from the brink of death. So thank GOD for his marvelous love, for his miracle mercy to the children he loves.

**Romans 12:1-2 CEV**   I beg you to offer your bodies to him as a living sacrifice, pure and pleasing. That's the most sensible way to serve God. Don't be like the people of this world, but let God change the way you think. Then you will know how to do everything that is good and pleasing to him.

**1 Corinthians 6:12 GNT**   Not everything is good for you. I could say that I am allowed to do anything, but I am not going to let anything make me its slave.

**1 Corinthians 6:19-20 ESV**   Do you not know that your body is a temple of the Holy Spirit within you, whom you have from God? You are not your own, for you were bought with a price. So glorify God in your body.

**1 Timothy 4:4-5 WEB**   For every creature of God is good, and nothing is to be rejected, if it is received with thanksgiving. For it is sanctified through the word of God and prayer.

# EMBARRASSMENT

**Isaiah 50:7 NKJV**  The Lord God will help Me; therefore I will not be disgraced; therefore I have set My face like a flint, and I know that I will not be ashamed.

**Isaiah 54:4 ESV**  Fear not, for you will not be ashamed; be not confounded, for you will not be disgraced; for you will forget the shame of your youth,

**Romans 1:16 TNIV**  I am not ashamed of the gospel, because it is the power of God that brings salvation to everyone who believes: first to the Jew, then to the Gentile.

**Romans 10:10-11 NCV**  We believe with our hearts, and so we are made right with God. And we declare with our mouths that we believe, and so we are saved. As the Scripture says, "Anyone who trusts in him will never be disappointed."

**2 Timothy 1:8 MSG**  Don't be embarrassed to speak up for our Master or for me, his prisoner. Take your share of suffering for the Message along with the rest of us. We can only keep on going, after all, by the power of God.

**2 Timothy 1:12 BBE**  I have no feeling of shame. For I have knowledge of him in whom I have faith, and I am certain that he is able to keep that which I have given into his care till that day.

**1 Peter 4:12-13 GNT**  Do not be surprised at the painful test you are suffering, as though something unusual were happening to you. Rather be glad that you are sharing Christ's sufferings, so that you may be full of joy when his glory is revealed.

**1 Peter 4:14 TNIV**  If you are insulted because of the name of Christ, you are blessed, for the Spirit of glory and of God rests on you.

**1 Peter 4:16 NCV**  If you suffer because you are a Christian, do not be ashamed. Praise God because you wear that name.

**Proverbs 15:30 MSG**   A twinkle in the eye means joy in the heart, and good news makes you feel fit as a fiddle.

**Romans 12:10 NLT**   Love each other with genuine affection, and take delight in honoring each other.

**Romans 15:13 ESV**   May the God of hope fill you with all joy and peace in believing, so that by the power of the Holy Spirit you may abound in hope.

**Ephesians 4:29 GNT**   Do not use harmful words, but only helpful words, the kind that build up and provide what is needed, so that what you say will do good to those who hear you.

**Philippians 2:1–4 ESV**   If there is any encouragement in Christ, any comfort from love, any participation in the Spirit, any affection and sympathy, complete my joy by being of the same mind, having the same love, being in full accord and of one mind. Do nothing from rivalry or conceit, but in humility count others more significant than yourselves. Let each of you look not only to his own interests, but also to the interests of others.

**1 Thessalonians 5:14 CEV**   Encourage anyone who feels left out, help all who are weak, and be patient with everyone.

**Hebrews 3:13 NCV**   Encourage each other every day while it is "today." Help each other so none of you will become hardened because sin has tricked you.

**Hebrews 10:23–25 TNIV**   Let us hold unswervingly to the hope we profess, for he who promised is faithful. And let us consider how we may spur one another on toward love and good deeds, not giving up meeting together, as some are in the habit of doing, but encouraging one another—and all the more as you see the Day approaching.

# END TIMES

**2 Thessalonians 1:7-8 NLT**   God will provide rest for you who are being persecuted and also for us when the Lord Jesus appears from heaven. He will come with his mighty angels, in flaming fire, bringing judgment on those who don't know God and on those who refuse to obey the Good News of our Lord Jesus.

**2 Timothy 3:1-5 CEV**   You can be certain that in the last days there will be some very hard times. People will love only themselves and money. They will be proud, stuck-up, rude, and disobedient to their parents. They will also be ungrateful, godless, heartless, and hateful. Their words will be cruel, and they will have no self-control or pity. These people will hate everything that is good. They will be sneaky, reckless, and puffed up with pride. Instead of loving God, they will love pleasure. Even though they will make a show of being religious, their religion won't be real. Don't have anything to do with such people.

**Revelation 3:10 NCV**   You have obeyed my teaching about not giving up your faith. So I will keep you from the time of trouble that will come to the whole world to test those who live on earth.

**Revelation 11:15-19 NIV**   The seventh angel sounded his trumpet, and there were loud voices in heaven, which said: "The kingdom of the world has become the kingdom of our Lord and of his Christ, and he will reign for ever and ever." And the twenty-four elders, who were seated on their thrones before God, fell on their faces and worshiped God, saying: "We give thanks to you, Lord God Almighty, the One who is and who was, because you have taken your great power and have begun to reign. The nations were angry; and your wrath has come. The time has come for judging the dead, and for rewarding your servants the prophets and your saints and those who reverence your name, both small and great—and for destroying those who destroy the earth." Then God's temple in heaven was opened, and within his temple was seen the ark of his covenant. And there came flashes of lightning, rumblings, peals of thunder, an earthquake and a great hailstorm.

**Revelation 22:20 ESV**   I am coming soon.

**1 Samuel 12:24 NKJV** Only fear the Lord, and serve Him in truth with all your heart; for consider what great things He has done for you.

**Psalm 19:7-9 NIV** The law of the Lord is perfect, reviving the soul. The statutes of the Lord are trustworthy, making wise the simple. The precepts of the Lord are right, giving joy to the heart. The commands of the Lord are radiant, giving light to the eyes. The fear of the Lord is pure, enduring forever.

**Psalm 23:4 CEV** I may walk through valleys as dark as death, but I won't be afraid. You are with me, and your shepherd's rod makes me feel safe.

**Psalm 31:24 NKJV** Be of good courage, and He shall strengthen your heart, all you who hope in the Lord.

**Isaiah 40:28-31 NCV** Surely you have heard. The Lord is the God who lives forever, who created all the world. He does not become tired or need to rest. No one can understand how great his wisdom is. He gives strength to those who are tired and more power to those who are weak. Even children become tired and need to rest, and young people trip and fall. But the people who trust the Lord will become strong again. They will rise up as an eagle in the sky; they will run and not need rest; they will walk and not become tired.

**Romans 12:12 NCV** Be joyful because you have hope. Be patient when trouble comes, and pray at all times.

**Hebrews 12:1-3 ESV** Let us run with endurance the race that is set before us, looking to Jesus, the founder and perfecter of our faith, who for the joy that was set before him endured the cross, despising the shame, and is seated at the right hand of the throne of God. Consider him who endured from sinners such hostility against himself, so that you may not grow weary or fainthearted.

**ENEMY**

**Exodus 15:6 NASB**   Your right hand, O Lᴏʀᴅ, is majestic in power, Your right hand, O Lᴏʀᴅ, shatters the enemy.

**Psalm 9:1–4 GNT**   I will praise you, Lord, with all my heart; I will tell of all the wonderful things you have done. I will sing with joy because of you. I will sing praise to you, Almighty God. My enemies turn back when you appear; they fall down and die. You are fair and honest in your judgments, and you have judged in my favor.

**Psalm 41:11–12 NASB**   I know that You are pleased with me, because my enemy does not shout in triumph over me. As for me, You uphold me in my integrity, and You set me in Your presence forever.

**Proverbs 16:7 NKJV**   When a man's ways please the Lᴏʀᴅ, He makes even his enemies to be at peace with him.

**Matthew 5:44–45 NCV**   I say to you, love your enemies. Pray for those who hurt you. If you do this, you will be true children of your Father in heaven.

**Matthew 18:21–22 ESV**   Peter came up and said to him, "Lord, how often will my brother sin against me, and I forgive him? As many as seven times?" Jesus said to him, "I do not say to you seven times, but seventy times seven."

**2 Thessalonians 3:14–15 TNIV**   Take special note of those who do not obey our instruction in this letter. Do not associate with them, in order that they may feel ashamed. Yet do not regard them as enemies, but warn them as fellow believers.

**James 4:4 NASB**   Whoever wishes to be a friend of the world makes himself an enemy of God.

**1 John 4:2–3 NCV**   Every spirit who confesses that Jesus Christ came to earth as a human is from God. And every spirit who refuses to say this about Jesus is not from God. It is the spirit of the enemy of Christ, which you have heard is coming, and now he is already in the world.

**Proverbs 14:6-8 CEV**   Make fun of wisdom, and you will never find it. But if you have understanding, knowledge comes easily. Stay away from fools, or you won't learn a thing. Wise people have enough sense to find their way, but stupid fools get lost.

**Isaiah 5:20-21 NKJV**   Woe to those who call evil good, and good evil; Who put darkness for light, and light for darkness; Who put bitter for sweet, and sweet for bitter! Woe to those who are wise in their own eyes, And prudent in their own sight!

**Matthew 5:28 CEV**   I tell you that if you look at another woman and want her, you are already unfaithful in your thoughts.

**Matthew 6:22-23 MSG**   Your eyes are windows into your body. If you open your eyes wide in wonder and belief, your body fills up with light. If you live squinty-eyed in greed and distrust, your body is a dank cellar.

**Romans 12:2 NCV**   Do not be shaped by this world; instead be changed within by a new way of thinking. Then you will be able to decide what God wants for you; you will know what is good and pleasing to him and what is perfect.

**Philippians 4:8 CEV**   Keep your minds on whatever is true, pure, right, holy, friendly, and proper. Don't ever stop thinking about what is truly worthwhile and worthy of praise.

**Colossians 3:1-2 BBE**   If then you have a new life with Christ, give your attention to the things of heaven, where Christ is seated at the right hand of God. Keep your mind on the higher things, not on the things of earth.

**1 Thessalonians 5:21-22 NASB**   Examine everything carefully; hold fast to that which is good; abstain from every form of evil.

# ETERNITY

**Matthew 10:32-33 TNIV**   Whoever publicly acknowledges me I will also acknowledge before my Father in heaven. But whoever publicly disowns me I will disown before my Father in heaven.

**Matthew 28:20 NCV**   Teach them to obey everything that I have taught you, and I will be with you always, even until the end of this age.

**John 3:16-18 TNIV**   God so loved the world that he gave his one and only Son, that whoever believes in him shall not perish but have eternal life. For God did not send his Son into the world to condemn the world, but to save the world through him. Whoever believes in him is not condemned, but whoever does not believe stands condemned already because they have not believed in the name of God's one and only Son.

**John 6:67-68 NRSV**   Jesus asked the twelve, "Do you also wish to go away?" Simon Peter answered him, "Lord, to whom can we go? You have the words of eternal life."

**John 11:25 MSG**   You don't have to wait for the End. I am, right now, Resurrection and Life. The one who believes in me, even though he or she dies, will live.

**Romans 6:22-23 BBE**   Being free from sin, and having been made servants to God, you have your fruit in that which is holy, and the end is eternal life. For the reward of sin is death; but what God freely gives is eternal life in Jesus Christ our Lord.

**1 Corinthians 2:9 GNT**   The scripture says, "What no one ever saw or heard, what no one ever thought could happen, is the very thing God prepared for those who love him."

**1 John 2:17 NASB**   The world is passing away, and also its lusts; but the one who does the will of God lives forever.

**Psalm 34:13-14 WEB**   Keep your tongue from evil, and your lips from speaking lies. Depart from evil, and do good. Seek peace, and pursue it.

**Psalm 37:1-5 NCV**   Don't be upset because of evil people. Don't be jealous of those who do wrong, because like the grass, they will soon dry up. Like green plants, they will soon die away. Trust the LORD and do good. Live in the land and feed on truth. Enjoy serving the LORD, and he will give you what you want. Depend on the LORD; trust him, and he will take care of you.

**Psalm 101:3-4 NCV**   I will not look at anything wicked. I hate those who turn against you; they will not be found near me. Let those who want to do wrong stay away from me; I will have nothing to do with evil.

**Proverbs 4:14-16 CEV**   Don't follow the bad example of cruel and evil people. Turn aside and keep going. Stay away from them. They can't sleep or rest until they do wrong or harm some innocent victim.

**Proverbs 16:6 NIV**   Through love and faithfulness sin is atoned for; through the fear of the LORD a man avoids evil.

**John 8:44 GNT**   You are the children of your father, the Devil, and you want to follow your father's desires. From the very beginning he was a murderer and has never been on the side of truth, because there is no truth in him. When he tells a lie, he is only doing what is natural to him, because he is a liar and the father of all lies.

**Romans 16:20 NIV**   The God of peace will crush Satan under your feet. The grace of our Lord Jesus Christ be with you.

**James 1:19-21 ESV**   Let every person be quick to hear, slow to speak, slow to anger; for the anger of man does not produce the righteousness of God. Therefore put away all filthiness and rampant wickedness and receive with meekness the implanted word, which is able to save your souls.

**Genesis 1:1–4 ESV**   In the beginning, God created the heavens and the earth. The earth was without form and void, and darkness was over the face of the deep. And the Spirit of God was hovering over the face of the waters. And God said, "Let there be light," and there was light. And God saw that the light was good. And God separated the light from the darkness.

**Genesis 1:20–22 NKJV**   Then God said, "Let the waters abound with an abundance of living creatures, and let birds fly above the earth across the face of the firmament of the heavens." So God created great sea creatures and every living thing that moves, with which the waters abounded, according to their kind, and every winged bird according to its kind. And God saw that it was good. And God blessed them, saying, "Be fruitful and multiply, and fill the waters in the seas, and let birds multiply on the earth."

**Isaiah 45:11–12 NIV**   This is what the LORD says—the Holy One of Israel, and its Maker: Concerning things to come, do you question me about my children, or give me orders about the work of my hands? It is I who made the earth and created mankind upon it. My own hands stretched out the heavens; I marshaled their starry hosts.

**Ecclesiastes 8:16–17 NCV**   I tried to understand all that happens on earth. I saw how busy people are, working day and night and hardly ever sleeping. I also saw all that God has done. Nobody can understand what God does here on earth. No matter how hard people try to understand it, they cannot. Even if wise people say they understand, they cannot; no one can really understand it.

**Romans 1:20–22 GNT**   Ever since God created the world, his invisible qualities, both his eternal power and his divine nature, have been clearly seen; they are perceived in the things that God has made. So those people have no excuse at all! They know God, but they do not give him the honor that belongs to him, nor do they thank him. Instead, their thoughts have become complete nonsense, and their empty minds are filled with darkness. They say they are wise, but they are fools.

# EXAMPLE (95)

**Psalm 39:1 NCV**   I will be careful how I act and will not sin by what I say. I will be careful what I say around wicked people.

**Proverbs 10:19-21 NKJV**   In the multitude of words sin is not lacking, but he who restrains his lips is wise. The tongue of the righteous is choice silver; the heart of the wicked is worth little. The lips of the righteous feed many.

**Romans 15:5-7 TNIV**   May the God who gives endurance and encouragement give you the same attitude of mind toward each other that Christ Jesus had, so that with one mind and one voice you may glorify the God and Father of our Lord Jesus Christ. Accept one another, then, just as Christ accepted you, in order to bring praise to God.

**1 Timothy 4:12 CEV**   Don't let anyone make fun of you, just because you are young. Set an example for other followers by what you say and do, as well as by your love, faith, and purity.

**Titus 1:7-9 ESV**   An overseer, as God's steward, must be above reproach. He must not be arrogant or quick-tempered or a drunkard or violent or greedy for gain, but hospitable, a lover of good, self-controlled, upright, holy, and disciplined. He must hold firm to the trustworthy word as taught, so that he may be able to give instruction in sound doctrine and also to rebuke those who contradict it.

**1 Peter 2:21-23 GNT**   It was to this that God called you, for Christ himself suffered for you and left you an example, so that you would follow in his steps. He committed no sin, and no one ever heard a lie come from his lips. When he was insulted, he did not answer back with an insult; when he suffered, he did not threaten, but placed his hopes in God, the righteous Judge.

**1 John 2:5-6 NCV**   If someone obeys God's teaching, then in that person God's love has truly reached its goal. This is how we can be sure we are living in God: Whoever says that he lives in God must live as Jesus lived.

# EXCELLENCE

**Psalm 8:1 NKJV**   O LORD, our Lord, How excellent is Your name in all the earth, who have set Your glory above the heavens!

**Psalm 45:2-4 NIV**   You are the most excellent of men and your lips have been anointed with grace, since God has blessed you forever. Gird your sword upon your side, O mighty one; clothe yourself with splendor and majesty. In your majesty ride forth victoriously in behalf of truth, humility and righteousness; let your right hand display awesome deeds.

**Proverbs 12:4 NKJV**   An excellent wife is the crown of her husband, but she who causes shame is like rottenness in his bones.

**Acts 20:19 NLT**   I have done the Lord's work humbly and with many tears. I have endured the trials that came to me from the plots of the Jews.

**2 Corinthians 4:7 NKJV**   We have this treasure in earthen vessels, that the excellence of the power may be of God and not of us.

**Philippians 3:8 NCV**   I think that all things are worth nothing compared with the greatness of knowing Christ Jesus my Lord. Because of him, I have lost all those things, and now I know they are worthless trash. This allows me to have Christ.

**Philippians 4:8 TNIV**   Finally, brothers and sisters, whatever is true, whatever is noble, whatever is right, whatever is pure, whatever is lovely, whatever is admirable—if anything is excellent or praiseworthy—think about such things.

**2 Peter 1:3-4 ESV**   His divine power has granted to us all things that pertain to life and godliness, through the knowledge of him who called us to his own glory and excellence, by which he has granted to us his precious and very great promises, so that through them you may become partakers of the divine nature, having escaped from the corruption that is in the world because of sinful desire.

**2 Chronicles 16:9 NIV**   The eyes of the Lᴏʀᴅ range throughout the earth to strengthen those whose hearts are fully committed to him.

**Psalm 13:3 CEV**   Please listen, Lᴏʀᴅ God, and answer my prayers. Make my eyes sparkle again.

**Psalm 25:15 NCV**   My eyes are always looking to the Lᴏʀᴅ for help. He will keep me from any traps.

**Psalm 101:3 ESV**   I will not set before my eyes anything that is worthless. I hate the work of those who fall away; it shall not cling to me.

**Psalm 101:6 NIV**   My eyes will be on the faithful in the land, that they may dwell with me; he whose walk is blameless will minister to me.

**Psalm 119:15-18 ESV**   I will meditate on your precepts and fix my eyes on your ways. I will delight in your statutes; I will not forget your word. Deal bountifully with your servant, that I may live and keep your word. Open my eyes, that I may behold wondrous things out of your law.

**Psalm 141:8 AMP**   My eyes are toward You, O God the Lord; in You do I trust and take refuge; pour not out my life nor leave it destitute and bare.

**Proverbs 6:12-14 NCV**   Some people are wicked and no good. They go around telling lies, winking with their eyes, tapping with their feet, and making signs with their fingers. They make evil plans in their hearts and are always starting arguments.

**Ezekiel 20:7-8 NIV**   Each of you, get rid of the vile images you have set your eyes on, and do not defile yourselves with the idols of Egypt. I am the Lᴏʀᴅ your God. "But they rebelled against me and would not listen to me; they did not get rid of the vile images they had set their eyes on, nor did they forsake the idols of Egypt. So I said I would pour out my wrath on them and spend my anger against them in Egypt."

**Psalm 40:2-3 ESV**    He drew me up from the pit of destruction, out of the miry bog, and set my feet upon a rock, making my steps secure. He put a new song in my mouth, a song of praise to our God. Many will see and fear, and put their trust in the LORD.

**Psalm 138:8 CEV**    You, LORD, will always treat me with kindness. Your love never fails. You have made us what we are. Don't give up on us now!

**Proverbs 24:16 AMP**    A righteous man falls seven times and rises again, but the wicked are overthrown by calamity.

**Jeremiah 8:4-5 NLT**    This is what the LORD says: "When people fall down, don't they get up again? When they discover they're on the wrong road, don't they turn back? Then why do these people stay on their self-destructive path?"

**John 17:25 AMP**    O just and righteous Father, although the world has not known You and has failed to recognize You and has never acknowledged You.

**2 Corinthians 12:9-10 ESV**    My grace is sufficient for you, for my power is made perfect in weakness. Therefore I will boast all the more gladly of my weaknesses, so that the power of Christ may rest upon me. For the sake of Christ, then, I am content with weaknesses, insults, hardships, persecutions, and calamities. For when I am weak, then I am strong.

**2 Corinthians 13:5 CEV**    Test yourselves and find out if you really are true to your faith. If you pass the test, you will discover that Christ is living in you. But if Christ isn't living in you, you have failed.

**Matthew 17:20 NIV**  Because you have so little faith. I tell you the truth, if you have faith as small as a mustard seed, you can say to this mountain, "Move from here to there" and it will move. Nothing will be impossible for you.

**Mark 11:24 NKJV**  Whatever things you ask when you pray, believe that you receive them.

**Romans 5:1–2 GNT**  Now that we have been put right with God through faith, we have peace with God through our Lord Jesus Christ. He has brought us by faith into this experience of God's grace, in which we now live.

**Romans 10:17 NCV**  Faith comes from hearing the Good News, and people hear the Good News when someone tells them about Christ.

**Romans 14:23 HCSB**  Everything that is not from faith is sin.

**1 Corinthians 16:13 NKJV**  Watch, stand fast in the faith, be brave, be strong.

**2 Corinthians 5:7 NIV**  We live by faith, not by sight.

**Ephesians 6:16 HCSB**  In every situation take the shield of faith, and with it you will be able to extinguish the flaming arrows of the evil one.

**Hebrews 10:23–24 NASB**  Let us hold fast the confession of our hope without wavering, for He who promised is faithful; and let us consider how to stimulate one another to love and good deeds.

**Hebrews 11:1 CEV**  Faith makes us sure of what we hope for and gives us proof of what we cannot see.

**Hebrews 11:6 CEV**  Without faith no one can please God. We must believe that God is real and that he rewards everyone who searches for him.

**Genesis 28:15 CEV**   Wherever you go, I will watch over you, then later I will bring you back to this land. I won't leave you—I will do all I have promised.

**2 Chronicles 7:16 ESV**   Now I have chosen and consecrated this house that my name may be there forever. My eyes and my heart will be there for all time.

**Psalm 89:1-2 ESV**   I will sing of the steadfast love of the LORD, forever; with my mouth I will make known your faithfulness to all generations. For I said, "Steadfast love will be built up forever; in the heavens you will establish your faithfulness."

**Psalm 119:64-65 HCSB**   LORD, the earth is filled with Your faithful love; teach me Your statutes. LORD, You have treated Your servant well, just as You promised.

**Isaiah 54:10 ESV**   "For the mountains may depart and the hills be removed, but my steadfast love shall not depart from you, and my covenant of peace shall not be removed," says the LORD, who has compassion on you.

**John 10:11 TNIV**   I am the good shepherd. The good shepherd lays down his life for the sheep.

**1 Thessalonians 5:23-24 ESV**   Now may the God of peace himself sanctify you completely, and may your whole spirit and soul and body be kept blameless at the coming of our Lord Jesus Christ. He who calls you is faithful; he will surely do it.

**2 Timothy 2:13 CEV**   If we are not faithful, he will still be faithful. Christ cannot deny who he is.

**2 Peter 3:9 NASB**   The Lord is not slow about His promise, as some count slowness, but is patient toward you, not wishing for any to perish but for all to come to repentance.

**Deuteronomy 26:17-19 HCSB**   Today you have affirmed that the LORD is your God and that you will walk in His ways, keep His statutes, commands, and ordinances, and obey Him. And today the LORD has affirmed that you are His special people as He promised you, that you are to keep all His commands, that He will put you far above all the nations He has made in praise, fame, and glory, and that you will be a holy people to the LORD your God as He promised.

**1 Chronicles 29:12 HCSB**   Riches and honor come from You, and You are the ruler of everything. In Your hand are power and might, and it is in Your hand to make great and to give strength to all.

**Psalm 3:3 ESV**   But you, O LORD, are a shield about me, my glory, and the lifter of my head.

**Psalm 84:10-11 NASB**   For a day in Your courts is better than a thousand outside. I would rather stand at the threshold of the house of my God than dwell in the tents of wickedness. For the LORD God is a sun and shield; the LORD gives grace and glory; no good thing does He withhold from those who walk uprightly.

**Isaiah 60:1 ESV**   Arise, shine, for your light has come, and the glory of the LORD has risen upon you.

**Jeremiah 9:24 CEV**   If you feel you must brag, then have enough sense to brag about worshiping me, the LORD.

**Daniel 12:3 NIV**   Those who are wise will shine like the brightness of the heavens, and those who lead many to righteousness, like the stars for ever and ever.

**1 Corinthians 10:31-33 NRSV**   Whether you eat or drink, or whatever you do, do everything for the glory of God. . . . just as I try to please everyone in everything I do, not seeking my own advantage, but that of many, so that they may be saved.

**Proverbs 11:29 MSG**   Exploit or abuse your family, and end up with a fistful of air; common sense tells you it's a stupid way to live.

**Proverbs 24:3-4 WEB**   Through wisdom a house is built; by understanding it is established; by knowledge the rooms are filled with all rare and beautiful treasure.

**Matthew 10:36-39 MSG**   Well-meaning family members can be your worst enemies. If you prefer father or mother over me, you don't deserve me. If you prefer son or daughter over me, you don't deserve me. If you don't go all the way with me, through thick and thin, you don't deserve me. If your first concern is to look after yourself, you'll never find yourself. But if you forget about yourself and look to me, you'll find both yourself and me.

**Matthew 12:25 GNT**   Any country that divides itself into groups which fight each other will not last very long. And any town or family that divides itself into groups which fight each other will fall apart.

**1 Corinthians 1:10 MSG**   I'll put it as urgently as I can: You must get along with each other. You must learn to be considerate of one another, cultivating a life in common.

**Ephesians 4:31-32 WEB**   Let all bitterness, wrath, anger, outcry, and slander, be put away from you, with all malice. And be kind to one another, tenderhearted, forgiving each other, just as God also in Christ forgave you.

**Ephesians 6:1-4 NIV**   Children, obey your parents in the Lord, for this is right. "Honor your father and mother"—which is the first commandment with a promise—"that it may go well with you and that you may enjoy long life on the earth." Fathers, do not exasperate your children; instead, bring them up in the training and instruction of the Lord.

**Colossians 3:12-14 ESV**   Put on then, as God's chosen ones, holy and beloved, compassionate hearts, kindness, humility, meekness, and patience, bearing with one another and, if one has a complaint against another, forgiving each other; as the Lord has forgiven you, so you also must forgive. And above all these put on love, which binds everything together in perfect harmony.

**Colossians 3:15-17 WEB**   Let the peace of Christ rule in your hearts, to which also you were called in one body; and be thankful. Let the word of Christ dwell in you richly; in all wisdom teaching and admonishing one another with psalms, hymns, and spiritual songs, singing with grace in your heart to God. Whatever you do, in word or in deed, do all in the name of the Lord Jesus, giving thanks to God, the Father, through him.

**Colossians 3:20-21 WEB**   Children, obey your parents in all things, for this pleases the Lord. Fathers, don't provoke your children, so that they won't be discouraged.

**1 Timothy 5:1-2 MSG**   Don't be harsh or impatient with an older man. Talk to him as you would your own father, and to the younger men as your brothers. Reverently honor an older woman as you would your mother, and the younger women as sisters.

**1 Timothy 5:3-4 ESV**   Honor widows who are truly widows. But if a widow has children or grandchildren, let them first learn to show godliness to their own household and to make some return to their parents, for this is pleasing in the sight of God.

**1 Timothy 5:8 TNIV**   Anyone who does not provide for their relatives, and especially for their own household, has denied the faith and is worse than an unbeliever.

**1 Peter 3:8-9 WEB**   Finally, be all like-minded, compassionate, loving as brothers, tenderhearted, courteous, not rendering evil for evil, or insult for insult; but instead blessing; knowing that to this were you called, that you may inherit a blessing.

# FATHER GOD

**Psalm 103:13-14 NASB**  Just as a father has compassion on his children, so the LORD has compassion on those who fear Him. For He Himself knows our frame; He is mindful that we are but dust.

**Psalm 145:8-9 ESV**  The LORD is gracious and merciful, slow to anger and abounding in steadfast love. The LORD is good to all, and his mercy is over all that he has made.

**Matthew 18:12-14 MSG**  Look at it this way. If someone has a hundred sheep and one of them wanders off, doesn't he leave the ninety-nine and go after the one? And if he finds it, doesn't he make far more over it than over the ninety-nine who stay put? Your Father in heaven feels the same way. He doesn't want to lose even one of these simple believers.

**John 15:9-11 ESV**  As the Father has loved me, so have I loved you. Abide in my love. If you keep my commandments, you will abide in my love, just as I have kept my Father's commandments and abide in his love. These things I have spoken to you, that my joy may be in you, and that your joy may be full.

**Romans 5:8 NIV**  God demonstrates his own love for us in this: While we were still sinners, Christ died for us.

**2 Corinthians 6:18 NIV**  I will be a Father to you, and you will be my sons and daughters, says the Lord Almighty.

**Ephesians 1:4-5 TNIV**  He chose us in him before the creation of the world to be holy and blameless in his sight. In love he predestined us for adoption to sonship through Jesus Christ, in accordance with his pleasure and will.

**Ephesians 3:17-19 TNIV**  I pray that you, being rooted and established in love, may have power, together with all the Lord's people, to grasp how wide and long and high and deep is the love of Christ, and to know this love that surpasses knowledge—that you may be filled to the measure of all the fullness of God.

**Deuteronomy 6:24 NCV**   The LORD ordered us to obey all these commands and to respect the LORD our God so that we will always do well and stay alive, as we are today.

**Deuteronomy 8:5-7 HCSB**   Keep in mind that the LORD your God has been disciplining you just as a man disciplines his son. So keep the commands of the LORD your God by walking in His ways and fearing Him. For the LORD your God is bringing you into a good land, a land with streams of water, springs, and deep water sources, flowing in both valleys and hills.

**Deuteronomy 10:20 NIV**   Fear the LORD your God and serve him. Hold fast to him and take your oaths in his name.

**Joshua 24:14 NASB**   Fear the LORD and serve Him in sincerity and truth; and put away the gods which your fathers served beyond the River and in Egypt, and serve the LORD.

**Psalm 25:12-13 ESV**   Who is the man who fears the LORD? Him will he instruct in the way that he should choose. His soul shall abide in well-being, and his offspring shall inherit the land.

**Psalm 33:8 NASB**   Let all the earth fear the LORD; let all the inhabitants of the world stand in awe of Him.

**Psalm 115:11 NLT**   All you who fear the LORD, trust the LORD! He is your helper and your shield.

**Psalm 128:1-2 NIV**   Blessed are all who fear the LORD, who walk in his ways. You will eat the fruit of your labor; blessings and prosperity will be yours.

**Proverbs 8:13 ESV**   The fear of the LORD is hatred of evil. Pride and arrogance and the way of evil and perverted speech I hate.

**Proverbs 10:27 MSG**   The Fear-of-GOD expands your life; a wicked life is a puny life.

# FLATTERY

**Proverbs 16:24 NLT**   Kind words are like honey—sweet to the soul and healthy for the body.

**Proverbs 26:23-25 GNT**   Insincere talk that hides what you are really thinking is like a fine glaze on a cheap clay pot. A hypocrite hides hate behind flattering words. They may sound fine, but don't believe him, because his heart is filled to the brim with hate.

**Proverbs 26:28 MSG**   Liars hate their victims; flatterers sabotage trust.

**Proverbs 27:1-2 NASB**   Do not boast about tomorrow, for you do not know what a day may bring forth. Let another praise you, and not your own mouth; a stranger, and not your own lips.

**Proverbs 28:23 NLT**   People appreciate honest criticism far more than flattery.

**Ephesians 4:25 MSG**   What this adds up to, then, is this: no more lies, no more pretense. Tell your neighbor the truth. In Christ's body we're all connected to each other, after all. When you lie to others, you end up lying to yourself.

**1 Thessalonians 2:4-8 NCV**   We speak the Good News because God tested us and trusted us to do it. When we speak, we are not trying to please people, but God, who tests our hearts. You know that we never tried to influence you by saying nice things about you. We were not trying to get your money; we had no selfishness to hide from you. God knows that this is true. We were not looking for human praise, from you or anyone else, even though as apostles of Christ we could have used our authority over you. But we were very gentle with you, like a mother caring for her little children. Because we loved you, we were happy to share not only God's Good News with you, but even our own lives. You had become so dear to us!

**1 John 3:18 NCV**   We should love people not only with words and talk, but by our actions and true caring.

**1 Chronicles 29:19 MSG**   Give my son Solomon an uncluttered and focused heart so that he can obey what you command, live by your directions and counsel, and carry through with building The Temple for which I have provided.

**Proverbs 4:25 NCV**   Keep your eyes focused on what is right, and look straight ahead to what is good.

**Matthew 6:33 NCV**   Seek first God's kingdom and what God wants. Then all your other needs will be met as well.

**Romans 8:6-7 MSG**   Obsession with self in these matters is a dead end; attention to God leads us out into the open, into a spacious, free life. Focusing on the self is the opposite of focusing on God. Anyone completely absorbed in self ignores God, ends up thinking more about self than God. That person ignores who God is and what he is doing.

**1 Corinthians 15:57-58 NKJV**   But thanks be to God, who gives us the victory through our Lord Jesus Christ. Therefore, my beloved brethren, be steadfast, immovable, always abounding in the work of the Lord, knowing that your labor is not in vain in the Lord.

**Philippians 3:13-15 MSG**   Friends, don't get me wrong: By no means do I count myself an expert in all of this, but I've got my eye on the goal, where God is beckoning us onward—to Jesus. . . . So let's keep focused on that goal, those of us who want everything God has for us. If any of you have something else in mind, something less than total commitment, God will clear your blurred vision—you'll see it yet! Now that we're on the right track, let's stay on it.

**2 Peter 1:5-8 CEV**   Do your best to improve your faith. You can do this by adding goodness, understanding, self-control, patience, devotion to God, concern for others, and love. If you keep growing in this way, it will show that what you know about our Lord Jesus Christ has made your lives useful and meaningful.

# FORGIVE

**Proverbs 19:11 CEV**   It's wise to be patient and show what you are like by forgiving others.

**Matthew 5:23–24 NCV**   So when you offer your gift to God at the altar, and you remember that your brother or sister has something against you, leave your gift there at the altar. Go and make peace with that person, and then come and offer your gift.

**Matthew 18:32–35 GNT**   So he called the servant in. "You worthless slave!" he said. "I forgave you the whole amount you owed me, just because you asked me to. You should have had mercy on your fellow servant, just as I had mercy on you. The king was very angry, and he sent the servant to jail to be punished until he should pay back the whole amount." And Jesus concluded, "That is how my Father in heaven will treat every one of you unless you forgive your brother from your heart."

**Luke 6:37 HCSB**   Forgive, and you will be forgiven.

**Luke 11:4 NCV**   Forgive us for our sins, because we forgive everyone who has done wrong to us.

**Luke 17:3–4 HCSB**   If your brother sins, rebuke him, and if he repents, forgive him. And if he sins against you seven times in a day, and comes back to you seven times, saying, "I repent," you must forgive him.

**Ephesians 4:32 NIV**   Be kind and compassionate to one another, forgiving each other, just as in Christ God forgave you.

**1 Peter 3:9 NCV**   Do not do wrong to repay a wrong, and do not insult to repay an insult. But repay with a blessing, because you yourselves were called to do this so that you might receive a blessing.

**1 Peter 4:8 NIV**   Above all, love each other deeply, because love covers over a multitude of sins.

**Psalm 25:11 CEV**   Be true to your name, LORD, by forgiving each one of my terrible sins.

**Psalm 86:5-7 NIV**   You are forgiving and good, O LORD, abounding in love to all who call to you. Hear my prayer, O LORD; listen to my cry for mercy. In the day of my trouble I will call to you, for you will answer me.

**Psalm 103:1-3 GNT**   Praise the Lord, my soul! All my being, praise his holy name! Praise the Lord, my soul, and do not forget how kind he is. He forgives all my sins and heals all my diseases.

**Psalm 103:8-12 NCV**   The LORD shows mercy and is kind. He does not become angry quickly, and he has great love. He will not always accuse us, and he will not be angry forever. He has not punished us as our sins should be punished; he has not repaid us for the evil we have done. As high as the sky is above the earth, so great is his love for those who respect him. He has taken our sins away from us as far as the east is from west.

**Jeremiah 31:34 HCSB**   I will forgive their wrongdoing and never again remember their sin.

**Matthew 6:14-15 TNIV**   If you forgive others when they sin against you, your heavenly Father will also forgive you. But if you do not forgive others their sins, your Father will not forgive your sins.

**Matthew 26:27-28 CEV**   Jesus picked up a cup of wine and gave thanks to God. He then gave it to his disciples and said, "Take this and drink it. This is my blood, and with it God makes his agreement with you. It will be poured out, so that many people will have their sins forgiven."

**Acts 8:22-23 CEV**   Get rid of these evil thoughts and ask God to forgive you. I can see that you are jealous and bound by your evil ways.

# FORTUNE-TELLING

**Leviticus 20:6 NCV**   I will be against anyone who goes to mediums and fortune-tellers for advice, because that person is being unfaithful to me. So I will cut him off from his people.

**Deuteronomy 18:10-12 HCSB**   No one among you is to make his son or daughter pass through the fire, practice divination, tell fortunes, interpret omens, practice sorcery, cast spells, consult a medium or a familiar spirit, or inquire of the dead. Everyone who does these things is detestable to the LORD.

**Isaiah 8:19 NCV**   Some people say, "Ask the mediums and fortune-tellers, who whisper and mutter, what to do." But I tell you that people should ask their God for help. Why should people who are still alive ask something from the dead?

**Isaiah 44:25-26 NLT**   I expose the false prophets as liars and make fools of fortune-tellers. I cause the wise to give bad advice, thus proving them to be fools. But I carry out the predictions of my prophets!

**Jeremiah 31:34 NIV**   I will forgive their wickedness and will remember their sins no more.

**Ezekiel 13:23 CEV**   I will no longer let these women give false messages and use magic, and I will free my people from their control. Then they will know that I, the LORD, have done these things.

**Zechariah 10:2 NCV**   Idols tell lies; fortune-tellers see false visions and tell about false dreams. The comfort they give is worth nothing.

**Acts 16:16 NKJV**   Now it happened, as we went to prayer, that a certain slave girl possessed with a spirit of divination met us, who brought her masters much profit by fortune-telling.

**2 Peter 3:9 NIV**   The Lord is not slow in keeping his promise, as some understand slowness. He is patient with you, not wanting anyone to perish, but everyone to come to repentance.

**Psalm 118:4-5 GNT**   Let all who worship him say, "His love is eternal." In my distress I called to the Lord; he answered me and set me free.

**Proverbs 11:6 NCV**   Doing right brings freedom to honest people, but those who are not trustworthy will be caught by their own desires.

**Isaiah 61:1 TNIV**   The Spirit of the Sovereign LORD is on me, because the LORD has anointed me to proclaim good news to the poor. He has sent me to bind up the brokenhearted, to proclaim freedom for the captives and release from darkness for the prisoners.

**Luke 1:68 NCV**   Let us praise the Lord, the God of Israel, because he has come to help his people and has given them freedom.

**John 8:32 ESV**   You will know the truth, and the truth will set you free.

**Romans 6:22 NKJV**   Now having been set free from sin, and having become slaves of God, you have your fruit to holiness, and the end, everlasting life.

**1 Corinthians 8:9 NIV**   Be careful, however, that the exercise of your freedom does not become a stumbling block to the weak.

**2 Corinthians 3:17 ESV**   Now the Lord is the Spirit, and where the Spirit of the Lord is, there is freedom.

**Galatians 5:1 NCV**   We have freedom now, because Christ made us free. So stand strong. Do not change and go back into the slavery of the law.

**James 1:25 CEV**   You must never stop looking at the perfect law that sets you free. God will bless you in everything you do, if you listen and obey, and don't just hear and forget.

**Job 10:12 BBE**   You have been kind to me, and your grace has been with me, and your care has kept my spirit safe.

**Psalm 25:14 ESV**   The friendship of the LORD is for those who fear him.

**Proverbs 12:26 NKJV**   The righteous should choose his friends carefully, for the way of the wicked leads them astray.

**Proverbs 13:20 WEB**   One who walks with wise men grows wise, but a companion of fools suffers harm.

**Proverbs 17:17 NASB**   A friend loves at all times.

**Proverbs 27:9 WEB**   Perfume and incense bring joy to the heart; so does earnest counsel from a man's friend.

**Proverbs 27:17 NLT**   As iron sharpens iron, so a friend sharpens a friend.

**John 15:12-13 WEB**   This is my commandment, that you love one another, even as I have loved you. Greater love has no one than this, that a man lay down his life for his friends.

**John 15:14-15 NIV**   You are my friends if you do what I command. I no longer call you servants, because a servant does not know his master's business. Instead, I have called you friends, for everything that I learned from my Father I have made known to you.

**Romans 12:16-17 NCV**   Live in peace with each other. Do not be proud, but make friends with those who seem unimportant. . . . If someone does wrong to you, do not pay him back by doing wrong to him. Try to do what everyone thinks is right.

**1 Corinthians 10:24 NLT**   Don't think only of your own good. Think of other Christians and what is best for them.

**Deuteronomy 4:30-31 NLT**   In the distant future, when you are suffering all these things, you will finally return to the Lord your God and listen to what he tells you. For the Lord your God is a merciful God; he will not abandon you or destroy you or forget the solemn covenant he made with your ancestors.

**Psalm 139:15-16 MSG**   You know exactly how I was made, bit by bit, how I was sculpted from nothing into something. Like an open book, you watched me grow from conception to birth; all the stages of my life were spread out before you, the days of my life all prepared before I'd even lived one day.

**Proverbs 23:15-18 ESV**   My son, if your heart is wise, my heart too will be glad. My inmost being will exult when your lips speak what is right. Let not your heart envy sinners, but continue in the fear of the Lord all the day. Surely there is a future, and your hope will not be cut off.

**Jeremiah 31:17 NCV**   "So there is hope for you in the future," says the Lord.

**Ephesians 2:7 NLT**   God can point to us in all future ages as examples of the incredible wealth of his grace and kindness toward us, as shown in all he has done for us who are united with Christ Jesus.

**Ephesians 2:10 NCV**   God has made us what we are. In Christ Jesus, God made us to do good works, which God planned in advance for us to live our lives doing.

**1 Peter 1:3-4 MSG**   What a God we have! And how fortunate we are to have him, this Father of our Master Jesus! Because Jesus was raised from the dead, we've been given a brand-new life and have everything to live for, including a future in heaven—and the future starts now! God is keeping careful watch over us and the future. The Day is coming when you'll have it all—life healed and whole.

**Proverbs 1:10-18 NCV**   If sinners try to lead you into sin, do not follow them. They will say, "Come with us. Let's ambush and kill someone; let's attack some innocent people just for fun. Let's swallow them alive, as death does; let's swallow them whole, as the grave does. We will take all kinds of valuable things and fill our houses with stolen goods. Come join us, and we will share with you stolen goods." My child, do not go along with them; do not do what they do. They are eager to do evil and are quick to kill. . . . Sinners will fall into their own traps; they will only catch themselves!

**Proverbs 1:29-33 GNT**   You have never had any use for knowledge and have always refused to obey the Lord. You have never wanted my advice or paid any attention when I corrected you. So then, you will get what you deserve, and your own actions will make you sick. Inexperienced people die because they reject wisdom. Stupid people are destroyed by their own lack of concern. But whoever listens to me will have security. He will be safe, with no reason to be afraid.

**Ezekiel 3:18-19 NCV**   When I say to the wicked, "You will surely die," you must warn them so they may live. If you don't speak out to warn the wicked to stop their evil ways, they will die in their sin. But I will hold you responsible for their death. If you warn the wicked and they do not turn from their wickedness or their evil ways, they will die because of their sin. But you will have saved your life.

**Galatians 5:13 NIV**   Do not use your freedom to indulge the sinful nature; rather, serve one another in love.

**Ephesians 4:22-24 NIV**   You were taught, with regard to your former way of life, to put off your old self, which is being corrupted by its deceitful desires; to be made new in the attitude of your minds; and to put on the new self, created to be like God in true righteousness and holiness.

**1 John 1:8-9 NKJV**   If we say that we have no sin, we deceive ourselves, and the truth is not in us. If we confess our sins, He is faithful and just to forgive us our sins.

**Numbers 13:31–33 NLT**   The other men who had explored the land with him disagreed. "We can't go up against them! They are stronger than we are!" So they spread this bad report about the land among the Israelites: "The land we traveled through and explored will devour anyone who goes to live there. All the people we saw were huge. We even saw giants there, the descendants of Anak. Next to them we felt like grasshoppers, and that's what they thought, too!"

**Deuteronomy 3:11 CEV**   King Og was the last of the Rephaim, and his coffin is in the town of Rabbah in Ammon. It is made of hard black rock and is thirteen and a half feet long and six feet wide.

**Deuteronomy 9:1–3 NLT**   Today you are about to cross the Jordan River to take over the land belonging to nations much greater and more powerful than you. They live in cities with walls that reach to the sky! The people are strong and tall—descendants of the famous Anakite giants. You've heard the saying, "Who can stand up to the Anakites?" But recognize today that the LORD your God is the one who will cross over ahead of you like a devouring fire to destroy them.

**1 Samuel 17:4–7 NCV**   The Philistines had a champion fighter from Gath named Goliath. He was about nine feet, four inches tall. He came out of the Philistine camp with a bronze helmet on his head and a coat of bronze armor that weighed about one hundred twenty-five pounds. He wore bronze protectors on his legs, and he had a bronze spear on his back. The wooden part of his larger spear was like a weaver's rod, and its blade weighed about fifteen pounds.

**1 Chronicles 20:4 NASB**   Now it came about after this, that war broke out at Gezer with the Philistines; then Sibbecai the Hushathite killed Sippai, one of the descendants of the giants, and they were subdued.

**1 Chronicles 20:6–7 NIV**   In still another battle, which took place at Gath, there was a huge man with six fingers on each hand and six toes on each foot—twenty-four in all. He also was descended from Rapha. When he taunted Israel, Jonathan son of Shimea, David's brother, killed him.

# GOALS

**Psalm 25:12 NLT**   Who are those who fear the LORD? He will show them the path they should choose.

**Psalm 27:4 NIV**   One thing I ask of the LORD, this is what I seek: that I may dwell in the house of the LORD all the days of my life, to gaze upon the beauty of the LORD and to seek him in his temple.

**Proverbs 3:5-7 NKJV**   Trust in the LORD with all your heart, And lean not on your own understanding; in all your ways acknowledge Him, and He shall direct your paths. Do not be wise in your own eyes; fear the LORD and depart from evil.

**Proverbs 23:4-5 NKJV**   Do not overwork to be rich; because of your own understanding, cease! Will you set your eyes on that which is not? For riches certainly make themselves wings; they fly away like an eagle toward heaven.

**Micah 6:8 NCV**   The LORD has told you, human, what is good; he has told you what he wants from you: to do what is right to other people, love being kind to others, and live humbly, obeying your God.

**2 Corinthians 5:9 TNIV**   We make it our goal to please him, whether we are at home in the body or away from it.

**Philippians 3:12-14 CEV**   I have not yet reached my goal, and I am not perfect. But Christ has taken hold of me. So I keep on running and struggling to take hold of the prize. My friends, I don't feel that I have already arrived. But I forget what is behind, and I struggle for what is ahead. I run toward the goal, so that I can win the prize of being called to heaven. This is the prize that God offers because of what Christ Jesus has done.

**James 3:17-18 TNIV**   The wisdom that comes from heaven is first of all pure; then peace-loving, considerate, submissive, full of mercy and good fruit, impartial and sincere. Peacemakers who sow in peace reap a harvest of righteousness.

**Exodus 18:11 NKJV** I know that the LORD is greater than all the gods.

**Deuteronomy 30:15-16 NLT** Now listen! Today I am giving you a choice between life and death, between prosperity and disaster. For I command you this day to love the LORD your God and to keep his commands, decrees, and regulations by walking in his ways. If you do this, you will live and multiply, and the LORD your God will bless you and the land you are about to enter and occupy.

**Psalm 116:5 NIV** The LORD is gracious and righteous; our God is full of compassion.

**Psalm 139:7-10 AMP** Where could I go from Your Spirit? Or where could I flee from Your presence? If I ascend up into heaven, You are there; if I make my bed in Sheol (the place of the dead), behold, You are there. If I take the wings of the morning or dwell in the uttermost parts of the sea, Even there shall Your hand lead me, and Your right hand shall hold me.

**Isaiah 45:5-7 NCV** I am the LORD. There is no other God; I am the only God. I will make you strong, even though you don't know me, so that everyone will know there is no other God. From the east to the west they will know I alone am the LORD. I made the light and the darkness. I bring peace, and I cause troubles. I, the LORD, do all these things.

**Romans 11:22 NLT** Notice how God is both kind and severe. He is severe toward those who disobeyed, but kind to you if you continue to trust in his kindness. But if you stop trusting, you also will be cut off.

**1 Corinthians 8:6 NLT** We know that there is only one God, the Father, who created everything, and we live for him. And there is only one Lord, Jesus Christ, through whom God made everything and through whom we have been given life.

**2 Corinthians 13:11 NKJV** Become complete. Be of good comfort, be of one mind, live in peace; and the God of love and peace will be with you.

**Leviticus 18:22 NLT**   Do not practice homosexuality, having sex with another man as with a woman. It is a detestable sin.

**Deuteronomy 18:11-13 NCV**   Don't let anyone try to control others with magic, and don't let them be mediums or try to talk with the spirits of dead people. The LORD hates anyone who does these things. Because the other nations do these things, the LORD your God will force them out of the land ahead of you. But you must be innocent in the presence of the LORD your God.

**Psalm 11:5 TNIV**   The LORD examines the righteous, but the wicked, those who love violence, he hates with a passion.

**Proverbs 6:16-19 AMP**   These six things the Lord hates, indeed, seven are an abomination to Him: A proud look [the spirit that makes one overestimate himself and underestimate others], a lying tongue, and hands that shed innocent blood, A heart that manufactures wicked thoughts and plans, feet that are swift in running to evil, A false witness who breathes out lies [even under oath], and he who sows discord among his brethren.

**Proverbs 12:22 AMP**   Lying lips are extremely disgusting and hateful to the Lord, but they who deal faithfully are His delight.

**Proverbs 15:26 AMP**   The thoughts of the wicked are shamefully vile and exceedingly offensive to the Lord, but the words of the pure are pleasing words to Him.

**Proverbs 16:5 TNIV**   The LORD detests all the proud of heart. Be sure of this: They will not go unpunished.

**Malachi 2:16 AMP**   For the Lord, the God of Israel, says: I hate divorce and marital separation and him who covers his garment [his wife] with violence.

**Psalm 34:8 NRSV**   O taste and see that the Lord is good; happy are those who take refuge in him.

**Psalm 84:11-12 NIV**   For the LORD God is a sun and shield; the LORD bestows favor and honor; no good thing does he withhold from those whose walk is blameless. O LORD Almighty, blessed is the man who trusts in you.

**Psalm 103:1-5 BBE**   Give praise to the Lord, O my soul; let everything in me give praise to his holy name. Give praise to the Lord, O my soul; let not all his blessings go from your memory. He has forgiveness for all your sins; he takes away all your diseases; He keeps back your life from destruction, crowning you with mercy and grace. He makes your mouth full of good things, so that your strength is made new again like the eagle's.

**Psalm 112:5 NIV**   Good will come to him who is generous and lends freely, who conducts his affairs with justice

**Micah 6:8 BBE**   He has made clear to you, O man, what is good; and what is desired from you by the Lord; only doing what is right, and loving mercy, and walking without pride before your God.

**Nahum 1:7 NLT**   The LORD is good. When trouble comes, he is a strong refuge. And he knows everyone who trusts in him.

**Matthew 19:17 TNIV**   "Why do you ask me about what is good?" Jesus replied. "There is only One who is good. If you want to enter life, keep the commandments."

**1 Peter 2:12 NLT**   Be careful to live properly among your unbelieving neighbors. Then even if they accuse you of doing wrong, they will see your honorable behavior, and they will give honor to God when he judges the world.

**Leviticus 19:16 NLT**   Do not spread slanderous gossip among your people.

**Psalm 141:3-4 NCV**   LORD, help me control my tongue; help me be careful about what I say. Take away my desire to do evil or to join others in doing wrong.

**Proverbs 20:19-20 NLT**   A gossip goes around telling secrets, so don't hang around with chatterers. If you insult your father or mother, your light will be snuffed out in total darkness.

**Proverbs 29:20 NKJV**   Do you see a man hasty in his words? There is more hope for a fool than for him.

**Matthew 12:34-35 NKJV**   Out of the abundance of the heart the mouth speaks. A good man out of the good treasure of his heart brings forth good things, and an evil man out of the evil treasure brings forth evil things.

**Colossians 4:6 NASB**   Let your speech always be with grace, as though seasoned with salt, so that you will know how you should respond to each person.

**James 1:26 NLT**   If you claim to be religious but don't control your tongue, you are just fooling yourself, and your religion is worthless.

**James 3:6-8 NCV**   The tongue is set on fire by hell, and it starts a fire that influences all of life. People can tame every kind of wild animal, bird, reptile, and fish, and they have tamed them, but no one can tame the tongue. It is wild and evil and full of deadly poison.

**James 4:11 WEB**   Don't speak against one another, brothers. He who speaks against a brother and judges his brother, speaks against the law and judges the law. But if you judge the law, you are not a doer of the law, but a judge.

**Luke 11:33-36 NASB**   No one, after lighting a lamp, puts it away in a cellar nor under a basket, but on the lampstand, so that those who enter may see the light. The eye is the lamp of your body; when your eye is clear, your whole body also is full of light; but when it is bad, your body also is full of darkness. Then watch out that the light in you is not darkness. If therefore your whole body is full of light, with no dark part in it, it will be wholly illumined, as when the lamp illumines you with its rays.

**Romans 12:2 MSG**   Don't become so well-adjusted to your culture that you fit into it without even thinking. Instead, fix your attention on God. You'll be changed from the inside out. Readily recognize what he wants from you, and quickly respond to it. Unlike the culture around you, always dragging you down to its level of immaturity, God brings the best out of you, develops well-formed maturity in you.

**2 Corinthians 6:17-18 ESV**   Go out from their midst, and be separate from them, says the Lord, and touch no unclean thing; then I will welcome you, and I will be a father to you, and you shall be sons and daughters to me, says the Lord Almighty.

**Ephesians 6:12 NIV**   Our struggle is not against flesh and blood, but against the rulers, against the authorities, against the powers of this dark world and against the spiritual forces of evil in the heavenly realms.

**1 Thessalonians 5:4-5 NASB**   You, brethren, are not in darkness, that the day would overtake you like a thief; for you are all sons of light and sons of day. We are not of night nor of darkness.

**1 John 1:5-6 NASB**   This is the message we have heard from Him and announce to you, that God is Light, and in Him there is no darkness at all. If we say that we have fellowship with Him and yet walk in the darkness, we lie and do not practice the truth.

# GRACE

**Nehemiah 9:16-17 NLT**   Our ancestors were proud and stubborn, and they paid no attention to your commands. They refused to obey and did not remember the miracles you had done for them. Instead, they became stubborn and appointed a leader to take them back to their slavery in Egypt! But you are a God of forgiveness, gracious and merciful, slow to become angry, and rich in unfailing love. You did not abandon them.

**Psalm 78:37-39 NCV**   Their hearts were not really loyal to God; they did not keep his agreement. Still God was merciful. He forgave their sins and did not destroy them. Many times he held back his anger and did not stir up all his anger. He remembered that they were only human, like a wind that blows and does not come back.

**Psalm 84:11 NASB**   The LORD God is a sun and shield; the LORD gives grace and glory; no good thing does He withhold from those who walk uprightly.

**Psalm 103:8-10 NCV**   The LORD shows mercy and is kind. He does not become angry quickly, and he has great love. He will not always accuse us, and he will not be angry forever. He has not punished us as our sins should be punished; he has not repaid us for the evil we have done.

**Isaiah 30:18 NIV**   The LORD longs to be gracious to you; he rises to show you compassion. For the LORD is a God of justice. Blessed are all who wait for him!

**John 1:16 GNT**   Out of the fullness of his grace he has blessed us all, giving us one blessing after another.

**Ephesians 1:7-9 NKJV**   In Him we have redemption through His blood, the forgiveness of sins, according to the riches of His grace which He made to abound toward us in all wisdom and prudence, having made known to us the mystery of His will, according to His good pleasure which He purposed in Himself.

**Leviticus 19:32 NIV**   Rise in the presence of the aged, show respect for the elderly and revere your God. I am the LORD.

**Job 12:12 NCV**   Older people are wise, and long life brings understanding.

**Psalm 145:4–7 NCV**   Parents will tell their children what you have done. They will retell your mighty acts, wonderful majesty, and glory. And I will think about your miracles. They will tell about the amazing things you do, and I will tell how great you are. They will remember your great goodness and will sing about your fairness.

**Proverbs 17:6 CEV**   Grandparents are proud of their grandchildren, and children should be proud of their parents.

**Jeremiah 31:25 NCV**   I will give rest and strength to those who are weak and tired.

**Mark 10:43 TNIV**   Whoever wants to become great among you must be your servant.

**1 Timothy 5:4 NIV**   If a widow has children or grandchildren, these should learn first of all to put their religion into practice by caring for their own family and so repaying their parents and grandparents, for this is pleasing to God.

**1 Timothy 5:8 TNIV**   Anyone who does not provide for their relatives, and especially for their own household, has denied the faith and is worse than an unbeliever.

**2 Timothy 1:5 NASB**   I am mindful of the sincere faith within you, which first dwelt in your grandmother Lois and your mother Eunice.

**1 Peter 3:8 MSG**   Summing up: Be agreeable, be sympathetic, be loving, be compassionate, be humble.

# GROW

**Psalm 105:24 NCV** The LORD made his people grow in number, and he made them stronger than their enemies.

**Ephesians 5:9-11 NCV** Light brings every kind of goodness, right living, and truth. Try to learn what pleases the Lord. Have nothing to do with the things done in darkness, which are not worth anything. But show that they are wrong.

**Colossians 1:23 CEV** You must stay deeply rooted and firm in your faith. You must not give up the hope you received when you heard the good news.

**1 Thessalonians 3:12-13 TNIV** May the Lord make your love increase and overflow for each other and for everyone else, just as ours does for you. May he strengthen your hearts so that you will be blameless and holy in the presence of our God and Father when our Lord Jesus comes with all his holy ones.

**1 Thessalonians 4:11-12 NLT** Make it your goal to live a quiet life, minding your own business and working with your hands, just as we instructed you before. Then people who are not Christians will respect the way you live, and you will not need to depend on others.

**2 Peter 1:5-9 TNIV** Make every effort to add to your faith goodness; and to goodness, knowledge; and to knowledge, self-control; and to self-control, perseverance; and to perseverance, godliness; and to godliness, mutual affection; and to mutual affection, love. For if you possess these qualities in increasing measure, they will keep you from being ineffective and unproductive in your knowledge of our Lord Jesus Christ. But if any of you do not have them, you are nearsighted and blind, and you have forgotten that you have been cleansed from your past sins.

**2 Peter 3:18 ESV** Grow in the grace and knowledge of our Lord and Savior Jesus Christ. To him be the glory both now and to the day of eternity. Amen.

**Exodus 15:13 TNIV**  In your unfailing love you will lead the people you have redeemed. In your strength you will guide them to your holy dwelling.

**Deuteronomy 32:12 NLT**  The LORD alone guided them; they followed no foreign gods.

**Psalm 5:7-8 CEV**  Because of your great mercy, I come to your house, LORD, and I am filled with wonder as I bow down to worship at your holy temple. You do what is right, and I ask you to guide me.

**Psalm 16:6-8 CEV**  You make my life pleasant, and my future is bright. I praise you, LORD, for being my guide. Even in the darkest night, your teachings fill my mind. I will always look to you, as you stand beside me and protect me from fear.

**Psalm 23:2-4 NLT**  He lets me rest in green meadows; he leads me beside peaceful streams. He renews my strength. He guides me along right paths, bringing honor to his name. Even when I walk through the darkest valley, I will not be afraid, for you are close beside me. Your rod and your staff protect and comfort me.

**Psalm 25:4-6 NIV**  Show me your ways, O LORD, teach me your paths; guide me in your truth and teach me, for you are God my Savior, and my hope is in you all day long. Remember, O LORD, your great mercy and love, for they are from of old.

**Psalm 25:9-10 NIV**  He guides the humble in what is right and teaches them his way. All the ways of the LORD are loving and faithful for those who keep the demands of his covenant.

**Psalm 32:8 NLT**  I will guide you along the best pathway for your life. I will advise you and watch over you.

**Deuteronomy 22:25-27 AMP**   If a man finds the betrothed maiden in the open country and the man seizes her and lies with her, then only the man who lay with her shall die. But you shall do nothing to the young woman; she has committed no sin punishable by death, for this is as when a man attacks and slays his neighbor, for he came upon her in the open country, and the betrothed girl cried out, but there was no one to save her.

**Psalm 6:8-10 ESV**   Depart from me, all you workers of evil, for the LORD has heard the sound of my weeping. The LORD has heard my plea; the LORD accepts my prayer. All my enemies shall be ashamed and greatly troubled; they shall turn back and be put to shame in a moment.

**Psalm 25:5 NIV**   Guide me in your truth and teach me, for you are God my Savior, and my hope is in you all day long.

**Psalm 34:4-5 NIV**   I sought the LORD, and he answered me; he delivered me from all my fears. Those who look to him are radiant; their faces are never covered with shame.

**Psalm 69:5 AMP**   O God, You know my folly and blundering; my sins and my guilt are not hidden from You.

**Psalm 103:12 AMP**   As far as the east is from the west, so far has He removed our transgressions from us.

**Proverbs 28:13 TNIV**   Those who conceal their sins do not prosper, but those who confess and renounce them find mercy.

**Hebrews 10:19-22 TNIV**   Since we have confidence to enter the Most Holy Place by the blood of Jesus, by a new and living way opened for us through the curtain, that is, his body, and since we have a great priest over the house of God, let us draw near to God with a sincere heart in full assurance of faith, having our hearts sprinkled to cleanse us from a guilty conscience and having our bodies washed with pure water.

**Proverbs 10:4 NKJV**   He who has a slack hand becomes poor, but the hand of the diligent makes rich.

**Romans 12:2 ESV**   Do not be conformed to this world, but be transformed by the renewal of your mind, that by testing you may discern what is the will of God, what is good and acceptable and perfect.

**1 Corinthians 6:19-20 CEV**   You surely know that your body is a temple where the Holy Spirit lives. The Spirit is in you and is a gift from God. You are no longer your own. God paid a great price for you. So use your body to honor God.

**1 Corinthians 15:33-34 NCV**   Do not be fooled: "Bad friends will ruin good habits." Come back to your right way of thinking and stop sinning. Some of you do not know God—I say this to shame you.

**Ephesians 4:17-22 CEV**   As a follower of the Lord, I order you to stop living like stupid, godless people. Their minds are in the dark, and they are stubborn and ignorant and have missed out on the life that comes from God. They no longer have any feelings about what is right, and they are so greedy that they do all kinds of indecent things. But that isn't what you were taught about Jesus Christ. He is the truth, and you heard about him and learned about him.

**Ephesians 5:18-19 NLT**   Don't be drunk with wine, because that will ruin your life. Instead, be filled with the Holy Spirit, singing psalms and hymns and spiritual songs among yourselves, and making music to the Lord in your hearts.

**1 Peter 4:1-2 MSG**   Since Jesus went through everything you're going through and more, learn to think like him. Think of your sufferings as a weaning from that old sinful habit of always expecting to get your own way. Then you'll be able to live out your days free to pursue what God wants instead of being tyrannized by what you want.

**Numbers 6:5 TNIV**   During the entire period of the Nazirite's vow, no razor may be used on their head. They must be holy until the period of their dedication to the LORD is over; they must let their hair grow long.

**Deuteronomy 14:1-2 NLT**   Since you are the people of the LORD your God, never cut yourselves or shave the hair above your foreheads in mourning for the dead. You have been set apart as holy to the LORD your God, and he has chosen you from all the nations of the earth to be his own special treasure.

**2 Samuel 14:26 NASB**   When he cut the hair of his head (and it was at the end of every year that he cut it, for it was heavy on him so he cut it), he weighed the hair of his head at 200 shekels by the king's weight.

**Job 1:20 NASB**   Job arose and tore his robe and shaved his head, and he fell to the ground and worshiped.

**Proverbs 20:29 ESV**   The glory of young men is their strength, but the splendor of old men is their gray hair.

**Matthew 10:30-31 NCV**   God even knows how many hairs are on your head. So don't be afraid. You are worth much more than many sparrows.

**Luke 7:38 TNIV**   As she stood behind him at his feet weeping, she began to wet his feet with her tears. Then she wiped them with her hair, kissed them and poured perfume on them.

**1 Corinthians 11:14-15 NASB**   Does not even nature itself teach you that if a man has long hair, it is a dishonor to him, but if a woman has long hair, it is a glory to her? For her hair is given to her for a covering.

**Job 22:21 NCV**   Obey God and be at peace with him; this is the way to happiness.

**Psalm 1:1–2 BBE**   Happy is the man who does not go in the company of sinners, or take his place in the way of evil-doers, or in the seat of those who do not give honour to the Lord. But whose delight is in the law of the Lord, and whose mind is on his law day and night.

**Psalm 2:12 NCV**   Happy are those who trust him for protection.

**Psalm 32:1–2 NCV**   Happy is the person whose sins are forgiven, whose wrongs are pardoned. Happy is the person whom the LORD does not consider guilty and in whom there is nothing false.

**Psalm 41:1 NRSV**   Happy are those who consider the poor; the Lord delivers them in the day of trouble.

**Psalm 84:4–5 BBE**   Happy are they whose resting-place is in your house: they will still be praising you. Happy is the man whose strength is in you.

**Psalm 89:15–17 NCV**   Happy are the people who know how to praise you. Lord, let them live in the light of your presence. In your name they rejoice and continually praise your goodness. You are their glorious strength.

**Psalm 106:3 BBE**   Happy are they whose decisions are upright, and he who does righteousness at all times.

**Romans 15:13 NLT**   Pray that God, who gives you hope, will keep you happy and full of peace as you believe in him. May you overflow with hope through the power of the Holy Spirit.

**Revelation 1:3 NCV**   Happy is the one who reads the words of God's message, and happy are the people who hear this message and do what is written in it. The time is near when all of this will happen.

**Leviticus 19:17 NKJV**   You shall not hate your brother in your heart.

**Proverbs 10:11-12 NKJV**   The mouth of the righteous is a well of life, but violence covers the mouth of the wicked. Hatred stirs up strife, but love covers all sins.

**Proverbs 15:17 AMP**   Better is a dinner of herbs where love is than a fatted ox and hatred with it.

**Matthew 5:43-44 ESV**   You have heard that it was said, "You shall love your neighbor and hate your enemy." But I say to you, Love your enemies and pray for those who persecute you.

**John 15:18-19 AMP**   If the world hates you, know that it hated Me before it hated you. If you belonged to the world, the world would treat you with affection and would love you as its own. But because you are not of the world [no longer one with it], but I have chosen (selected) you out of the world, the world hates (detests) you.

**Romans 1:29-30 NCV**   They gossip and say evil things about each other. They hate God. They are rude and conceited and brag about themselves. They invent ways of doing evil. They do not obey their parents.

**1 John 2:9-11 ESV**   Whoever says he is in the light and hates his brother is still in darkness. Whoever loves his brother abides in the light, and in him there is no cause for stumbling. But whoever hates his brother is in the darkness and walks in the darkness, and does not know where he is going, because the darkness has blinded his eyes.

**1 John 3:14-16 ESV**   We know that we have passed out of death into life, because we love the brothers. Whoever does not love abides in death. Everyone who hates his brother is a murderer, and you know that no murderer has eternal life abiding in him. By this we know love, that he laid down his life for us, and we ought to lay down our lives for the brothers.

**2 Kings 20:2-6 NCV**   Hezekiah turned toward the wall and prayed to the LORD, "LORD, please remember that I have always obeyed you. I have given myself completely to you and have done what you said was right." . . . "This is what the LORD, the God of your ancestor David, says: I have heard your prayer and seen your tears, so I will heal you. Three days from now you will go up to the Temple of the LORD. I will add fifteen years to your life."

**Psalm 41:3 NCV**   The LORD will give them strength when they are sick, and he will make them well again.

**Psalm 30:2 TNIV**   LORD my God, I called to you for help, and you healed me.

**Psalm 73:25-26 TNIV**   Whom have I in heaven but you? And earth has nothing I desire besides you. My flesh and my heart may fail, but God is the strength of my heart and my portion forever.

**Psalm 103:3-4 CEV**   The LORD forgives our sins, heals us when we are sick, and protects us from death. His kindness and love are a crown on our heads.

**Jeremiah 17:14 NCV**   LORD, heal me, and I will truly be healed. Save me, and I will truly be saved. You are the one I praise.

**Matthew 9:22 CEV**   Jesus turned. He saw the woman and said, "Don't worry! You are now well because of your faith." At that moment she was healed.

**James 5:14-16 ESV**   Is anyone among you sick? Let him call for the elders of the church, and let them pray over him, anointing him with oil in the name of the Lord. And the prayer of faith will save the one who is sick, and the Lord will raise him up. And if he has committed sins, he will be forgiven. Therefore, confess your sins to one another and pray for one another, that you may be healed. The prayer of a righteous person has great power as it is working.

# HEALTH

**1 Samuel 25:6 NIV**   Long life to you! Good health to you and your household! And good health to all that is yours!

**Psalm 18:24 NCV**   The LORD rewarded me because I did what was right, because I did what the LORD said was right.

**Psalm 41:4 NASB**   As for me, I said, "O LORD, be gracious to me; heal my soul, for I have sinned against You."

**Proverbs 3:7-8 TNIV**   Do not be wise in your own eyes; fear the LORD and shun evil. This will bring health to your body and nourishment to your bones.

**Proverbs 14:30 CEV**   It's healthy to be content, but envy can eat you up.

**Proverbs 16:24 ESV**   Gracious words are like a honeycomb, sweetness to the soul and health to the body.

**Proverbs 18:14 TNIV**   The human spirit can endure in sickness, but a crushed spirit who can bear?

**Jeremiah 30:17 NCV**   "I will bring back your health and heal your injuries," says the LORD.

**Luke 11:34-35 TNIV**   Your eye is the lamp of your body. When your eyes are healthy, your whole body also is full of light. But when they are unhealthy, your body also is full of darkness. See to it, then, that the light within you is not darkness.

**1 Corinthians 6:19-20 CEV**   You surely know that your body is a temple where the Holy Spirit lives. The Spirit is in you and is a gift from God. You are no longer your own. God paid a great price for you. So use your body to honor God.

**3 John 1:2 TNIV**   Dear friend, I pray that you may enjoy good health and that all may go well with you, even as your soul is getting along well.

**1 Samuel 16:7 NKJV**  The Lord said to Samuel, "Do not look at his appearance or at the height of his stature, because I have refused him. For the Lord does not see as man sees; for man looks at the outward appearance, but the Lord looks at the heart."

**1 Kings 8:61 NKJV**  Let your heart therefore be loyal to the Lord our God.

**Psalm 37:4 NRSV**  Take delight in the Lord, and he will give you the desires of your heart.

**Psalm 139:1-3 NCV**  Lord, you have examined me and know all about me. You know when I sit down and when I get up. You know my thoughts before I think them. You know where I go and where I lie down. You know everything I do.

**Proverbs 4:20-23 NIV**  My son, pay attention to what I say; listen closely to my words. Do not let them out of your sight, keep them within your heart; for they are life to those who find them and health to a man's whole body. Above all else, guard your heart, for it is the wellspring of life.

**Proverbs 27:19 NKJV**  As in water face reflects face, so a man's heart reveals the man.

**Proverbs 28:25-26 NKJV**  He who is of a proud heart stirs up strife, but he who trusts in the Lord will be prospered. He who trusts in his own heart is a fool, but whoever walks wisely will be delivered.

**Jeremiah 24:7 HCSB**  I will give them a heart to know Me, that I am the LORD. They will be My people, and I will be their God.

**Jeremiah 29:13-14 NIV**  You will seek me and find me when you seek me with all your heart. I will be found by you.

**Matthew 6:21 ESV**  For where your treasure is, there your heart will be also.

# HEARTACHE

**Psalm 34:17-20 HCSB**  The righteous cry out, and the LORD hears, and delivers them from all their troubles. The LORD is near the brokenhearted; He saves those crushed in spirit. Many adversities come to the one who is righteous, but the LORD delivers him from them all. He protects all his bones; not one of them is broken.

**Psalm 38:6-9 NASB**  I am bent over and greatly bowed down; I go mourning all day long. For my loins are filled with burning, and there is no soundness in my flesh. I am benumbed and badly crushed; I groan because of the agitation of my heart. Lord, all my desire is before You; and my sighing is not hidden from You.

**Psalm 73:21-26 NKJV**  Thus my heart was grieved, and I was vexed in my mind. I was so foolish and ignorant; I was like a beast before You. Nevertheless I am continually with You; You hold me by my right hand. You will guide me with Your counsel, and afterward receive me to glory. Whom have I in heaven but You? And there is none upon earth that I desire besides You. My flesh and my heart fail; but God is the strength of my heart and my portion forever.

**Psalm 147:3 CEV**  He renews our hopes and heals our bodies.

**Psalm 147:3 HCSB**  He heals the brokenhearted and binds up their wounds.

**Proverbs 15:13 ESV**  A glad heart makes a cheerful face, but by sorrow of heart the spirit is crushed.

**John 14:1 ESV**  Let not your hearts be troubled. Believe in God; believe also in me.

**2 Corinthians 4:8-9 GNT**  We are often troubled, but not crushed; sometimes in doubt, but never in despair; there are many enemies, but we are never without a friend; and though badly hurt at times, we are not destroyed.

**Psalm 103:19 NLT**   The LORD has made the heavens his throne; from there he rules over everything.

**Psalm 115:16 NIV**   The highest heavens belong to the LORD, but the earth he has given to man.

**John 14:2-4 CEV**   There are many rooms in my Father's house. I wouldn't tell you this, unless it was true. I am going there to prepare a place for each of you. After I have done this, I will come back and take you with me. Then we will be together. You know the way to where I am going.

**Revelation 21:22-27 NCV**   I did not see a temple in the city, because the Lord God Almighty and the Lamb are the city's temple. The city does not need the sun or the moon to shine on it, because the glory of God is its light, and the Lamb is the city's lamp. By its light the people of the world will walk, and the kings of the earth will bring their glory into it. The city's gates will never be shut on any day, because there is no night there. The glory and the honor of the nations will be brought into it. Nothing unclean and no one who does shameful things or tells lies will ever go into it. Only those whose names are written in the Lamb's book of life will enter the city.

**Revelation 22:1-5 HCSB**   He showed me the river of living water, sparkling like crystal, flowing from the throne of God and of the Lamb down the middle of the broad street of the city. On both sides of the river was the tree of life bearing 12 kinds of fruit, producing its fruit every month. The leaves of the tree are for healing the nations, and there will no longer be any curse. The throne of God and of the Lamb will be in the city, and His servants will serve Him. They will see His face, and His name will be on their foreheads. Night will no longer exist, and people will not need lamplight or sunlight, because the Lord God will give them light. And they will reign forever and ever.

**Revelation 7:14-17 TNIV**   These are they who have come out of the great tribulation; they have washed their robes and made them white in the blood of the Lamb. Therefore, they are before the throne of God and serve him day and night in his temple; and he who sits on the throne will spread his tent over them. Never again will they hunger; never again will they thirst. The sun will not beat down on them, nor any scorching heat. For the Lamb at the center before the throne will be their shepherd; he will lead them to springs of living water. And God will wipe away every tear from their eyes.

**Revelation 14:2-5 CEV**   I heard a sound from heaven that was like a roaring flood or loud thunder or even like the music of harps. And a new song was being sung in front of God's throne and in front of the four living creatures and the elders. No one could learn that song, except the one hundred forty-four thousand who had been rescued from the earth. All of these are pure virgins, and they follow the Lamb wherever he leads. They have been rescued to be presented to God and the Lamb as the most precious people on earth. They never tell lies, and they are innocent.

**Revelation 15:1-5 TNIV**   I saw in heaven another great and marvelous sign: seven angels with the seven last plagues—last, because with them God's wrath is completed. And I saw what looked like a sea of glass glowing with fire and, standing beside the sea, those who had been victorious over the beast and its image and over the number of its name. They held harps given them by God and sang the song of God's servant Moses and of the Lamb: "Great and marvelous are your deeds, Lord God Almighty. Just and true are your ways, King of the nations. Who will not fear you, Lord, and bring glory to your name? For you alone are holy. All nations will come and worship before you, for your righteous acts have been revealed." After this I looked, and I saw in heaven the temple—that is, the tabernacle of the covenant law—and it was opened.

**Revelation 22:3 NLT**   No longer will there be a curse upon anything. For the throne of God and of the Lamb will be there, and his servants will worship him.

**Romans 8:18-21 ESV**   I consider that the sufferings of this present time are not worth comparing with the glory that is to be revealed to us. For the creation waits with eager longing for the revealing of the sons of God. For the creation was subjected to futility, not willingly, but because of him who subjected it, in hope that the creation itself will be set free from its bondage to corruption and obtain the freedom of the glory of the children of God.

**1 Corinthians 15:43-44 NLT**   Our bodies are buried in brokenness, but they will be raised in glory. They are buried in weakness, but they will be raised in strength. They are buried as natural human bodies, but they will be raised as spiritual bodies. For just as there are natural bodies, there are also spiritual bodies.

**1 Corinthians 15:45-49 CEV**   The first man was named Adam, and the Scriptures tell us that he was a living person. But Jesus, who may be called the last Adam, is a life-giving spirit. We see that the one with a spiritual body did not come first. He came after the one who had a physical body. The first man was made from the dust of the earth, but the second man came from heaven. Everyone on earth has a body like the body of the one who was made from the dust of the earth. And everyone in heaven has a body like the body of the one who came from heaven. Just as we are like the one who was made out of earth, we will be like the one who came from heaven.

**2 Corinthians 5:1-3 CEV**   Our bodies are like tents that we live in here on earth. But when these tents are destroyed, we know that God will give each of us a place to live. These homes will not be buildings that someone has made, but they are in heaven and will last forever. While we are here on earth, we sigh because we want to live in that heavenly home. We want to put it on like clothes and not be naked.

**1 John 3:2-3 NCV**   Dear friends, now we are children of God, and we have not yet been shown what we will be in the future. But we know that when Christ comes again, we will be like him, because we will see him as he really is. Christ is pure, and all who have this hope in Christ keep themselves pure like Christ.

**Matthew 7:13 NCV**   Enter through the narrow gate. The gate is wide and the road is wide that leads to hell, and many people enter through that gate.

**Matthew 10:28 NIV**   Do not be afraid of those who kill the body but cannot kill the soul. Rather, be afraid of the One who can destroy both soul and body in hell.

**Matthew 25:41–42 NCV**   Then the King will say to those on his left, "Go away from me. You will be punished. Go into the fire that burns forever that was prepared for the devil and his angels. I was hungry, and you gave me nothing to eat. I was thirsty, and you gave me nothing to drink."

**Mark 9:48–49 NCV**   In hell the worm does not die; the fire is never put out. Every person will be salted with fire.

**2 Thessalonians 1:8–10 TNIV**   He will punish those who do not know God and do not obey the gospel of our Lord Jesus. They will be punished with everlasting destruction and shut out from the presence of the Lord and from the glory of his might on the day he comes to be glorified in his holy people and to be marveled at among all those who have believed. This includes you, because you believed our testimony to you.

**Revelation 14:10–11 NCV**   That person will be put in pain with burning sulfur before the holy angels and the Lamb. And the smoke from their burning pain will rise forever and ever. There will be no rest, day or night, for those who worship the beast and his idol or who get the mark of his name.

**Revelation 21:7–8 ESV**   The one who conquers will have this heritage, and I will be his God and he will be my son. But as for the cowardly, the faithless, the detestable, as for murderers, the sexually immoral, sorcerers, idolaters, and all liars, their portion will be in the lake that burns with fire and sulfur, which is the second death.

**Psalm 22:19-21 NIV**   O Lord, be not far off; O my Strength, come quickly to help me. Deliver my life from the sword, my precious life from the power of the dogs. Rescue me from the mouth of the lions; save me from the horns of the wild oxen.

**Psalm 59:10 NCV**   My God loves me, and he goes in front of me. He will help me defeat my enemies.

**Psalm 68:19 NCV**   Praise the Lord, God our Savior, who helps us every day.

**Psalm 72:12-14 NCV**   He will help the poor when they cry out and will save the needy when no one else will help. He will be kind to the weak and poor, and he will save their lives. He will save them from cruel people who try to hurt them, because their lives are precious to him.

**Psalm 102:1-2 WEB**   Hear my prayer, Yahweh! Let my cry come to you. Don't hide your face from me in the day of my distress. Turn your ear to me. Answer me quickly in the day when I call.

**Psalm 121:1-2 NKJV**   I will lift up my eyes to the hills—from whence comes my help? My help comes from the Lord, who made heaven and earth.

**Psalm 144:7 NLT**   Reach down from heaven and rescue me; rescue me from deep waters, from the power of my enemies.

**John 14:1 NCV**   Jesus said, "Don't let your hearts be troubled. Trust in God, and trust in me."

**1 Corinthians 10:13 NLT**   The temptations in your life are no different from what others experience. And God is faithful. He will not allow the temptation to be more than you can stand.

**Ephesians 3:12 NCV**   In Christ we can come before God with freedom and without fear. We can do this through faith in Christ.

**Exodus 26:1 NCV**   Have a skilled craftsman sew designs of creatures with wings on the pieces of cloth.

**Exodus 31:3-5 NCV**   I have filled Bezalel with the Spirit of God and have given him the skill, ability, and knowledge to do all kinds of work. He is able to design pieces to be made from gold, silver, and bronze, to cut jewels and put them in metal, to carve wood, and to do all kinds of work.

**Exodus 35:25 BBE**   All the women who were expert with their hands, made cloth, and gave the work of their hands, blue and purple and red and the best linen.

**Deuteronomy 15:10 ESV**   The LORD your God will bless you in all your work and in all that you undertake.

**Psalm 139:3 BBE**   You keep watch over my steps and my sleep, and have knowledge of all my ways.

**Luke 6:45 NKJV**   A good man out of the good treasure of his heart brings forth good; and an evil man out of the evil treasure of his heart brings forth evil.

**Luke 12:31 BBE**   Let your chief care be for his kingdom, and these other things will be given to you in addition.

**2 Corinthians 10:5 NLT**   We destroy every proud obstacle that keeps people from knowing God.

**Ephesians 5:15-17 WEB**   Watch carefully how you walk, not as unwise, but as wise; redeeming the time, because the days are evil. Therefore don't be foolish, but understand what the will of the Lord is.

**Ephesians 5:19 TNIV**   Sing and make music from your heart to the Lord.

**Proverbs 14:1-3 NIV**   The wise woman builds her house, but with her own hands the foolish one tears hers down. He whose walk is upright fears the LORD, but he whose ways are devious despises him. A fool's talk brings a rod to his back, but the lips of the wise protect them.

**1 Thessalonians 4:7-8 ESV**   God has not called us for impurity, but in holiness. Therefore whoever disregards this, disregards not man but God, who gives his Holy Spirit to you.

**1 Timothy 4:7 NASB**   Discipline yourself for the purpose of godliness.

**2 Timothy 1:9 CEV**   God saved us and chose us to be his holy people. We did nothing to deserve this, but God planned it because he is so kind.

**Titus 2:11-12 WEB**   The grace of God has appeared, bringing salvation to all men, instructing us to the intent that, denying ungodliness and worldly lusts, we would live soberly, righteously, and godly in this present world.

**Hebrews 12:14-15 TNIV**   Make every effort to live in peace with everyone and to be holy; without holiness no one will see the Lord. See to it that no one falls short of the grace of God and that no bitter root grows up to cause trouble and defile many.

**1 Peter 3:15-16 NCV**   Respect Christ as the holy Lord in your hearts. Always be ready to answer everyone who asks you to explain about the hope you have, but answer in a gentle way and with respect. Keep a clear conscience so that those who speak evil of your good life in Christ will be made ashamed.

**2 Peter 3:11-12 MSG**   Since everything here today might well be gone tomorrow, do you see how essential it is to live a holy life?

# HOLY SPIRIT

**John 14:16-17 AMP** I will ask the Father, and He will give you another Comforter (Counselor, Helper, Intercessor, Advocate, Strengthener, and Standby), that He may remain with you forever—The Spirit of Truth, Whom the world cannot receive (welcome, take to its heart), because it does not see Him or know and recognize Him. But you know and recognize Him, for He lives with you [constantly] and will be in you.

**Romans 5:5 ESV** God's love has been poured into our hearts through the Holy Spirit who has been given to us.

**Acts 15:8-9 TNIV** God, who knows the heart, showed that he accepted them by giving the Holy Spirit to them, just as he did to us. He did not discriminate between us and them, for he purified their hearts by faith.

**Galatians 5:22-23 NLT** The Holy Spirit produces this kind of fruit in our lives: love, joy, peace, patience, kindness, goodness, faithfulness, gentleness, and self-control. There is no law against these things!

**Ephesians 4:29-31 TNIV** Do not let any unwholesome talk come out of your mouths, but only what is helpful for building others up according to their needs, that it may benefit those who listen. And do not grieve the Holy Spirit of God, with whom you were sealed for the day of redemption. Get rid of all bitterness, rage and anger, brawling and slander, along with every form of malice.

**2 Timothy 1:7-8 CEV** God's Spirit doesn't make cowards out of us. The Spirit gives us power, love, and self-control. Don't be ashamed to speak for our Lord.

**Titus 3:4-6 NCV** When the kindness and love of God our Savior was shown, he saved us because of his mercy. It was not because of good deeds we did to be right with him. He saved us through the washing that made us new people through the Holy Spirit. God poured out richly upon us that Holy Spirit through Jesus Christ our Savior.

**Job 22:21-23 NIV**   Submit to God and be at peace with him; in this way prosperity will come to you. Accept instruction from his mouth and lay up his words in your heart. If you return to the Almighty, you will be restored.

**Romans 1:24-27 TNIV**   They exchanged the truth about God for a lie, and worshiped and served created things rather than the Creator—who is forever praised. Amen. Because of this, God gave them over to shameful lusts. Even their women exchanged natural sexual relations for unnatural ones. In the same way the men also abandoned natural relations with women and were inflamed with lust for one another. Men committed shameful acts with other men, and received in themselves the due penalty for their error.

**1 Thessalonians 5:23 NIV**   May God himself, the God of peace, sanctify you through and through. May your whole spirit, soul and body be kept blameless at the coming of our Lord Jesus Christ.

**1 Timothy 1:8-11 CEV**   We know that the Law is good, if it is used in the right way. We also understand that it wasn't given to control people who please God, but to control lawbreakers, criminals, godless people, and sinners. It is for wicked and evil people, and for murderers, who would even kill their own parents. The Law was written for people who are sexual perverts or who live as homosexuals or are kidnappers or liars or won't tell the truth in court. It is for anything else that opposes the correct teaching of the good news that the glorious and wonderful God has given me.

**James 1:21-24 CEV**   You must stop doing anything immoral or evil. Instead be humble and accept the message that is planted in you to save you. Obey God's message! Don't fool yourselves by just listening to it. If you hear the message and don't obey it, you are like people who stare at themselves in a mirror and forget what they look like as soon as they leave.

**HOPE**

**Psalm 10:17 CEV**   You listen to the longings of those who suffer. You offer them hope, and you pay attention to their cries for help.

**Psalm 25:4-5 TNIV**   Show me your ways, Lord, teach me your paths. Guide me in your truth and teach me, for you are God my Savior, and my hope is in you all day long.

**Psalm 146:5-8 ESV**   Blessed is he whose help is the God of Jacob, whose hope is in the Lord his God, who made heaven and earth, the sea, and all that is in them, who keeps faith forever; who executes justice for the oppressed, who gives food to the hungry. The Lord sets the prisoners free; the Lord opens the eyes of the blind. The Lord lifts up those who are bowed down; the Lord loves the righteous.

**Psalm 147:11 ESV**   The Lord takes pleasure in those who fear him, in those who hope in his steadfast love.

**Jeremiah 31:3-4 NCV**   From far away the Lord appeared to his people and said, "I love you people with a love that will last forever. That is why I have continued showing you kindness. People of Israel, I will build you up again, and you will be rebuilt. You will pick up your tambourines again and dance with those who are joyful."

**Lamentations 3:21-23 CEV**   I remember something that fills me with hope. The LORD's kindness never fails! If he had not been merciful, we would have been destroyed. The LORD can always be trusted to show mercy each morning.

**Luke 1:78 CEV**   God's love and kindness will shine upon us like the sun that rises in the sky.

**Romans 15:13 NCV**   I pray that the God who gives hope will fill you with much joy and peace while you trust in him. Then your hope will overflow by the power of the Holy Spirit.

**Genesis 1:27 WEB**   God created man in his own image. In God's image he created him; male and female he created them.

**1 Samuel 16:7 TNIV**   The Lord does not look at the things human beings look at. People look at the outward appearance, but the Lord looks at the heart.

**1 Corinthians 8:4-6 WEB**   We know that no idol is anything in the world, and that there is no other God but one. For though there are things that are called "gods," whether in the heavens or on earth; as there are many "gods" and many "lords"; yet to us there is one God, the Father, of whom are all things, and we to him; and one Lord, Jesus Christ, through whom are all things, and we through him.

**Galatians 2:20-21 NIV**   I have been crucified with Christ and I no longer live, but Christ lives in me. The life I live in the body, I live by faith in the Son of God, who loved me and gave himself for me. I do not set aside the grace of God, for if righteousness could be gained through the law, Christ died for nothing!

**Ephesians 2:10 WEB**   We are his workmanship, created in Christ Jesus for good works, which God prepared before that we would walk in them.

**Philippians 1:6 BBE**   I am certain of this very thing, that he by whom the good work was started in you will make it complete till the day of Jesus Christ.

**Philippians 2:3-5 NCV**   When you do things, do not let selfishness or pride be your guide. Instead, be humble and give more honor to others than to yourselves. Do not be interested only in your own life, but be interested in the lives of others. In your lives you must think and act like Christ Jesus.

**James 1:18 NCV**   God decided to give us life through the word of truth so we might be the most important of all the things he made.

# INFLUENCE

**1 Kings 21:25 NCV**   There was no one like Ahab who had chosen so often to do what the LORD said was wrong, because his wife Jezebel influenced him to do evil.

**2 Chronicles 19:7 NCV**   Now let each of you fear the LORD. Watch what you do, because the LORD our God wants people to be fair. He wants all people to be treated the same, and he doesn't want decisions influenced by money.

**Job 31:21–23 MSG**   If I've ever used my strength and influence to take advantage of the unfortunate, go ahead, break both my arms, cut off all my fingers! The fear of God has kept me from these things—how else could I ever face him?

**Daniel 12:3 NASB**   Those who have insight will shine brightly like the brightness of the expanse of heaven, and those who lead the many to righteousness, like the stars forever and ever.

**Matthew 5:14 NKJV**   You are the light of the world.

**John 15:12-13 ESV**   This is my commandment, that you love one another as I have loved you. Greater love has no one than this, that someone lay down his life for his friends.

**Romans 10:14 ESV**   How are they to hear without someone preaching?

**1 Corinthians 1:26–27 NCV**   Not many of you had great influence. Not many of you came from important families. But God chose the foolish things of the world to shame the wise, and he chose the weak things of the world to shame the strong.

**1 Peter 2:9 MSG**   You are the ones chosen by God, chosen for the high calling of priestly work, chosen to be a holy people, God's instruments to do his work and speak out for him, to tell others of the night-and-day difference he made for you.

# INSTRUCTIONS (147)

**Matthew 7:12 TNIV**   Do to others what you would have them do to you.

**Matthew 9:38 CEV**   Ask the Lord in charge of the harvest to send out workers to bring it in.

**Romans 14:13 GNT**   Never to do anything that would make others stumble or fall into sin.

**Philippians 2:16 TNIV**   Hold firmly to the word of life.

**Philippians 4:6 NLT**   Tell God what you need, and thank him for all he has done.

**Colossians 3:13 NCV**   Get along with each other, and forgive each other.

**Colossians 3:17 NKJV**   Do all in the name of the Lord Jesus.

**1 Thessalonians 5:16-18 ESV**   Rejoice always, pray without ceasing, give thanks in all circumstances.

**1 Thessalonians 5:21 NASB**   Examine everything carefully; hold fast to that which is good.

**1 Timothy 4:13 HCSB**   Give your attention to public reading, exhortation, and teaching.

**Hebrews 10:35 CEV**   Keep on being brave! It will bring you great rewards.

**1 Peter 3:15 NIV**   In your hearts set apart Christ as Lord.

**1 Peter 5:7 NLT**   Give all your worries and cares to God, for he cares about you.

# INTEGRITY

**2 Samuel 22:21-23 BBE** The Lord gives me the reward of my righteousness, because my hands are clean before him. For I have kept the ways of the Lord; I have not been turned away in sin from my God. For all his decisions were before me, and I did not put away his laws from me.

**1 Chronicles 29:17-18 NIV** I know, my God, that you test the heart and are pleased with integrity. All these things have I given willingly and with honest intent. And now I have seen with joy how willingly your people who are here have given to you. O LORD, God of our fathers Abraham, Isaac and Israel, keep this desire in the hearts of your people forever, and keep their hearts loyal to you.

**Psalm 15:1-3 NASB** LORD, who may abide in Your tent? Who may dwell on Your holy hill? He who walks with integrity, and works righteousness, and speaks truth in his heart. He does not slander with his tongue, nor does evil to his neighbor, nor takes up a reproach against his friend.

**Job 1:1 MSG** Job was a man who lived in Uz. He was honest inside and out, a man of his word, who was totally devoted to God and hated evil with a passion.

**Job 8:5-7 ESV** If you will seek God and plead with the Almighty for mercy, if you are pure and upright, surely then he will rouse himself for you and restore your rightful habitation. And though your beginning was small, your latter days will be very great.

**Psalm 25:20-21 HCSB** Guard me and deliver me; do not let me be put to shame, for I take refuge in You. May integrity and uprightness keep me, for I wait for You.

**1 Timothy 4:11 MSG** Teach believers with your life: by word, by demeanor, by love, by faith, by integrity.

**Deuteronomy 4:9 BBE**   Only take care, and keep watch on your soul, for fear that the things which your eyes have seen go from your memory and from your heart all the days of your life.

**2 Samuel 22:25 BBE**   The Lord has given me the reward of my righteousness, because my hands are clean in his eyes.

**Psalm 25:15 CEV**   I always look to you, because you rescue me from every trap.

**Psalm 25:20-21 TNIV**   Guard my life and rescue me; do not let me be put to shame, for I take refuge in you. May integrity and uprightness protect me.

**Psalm 101:2-4 NCV**   I will be careful to live an innocent life. When will you come to me? I will live an innocent life in my house. I will not look at anything wicked. I hate those who turn against you; they will not be found near me. Let those who want to do wrong stay away from me; I will have nothing to do with evil.

**Psalm 139:23-24 ESV**   Search me, O God, and know my heart! Try me and know my thoughts! And see if there be any grievous way in me, and lead me in the way everlasting!

**Matthew 26:41 ESV**   Watch and pray that you may not enter into temptation. The spirit indeed is willing, but the flesh is weak.

**Colossians 3:1-2 BBE**   If then you have a new life with Christ, give your attention to the things of heaven, where Christ is seated at the right hand of God. Keep your mind on the higher things, not on the things of earth.

**2 Thessalonians 3:13 GNT**   You, friends, must not become tired of doing good.

**1 Peter 5:8 NIV**   Be self-controlled and alert. Your enemy the devil prowls around like a roaring lion looking for someone to devour.

**Deuteronomy 32:20-21 NLT** They are a twisted generation, children without integrity. They have roused my jealousy by worshiping things that are not God; they have provoked my anger with their useless idols.

**Proverbs 23:17-18 NLT** Don't envy sinners, but always continue to fear the LORD. You will be rewarded for this; your hope will not be disappointed.

**Proverbs 24:19-20 CEV** Don't let evil people worry you or make you jealous. They will soon be gone like the flame of a lamp that burns out.

**Romans 13:13-14 NASB** Let us behave properly as in the day, not in carousing and drunkenness, not in sexual promiscuity and sensuality, not in strife and jealousy. But put on the Lord Jesus Christ, and make no provision for the flesh in regard to its lusts.

**1 Timothy 6:4-5 NCV** This person is full of pride and understands nothing, but is sick with a love for arguing and fighting about words. This brings jealousy, fighting, speaking against others, evil mistrust, and constant quarrels from those who have evil minds and have lost the truth. They think that serving God is a way to get rich.

**James 4:2-3 NASB** You lust and do not have; so you commit murder. You are envious and cannot obtain; so you fight and quarrel. You do not have because you do not ask. You ask and do not receive, because you ask with wrong motives, so that you may spend it on your pleasures.

**James 3:14-16 NCV** If you are selfish and have bitter jealousy in your hearts, do not brag. Your bragging is a lie that hides the truth. That kind of "wisdom" does not come from God but from the world. It is not spiritual; it is from the devil. Where jealousy and selfishness are, there will be confusion and every kind of evil.

**Matthew 1:18-21 ESV**   Now the birth of Jesus Christ took place in this way. When his mother Mary had been betrothed to Joseph, before they came together she was found to be with child from the Holy Spirit. And her husband Joseph, being a just man and unwilling to put her to shame, resolved to divorce her quietly. But as he considered these things, behold, an angel of the Lord appeared to him in a dream, saying, "Joseph, son of David, do not fear to take Mary as your wife, for that which is conceived in her is from the Holy Spirit. She will bear a son, and you shall call his name Jesus, for he will save his people from their sins."

**Matthew 28:20 TNIV**   I am with you always.

**Luke 23:44-48 BBE**   And it was now about the sixth hour; and all the land was dark till the ninth hour; The light of the sun went out, and the curtain in the Temple was parted in two. And Jesus gave a loud cry and said, Father, into your hands I give my spirit: and when he had said this, he gave up his spirit. And when the captain saw what was done, he gave praise to God, saying, Without doubt this was an upright man. And all the people who had come together to see it, when they saw the things which were done, went back again making signs of grief.

**John 1:14 CEV**   The Word became a human being and lived here with us. We saw his true glory, the glory of the only Son of the Father. From him all the kindness and all the truth of God have come down to us.

**John 8:12 NKJV**   I am the light of the world.

**John 10:9 CEV**   I am the gate.

**Acts 4:11-12 NLT**   For Jesus is the one referred to in the Scriptures, where it says, "The stone that you builders rejected has now become the cornerstone." There is salvation in no one else! God has given no other name under heaven by which we must be saved.

**Romans 5:1-2 NCV**   Since we have been made right with God by our faith, we have peace with God. This happened through our Lord Jesus

Christ, who through our faith has brought us into that blessing of God's grace that we now enjoy.

**Colossians 2:5-7 NCV**   I am happy to see your good lives and your strong faith in Christ. As you received Christ Jesus the Lord, so continue to live in him. Keep your roots deep in him and have your lives built on him. Be strong in the faith, just as you were taught, and always be thankful.

**2 Timothy 1:9-10 CEV**   Even before time began God planned for Christ Jesus to show kindness to us. Now Christ Jesus has come to show us the kindness of God. Christ our Savior defeated death and brought us the good news. It shines like a light and offers life that never ends.

**Hebrews 1:2-3 NCV**   God has spoken to us through his Son. God has chosen his Son to own all things, and through him he made the world. The Son reflects the glory of God and shows exactly what God is like.

**Hebrews 2:17 NLT**   It was necessary for him to be made in every respect like us, his brothers and sisters, so that he could be our merciful and faithful High Priest before God. Then he could offer a sacrifice that would take away the sins of the people.

**Hebrews 4:15-16 CEV**   Jesus understands every weakness of ours, because he was tempted in every way that we are. But he did not sin! So whenever we are in need, we should come bravely before the throne of our merciful God. There we will be treated with undeserved kindness, and we will find help.

**Revelation 1:17 NLT**   I am the First and the Last.

**Revelation 22:20 ESV**   I am coming soon.

**Psalm 16:10-13 CEV**  I am your chosen one. You won't leave me in the grave or let my body decay. You have shown me the path to life, and you make me glad by being near to me. Sitting at your right side, I will always be joyful.

**Psalm 22:26 NLT**  All who seek the LORD will praise him. Their hearts will rejoice with everlasting joy.

**Psalm 27:1 CEV**  You, LORD, are the light that keeps me safe. I am not afraid of anyone. You protect me, and I have no fears.

**Psalm 32:1 NLT**  Oh, what joy for those whose disobedience is forgiven, whose sin is put out of sight!

**Psalm 40:8-9 NLT**  I take joy in doing your will, my God, for your instructions are written on my heart. I have told all your people about your justice. I have not been afraid to speak out, as you, O LORD, well know.

**Psalm 106:3 HCSB**  How happy are those who uphold justice, who practice righteousness at all times.

**Acts 14:17 NCV**  He proved he is real by showing kindness, by giving you rain from heaven and crops at the right times, by giving you food and filling your hearts with joy.

**Romans 12:15 NCV**  Be happy with those who are happy, and be sad with those who are sad.

**James 1:2-3 NKJV**  My brethren, count it all joy when you fall into various trials, knowing that the testing of your faith produces patience.

**Nehemiah 9:17 NKJV** You are God, ready to pardon, gracious and merciful, slow to anger, abundant in kindness, and did not forsake them.

**Job 6:14 NCV** A person's friends should be kind to him when he is in trouble, even if he stops fearing the Almighty.

**Job 10:12 CEV** You, the source of my life, showered me with kindness and watched over me.

**Psalm 5:12 CEV** Our LORD, you bless those who live right, and you shield them with your kindness.

**Proverbs 3:1–4 NASB** My son, do not forget my teaching, but let your heart keep my commandments; for length of days and years of life and peace they will add to you. Do not let kindness and truth leave you; bind them around your neck, write them on the tablet of your heart. So you will find favor and good repute in the sight of God and man.

**Proverbs 14:21 NIV** Blessed is he who is kind to the needy.

**Romans 2:4 NCV** He has been very kind and patient, waiting for you to change, but you think nothing of his kindness. Perhaps you do not understand that God is kind to you so you will change your hearts and lives.

**Ephesians 4:32 NCV** Be kind and loving to each other, and forgive each other just as God forgave you in Christ.

**Philemon 1:14 CEV** I won't do anything unless you agree to it first. I want your act of kindness to come from your heart, and not be something you feel forced to do.

**1 Kings 19:20 NIV**   Elisha then left his oxen and ran after Elijah. "Let me kiss my father and mother good-by," he said, "and then I will come with you."

**Job 31:26–28 NASB**   If I have looked at the sun when it shone or the moon going in splendor, and my heart became secretly enticed, and my hand threw a kiss from my mouth, that too would have been an iniquity calling for judgment, for I would have denied God above.

**Psalm 85:10 NLT**   Unfailing love and truth have met together. Righteousness and peace have kissed!

**Proverbs 24:26 NIV**   An honest answer is like a kiss on the lips.

**Proverbs 27:6 ESV**   Faithful are the wounds of a friend; profuse are the kisses of an enemy.

**Song of Solomon 4:11 NASB**   Your lips, my bride, drip honey; honey and milk are under your tongue, and the fragrance of your garments is like the fragrance of Lebanon.

**Hosea 13:2 CEV**   Now you continue to sin by designing and making idols of silver in the shape of calves. You are told to sacrifice to these idols—yes, even to kiss them.

**Luke 7:38 CEV**   She came and stood behind Jesus. She cried and started washing his feet with her tears and drying them with her hair. The woman kissed his feet and poured the perfume on them.

**Luke 22:48 NKJV**   Jesus said to him, "Judas, are you betraying the Son of Man with a kiss?"

**1 Thessalonians 5:26 NCV**   Give each other a holy kiss when you meet.

**Romans 12:6-8 NIV** We have different gifts, according to the grace given us. If a man's gift is prophesying, let him use it in proportion to his faith. If it is serving, let him serve; if it is teaching, let him teach; if it is encouraging, let him encourage; if it is contributing to the needs of others, let him give generously; if it is leadership, let him govern diligently; if it is showing mercy, let him do it cheerfully.

**1 Timothy 3:1-3 ESV** If anyone aspires to the office of overseer, he desires a noble task. Therefore an overseer must be above reproach, the husband of one wife, sober-minded, self-controlled, respectable, hospitable, able to teach, not a drunkard, not violent but gentle, not quarrelsome, not a lover of money.

**Hebrews 2:10-11 NCV** God is the One who made all things, and all things are for his glory. He wanted to have many children share his glory, so he made the One who leads people to salvation perfect through suffering. Jesus, who makes people holy, and those who are made holy are from the same family. So he is not ashamed to call them his brothers and sisters.

**Hebrews 13:17 WEB** Obey those who have the rule over you, and submit to them, for they watch on behalf of your souls, as those who will give account, that they may do this with joy, and not with groaning, for that would be unprofitable for you.

**1 Peter 5:2-4 NLT** Care for the flock that God has entrusted to you. Watch over it willingly, not grudgingly—not for what you will get out of it, but because you are eager to serve God. Don't lord it over the people assigned to your care, but lead them by your own good example. And when the Great Shepherd appears, you will receive a crown of never-ending glory and honor.

**1 Peter 5:5 ESV** Be subject to the elders. Clothe yourselves, all of you, with humility toward one another, for "God opposes the proud but gives grace to the humble."

**Exodus 4:10-12 NCV** Moses said to the LORD, "Please, Lord, I have never been a skilled speaker. Even now, after talking to you, I cannot speak well. I speak slowly and can't find the best words." Then the LORD said to him, "Who made a person's mouth? And who makes someone deaf or not able to speak? Or who gives a person sight or blindness? It is I, the LORD. Now go! I will help you speak, and I will teach you what to say."

**Psalm 37:23-24 CEV** If you do what the LORD wants, he will make certain each step you take is sure. The LORD will hold your hand, and if you stumble, you still won't fall.

**Psalm 138:8 NLT** The LORD will work out his plans for my life—for your faithful love, O LORD, endures forever. Don't abandon me, for you made me.

**Proverbs 1:7 MSG** Start with GOD—the first step in learning is bowing down to GOD; only fools thumb their noses at such wisdom and learning.

**Jeremiah 29:11 ESV** I know the plans I have for you, declares the LORD, plans for welfare and not for evil, to give you a future and a hope.

**John 14:26 ESV** The Helper, the Holy Spirit, whom the Father will send in my name, he will teach you all things and bring to your remembrance all that I have said to you.

**Ephesians 3:20 NCV** With God's power working in us, God can do much, much more than anything we can ask or imagine.

**Philippians 1:6 NASB** I am confident of this very thing, that He who began a good work in you will perfect it until the day of Christ Jesus.

**Psalm 95:2 NIV**   Let us come before him with thanksgiving and extol him with music and song.

**Psalm 132:7 NIV**   Let us go to his dwelling place; let us worship at his footstool.

**Isaiah 2:5 NASB**   Let us walk in the light of the LORD.

**Jeremiah 5:24 NLT**   Let us live in awe of the LORD our God.

**Hosea 6:3 ESV**   Let us press on to know the LORD.

**Romans 14:13 NASB**   Let us not judge one another anymore.

**Romans 14:19 TNIV**   Let us therefore make every effort to do what leads to peace and to mutual edification.

**Galatians 5:25 TNIV**   Let us keep in step with the Spirit.

**Galatians 6:9 AMP**   Let us not lose heart and grow weary and faint in acting nobly and doing right, for in due time and at the appointed season we shall reap, if we do not loosen and relax our courage and faint.

**1 Thessalonians 5:8 NIV**   Let us be self-controlled, putting on faith and love as a breastplate, and the hope of salvation as a helmet.

**Hebrews 4:14 TNIV**   Let us hold firmly to the faith we profess.

**Hebrews 12:1 NCV**   Let us run the race that is before us and never give up.

**Hebrews 12:2 NIV**   Let us fix our eyes on Jesus, the author and perfecter of our faith, who for the joy set before him endured the cross.

**1 John 3:18 ESV**   Let us not love in word or talk but in deed and in truth.

**Proverbs 10:5 NLT**  A wise youth harvests in the summer, but one who sleeps during harvest is a disgrace.

**Ephesians 4:1-3 NCV**  I urge you who have been chosen by God to live up to the life to which God called you. Always be humble, gentle, and patient, accepting each other in love. You are joined together with peace through the Spirit, so make every effort to continue together in this way.

**Ephesians 5:1-2 NCV**  You are God's children whom he loves, so try to be like him. Live a life of love just as Christ loved us.

**2 Timothy 3:2-5 TNIV**  People will be lovers of themselves, lovers of money, boastful, proud, abusive, disobedient to their parents, ungrateful, unholy, without love, unforgiving, slanderous, without self-control, brutal, not lovers of the good, treacherous, rash, conceited, lovers of pleasure rather than lovers of God—having a form of godliness but denying its power. Have nothing to do with such people.

**Hebrews 3:14 NLT**  If we are faithful to the end, trusting God just as firmly as when we first believed, we will share in all that belongs to Christ.

**2 Peter 1:5-9 CEV**  Do your best to improve your faith. You can do this by adding goodness, understanding, self-control, patience, devotion to God, concern for others, and love. If you keep growing in this way, it will show that what you know about our Lord Jesus Christ has made your lives useful and meaningful. But if you don't grow, you are like someone who is nearsighted or blind, and you have forgotten that your past sins are forgiven.

**2 Peter 3:11-14 CEV**  You should serve and honor God by the way you live. You should look forward to the day when God judges everyone. . . . You should make certain that the Lord finds you pure, spotless, and living at peace.

**Deuteronomy 8:18-20 CEV**   Remember that the LORD your God gives you the strength to make a living. That's how he keeps the promise he made to your ancestors. But I'm warning you—if you forget the LORD your God and worship other gods, the LORD will destroy you, just as he destroyed the nations you fought.

**Psalm 5:3 CEV**   Each morning you listen to my prayer, as I bring my requests to you and wait for your reply.

**Proverbs 1:20-27 NCV**   Wisdom is like a woman shouting in the street; she raises her voice in the city squares. She cries out in the noisy street and shouts at the city gates: "You fools, how long will you be foolish? How long will you make fun of wisdom and hate knowledge? If only you had listened when I corrected you, I would have told you what's in my heart; I would have told you what I am thinking. I called, but you refused to listen; I held out my hand, but you paid no attention. You did not follow my advice and did not listen when I corrected you. So I will laugh when you are in trouble. I will make fun when disaster strikes you, when disaster comes over you like a storm, when trouble strikes you like a whirlwind, when pain and trouble overwhelm you."

**Zechariah 1:3-4 NLT**   "Return to me, and I will return to you, says the LORD Almighty." Do not be like your ancestors who would not listen when the earlier prophets said to them, "This is what the LORD Almighty says: Turn from your evil ways and stop all your evil practices."

**Luke 11:28 GNT**   Happy are those who hear the word of God and obey it!

**Ephesians 5:10 NCV**   Try to learn what pleases the Lord.

**James 1:19 NIV**   Everyone should be quick to listen, slow to speak and slow to become angry.

**Joshua 1:9 NCV**   Remember that I commanded you to be strong and brave. Don't be afraid, because the LORD your God will be with you everywhere you go.

**Psalm 9:9-10 NCV**   The LORD defends those who suffer; he defends them in times of trouble. Those who know the LORD trust him, because he will not leave those who come to him.

**Psalm 25:16-18 NIV**   Turn to me and be gracious to me, for I am lonely and afflicted. The troubles of my heart have multiplied; free me from my anguish. Look upon my affliction and my distress and take away all my sins.

**Psalm 27:10 MSG**   My father and mother walked out and left me, but God took me in.

**Psalm 68:5-6 BBE**   A father to those who have no father, a judge of the widows, is God in his holy place. Those who are without friends, God puts in families; he makes free those who are in chains; but those who are turned away from him are given a dry land.

**Psalm 142:4-7 CEV**   Even if you look, you won't see anyone who cares enough to walk beside me. There is no place to hide, and no one who really cares. I pray to you, LORD! You are my place of safety, and you are my choice in the land of the living. Please answer my prayer. I am completely helpless. Help! They are chasing me, and they are too strong. Rescue me from this prison, so I can praise your name. And when your people notice your wonderful kindness to me, they will rush to my side.

**Colossians 2:10 NKJV**   You are complete in Him.

**Hebrews 13:5-6 TNIV**   Be content with what you have, because God has said, "Never will I leave you; never will I forsake you." So we say with confidence, "The Lord is my helper; I will not be afraid. What can human beings do to me?"

**Psalm 10:17 NKJV**   Lord, You have heard the desire of the humble; You will prepare their heart; You will cause Your ear to hear.

**Psalm 20:4 NKJV**   May He grant you according to your heart's desire, and fulfill all your purpose.

**Psalm 38:9-15 ESV**   O Lord, all my longing is before you; my sighing is not hidden from you. My heart throbs; my strength fails me, and the light of my eyes—it also has gone from me. My friends and companions stand aloof from my plague, and my nearest kin stand far off. Those who seek my life lay their snares; those who seek my hurt speak of ruin and meditate treachery all day long. But I am like a deaf man; I do not hear, like a mute man who does not open his mouth. I have become like a man who does not hear, and in whose mouth are no rebukes. But for you, O Lord, do I wait; it is you, O Lord my God, who will answer.

**Psalm 40:8 NIV**   I desire to do your will, O my God; your law is within my heart.

**Psalm 42:1-5 GNT**   As a deer longs for a stream of cool water, so I long for you, O God. I thirst for you, the living God. When can I go and worship in your presence? Day and night I cry, and tears are my only food; all the time my enemies ask me, "Where is your God?" My heart breaks when I remember the past, when I went with the crowds to the house of God and led them as they walked along, a happy crowd, singing and shouting praise to God. Why am I so sad? Why am I so troubled? I will put my hope in God, and once again I will praise him, my savior and my God.

**Proverbs 11:27-28 NCV**   Whoever looks for good will find kindness, but whoever looks for evil will find trouble. Those who trust in riches will be ruined, but a good person will be healthy like a green leaf.

**Isaiah 58:11 WEB**   Yahweh will guide you continually, and satisfy your soul in dry places, and make strong your bones; and you shall be like a watered garden, and like a spring of water, whose waters don't fail.

**Exodus 20:3-5 TNIV**  You shall have no other gods before me. You shall not make for yourself an image in the form of anything in heaven above or on the earth beneath or in the waters below. You shall not bow down to them or worship them; for I, the LORD your God, am a jealous God.

**1 Chronicles 16:25 ESV**  Great is the LORD, and greatly to be praised, and he is to be held in awe above all gods.

**Psalm 68:19 NLT**  Praise the Lord; praise God our savior! For each day he carries us in his arms.

**Psalm 86:5 ESV**  You, O Lord, are good and forgiving, abounding in steadfast love to all who call upon you.

**Psalm 146:5-10 CEV**  The LORD God of Jacob blesses everyone who trusts him and depends on him. God made heaven and earth; he created the sea and everything else. God always keeps his word. He gives justice to the poor and food to the hungry. The LORD sets prisoners free and heals blind eyes. He gives a helping hand to everyone who falls. The LORD loves good people and looks after strangers. He defends the rights of orphans and widows, but destroys the wicked. The LORD God of Zion will rule forever! Shout praises to the LORD.

**Romans 14:8 NIV**  If we live, we live to the Lord; and if we die, we die to the Lord. So, whether we live or die, we belong to the Lord.

**Luke 6:46 ESV**  Why do you call me "Lord, Lord," and not do what I tell you?

**Acts 17:23-25 ESV**  As I passed along and observed the objects of your worship, I found also an altar with this inscription, "To the unknown god." What therefore you worship as unknown, this I proclaim to you. The God who made the world and everything in it, being Lord of heaven and earth, does not live in temples made by man, nor is he served by human hands, as though he needed anything, since he himself gives to all mankind life and breath and everything.

**LOVE**

**Proverbs 17:9 ESV**   Whoever covers an offense seeks love, but he who repeats a matter separates close friends.

**Proverbs 30:18-19 CEV**   There are three or four things I cannot understand: How eagles fly so high or snakes crawl on rocks, how ships sail the ocean or people fall in love.

**Luke 10:27 ESV**   You shall love the Lord your God with all your heart and with all your soul and with all your strength and with all your mind, and your neighbor as yourself.

**John 13:34-35 TNIV**   A new command I give you: Love one another. As I have loved you, so you must love one another. By this everyone will know that you are my disciples, if you love one another.

**Romans 12:9-10 NCV**   Your love must be real. Hate what is evil, and hold on to what is good. Love each other like brothers and sisters. Give each other more honor than you want for yourselves.

**1 Corinthians 13:13 NKJV**   Now abide faith, hope, love, these three; but the greatest of these is love.

**1 Thessalonians 3:12 NLT**   May the Lord make your love for one another and for all people grow and overflow, just as our love for you overflows.

**1 John 3:17-18 ESV**   If anyone has the world's goods and sees his brother in need, yet closes his heart against him, how does God's love abide in him? Little children, let us not love in word or talk but in deed and in truth.

**1 John 4:17-19 CEV**   If we truly love others and live as Christ did in this world, we won't be worried about the day of judgment. A real love for others will chase those worries away. The thought of being punished is what makes us afraid. It shows that we have not really learned to love. We love because God loved us first.

**Proverbs 6:16-19 MSG** Here are six things God hates, and one more that he loathes with a passion: eyes that are arrogant, a tongue that lies, hands that murder the innocent, a heart that hatches evil plots, feet that race down a wicked track, a mouth that lies under oath, a troublemaker in the family.

**Proverbs 11:11 HCSB** A city is built up by the blessing of the upright, but it is torn down by the mouth of the wicked.

**Proverbs 12:18-19 NKJV** There is one who speaks like the piercings of a sword, But the tongue of the wise promotes health. The truthful lip shall be established forever, But a lying tongue is but for a moment.

**Proverbs 12:22 NCV** The LORD hates those who tell lies but is pleased with those who keep their promises.

**Proverbs 12:22 NRSV** Lying lips are an abomination to the Lord, but those who act faithfully are his delight.

**Proverbs 19:9 MSG** The person who tells lies gets caught; the person who spreads rumors is ruined.

**Colossians 3:9-10 WEB** Don't lie to one another, seeing that you have put off the old man with his doings, and have put on the new man, that is being renewed in knowledge after the image of his Creator.

**1 Peter 3:10 ESV** Whoever desires to love life and see good days, let him keep his tongue from evil and his lips from speaking deceit.

**Revelation 21:8 NIV** But the cowardly, the unbelieving, the vile, the murderers, the sexually immoral, those who practice magic arts, the idolaters and all liars—their place will be in the fiery lake of burning sulfur. This is the second death.

**Genesis 41:8 TNIV**   In the morning his mind was troubled, so he sent for all the magicians and wise men of Egypt. Pharaoh told them his dreams, but no one could interpret them for him.

**Exodus 7:22 NLT**   But again the magicians of Egypt used their magic, and they, too, turned water into blood. So Pharaoh's heart remained hard. He refused to listen to Moses and Aaron, just as the Lord had predicted.

**Exodus 8:18–19 NCV**   Using their tricks, the magicians tried to do the same thing, but they could not make the dust change into gnats. The gnats remained on the people and animals. So the magicians told the king that the power of God had done this.

**Numbers 23:21–23 MSG**   God is with them, and they're with him, shouting praises to their King. God brought them out of Egypt, rampaging like a wild ox. No magic spells can bind Jacob, no incantations can hold back Israel. People will look at Jacob and Israel and say, "What a great thing has God done!"

**Deuteronomy 18:10–12 NCV**   Don't let anyone use magic or witchcraft, or try to explain the meaning of signs. Don't let anyone try to control others with magic, and don't let them be mediums or try to talk with the spirits of dead people. The Lord hates anyone who does these things.

**2 Kings 17:17 MSG**   They indulged in all the black arts of magic and sorcery. In short, they prostituted themselves to every kind of evil available to them. And God had had enough.

**Ezekiel 13:18 NLT**   This is what the Sovereign Lord says: What sorrow awaits you women who are ensnaring the souls of my people, young and old alike. You tie magic charms on their wrists and furnish them with magic veils. Do you think you can trap others without bringing destruction on yourselves?

**Genesis 2:18 TNIV** The LORD God said, "It is not good for the man to be alone. I will make a helper suitable for him."

**Deuteronomy 24:5 NIV** If a man has recently married, he must not be sent to war or have any other duty laid on him. For one year he is to be free to stay at home and bring happiness to the wife he has married.

**Proverbs 5:19-21 NCV** She is as lovely and graceful as a deer. Let her love always make you happy; let her love always hold you captive. My son, don't be held captive by a woman who takes part in adultery. Don't hug another man's wife. The LORD sees everything you do, and he watches where you go.

**Matthew 5:32 NIV** I tell you that anyone who divorces his wife, except for marital unfaithfulness, causes her to become and adulteress, and anyone who marries the divorced woman commits adultery.

**Mark 10:6-9 ESV** From the beginning of creation, God made them male and female. Therefore a man shall leave his father and mother and hold fast to his wife, and the two shall become one flesh. So they are no longer two but one flesh. What therefore God has joined together, let not man separate.

**2 Corinthians 6:14 NCV** You are not the same as those who do not believe. So do not join yourselves to them. Good and bad do not belong together. Light and darkness cannot share together.

**Ephesians 4:2-3 NCV** Always be humble, gentle, and patient, accepting each other in love. You are joined together with peace through the Spirit, so make every effort to continue together in this way.

**Colossians 3:18-19 NIV** Wives, submit yourselves to your husbands, as is fitting in the Lord. Husbands, love your wives and do not be harsh with them.

**Hebrews 13:4 NKJV** Marriage is honorable among all, and the bed undefiled; but fornicators and adulterers God will judge.

**Luke 8:14 NLT**   The seeds that fell among the thorns represent those who hear the message, but all too quickly the message is crowded out by the cares and riches and pleasures of this life. And so they never grow into maturity.

**John 14:12 ESV**   I say to you, whoever believes in me will also do the works that I do; and greater works than these will he do, because I am going to the Father.

**2 Corinthians 13:11 NLT**   Be joyful. Grow to maturity. Encourage each other. Live in harmony and peace. Then the God of love and peace will be with you.

**Ephesians 4:13–14 NCV**   We must become like a mature person, growing until we become like Christ and have his perfection. Then we will no longer be babies. We will not be tossed about like a ship that the waves carry one way and then another. We will not be influenced by every new teaching we hear from people who are trying to fool us. They make plans and try any kind of trick to fool people into following the wrong path.

**Colossians 1:9–12 TNIV**   We have not stopped praying for you. We continually ask God to fill you with the knowledge of his will through all the wisdom and understanding that the Spirit gives, so that you may live a life worthy of the Lord and please him in every way: bearing fruit in every good work, growing in the knowledge of God, being strengthened with all power according to his glorious might so that you may have great endurance and patience, and giving joyful thanks to the Father, who has qualified you to share in the inheritance of his people in the kingdom of light.

**Colossians 4:12 TNIV**   He is always wrestling in prayer for you, that you may stand firm in all the will of God, mature and fully assured.

**1 Timothy 4:12 NASB**   Let no one look down on your youthfulness, but rather in speech, conduct, love, faith and purity, show yourself an example of those who believe.

**Psalm 19:14 NRSV**   Let the words of my mouth and the meditation of my heart be acceptable to you, O Lord, my rock and my redeemer.

**Psalm 27:8 NRSV**   "Come," my heart says, "seek his face!" Your face, Lord, do I seek.

**Psalm 37:7-8 TNIV**   Be still before the Lord and wait patiently for him; do not fret when people succeed in their ways, when they carry out their wicked schemes. Refrain from anger and turn from wrath; do not fret— it leads only to evil.

**Psalm 77:11-13 NIV**   I will remember the deeds of the Lord; yes, I will remember your miracles of long ago. I will meditate on all your works and consider all your mighty deeds. Your ways, O God, are holy. What god is so great as our God?

**Psalm 119:27-29 TNIV**   Cause me to understand the way of your precepts, that I may meditate on your wonderful deeds. My soul is weary with sorrow; strengthen me according to your word. Keep me from deceitful ways; be gracious to me and teach me your law.

**Psalm 119:97-99 GNT**   How I love your law! I think about it all day long. Your commandment is with me all the time and makes me wiser than my enemies. I understand more than all my teachers, because I meditate on your instructions.

**Philippians 4:8-9 NKJV**   Brethren, whatever things are true, whatever things are noble, whatever things are just, whatever things are pure, whatever things are lovely, whatever things are of good report, if there is any virtue and if there is anything praiseworthy—meditate on these things. The things which you learned and received and heard and saw in me, these do, and the God of peace will be with you.

**Isaiah 54:10 NKJV** "The mountains shall depart and the hills be removed, but My kindness shall not depart from you, nor shall My covenant of peace be removed," says the LORD, who has mercy on you.

**Isaiah 63:7 NCV** I will tell about the LORD's kindness and praise him for everything he has done. I will praise the LORD for the many good things he has given us and for his goodness to the people of Israel. He has shown great mercy to us and has been very kind to us.

**Daniel 9:9 NCV** Lord our God, you show us mercy and forgive us even though we have turned against you.

**Micah 6:8 TNIV** He has shown all you people what is good. And what does the LORD require of you? To act justly and to love mercy and to walk humbly with your God.

**Ephesians 2:4-5 CEV** God was merciful! We were dead because of our sins, but God loved us so much that he made us alive with Christ, and God's wonderful kindness is what saves you.

**1 Timothy 1:12-14 CEV** I thank Christ Jesus our Lord. He has given me the strength for my work because he knew that he could trust me. I used to say terrible and insulting things about him, and I was cruel. But he had mercy on me because I didn't know what I was doing, and I had not yet put my faith in him. Christ Jesus our Lord was very kind to me. He has greatly blessed my life with faith and love just like his own.

**Hebrews 4:15-17 CEV** Jesus understands every weakness of ours, because he was tempted in every way that we are. But he did not sin! So whenever we are in need, we should come bravely before the throne of our merciful God. There we will be treated with undeserved kindness, and we will find help.

**Genesis 1:2-3 TNIV**  Now the earth was formless and empty, darkness was over the surface of the deep, and the Spirit of God was hovering over the waters. And God said, "Let there be light," and there was light.

**Exodus 3:2 ESV**  The angel of the Lord appeared to him in a flame of fire out of the midst of a bush. He looked, and behold, the bush was burning, yet it was not consumed.

**Exodus 7:10 NCV**  Aaron threw his walking stick down in front of the king and his officers, and it became a snake.

**Nehemiah 9:17 NIV**  They refused to listen and failed to remember the miracles you performed among them. They became stiff-necked and in their rebellion appointed a leader in order to return to their slavery. But you are a forgiving God, gracious and compassionate, slow to anger and abounding in love. Therefore you did not desert them.

**Matthew 8:15-16 ESV**  He touched her hand, and the fever left her, and she rose and began to serve him. That evening they brought to him many who were oppressed by demons, and he cast out the spirits with a word and healed all who were sick.

**Matthew 8:24-26 NCV**  A great storm arose on the lake so that waves covered the boat, but Jesus was sleeping. His followers went to him and woke him, saying, "Lord, save us! We will drown!" Jesus answered, "Why are you afraid? You don't have enough faith." Then Jesus got up and gave a command to the wind and the waves, and it became completely calm.

**Matthew 14:25-27 NCV**  Between three and six o'clock in the morning, Jesus came to them, walking on the water. When his followers saw him walking on the water, they were afraid. They said, "It's a ghost!" and cried out in fear. But Jesus quickly spoke to them, "Have courage! It is I. Do not be afraid."

**Proverbs 3:9-10 NASB**   Honor the LORD from your wealth and from the first of all your produce; so your barns will be filled with plenty and your vats will overflow with new wine.

**Proverbs 20:21 NIV**   An inheritance quickly gained at the beginning will not be blessed at the end.

**Proverbs 23:4 GNT**   Be wise enough not to wear yourself out trying to get rich.

**Proverbs 28:11 HCSB**   A rich man is wise in his own eyes, but a poor man who has discernment sees through him.

**Proverbs 28:20 NASB**   A faithful man will abound with blessings, but he who makes haste to be rich will not go unpunished.

**Luke 12:15 CEV**   Don't be greedy! Owning a lot of things won't make your life safe.

**1 Timothy 6:7-10 CEV**   We didn't bring anything into this world, and we won't take anything with us when we leave. So we should be satisfied just to have food and clothes. People who want to be rich fall into all sorts of temptations and traps. They are caught by foolish and harmful desires that drag them down and destroy them. The love of money causes all kinds of trouble. Some people want money so much that they have given up their faith and caused themselves a lot of pain.

**Hebrews 13:5 TNIV**   Keep your lives free from the love of money and be content with what you have, because God has said, "Never will I leave you; never will I forsake you."

**James 1:9-11 NCV**   Believers who are poor should take pride that God has made them spiritually rich. Those who are rich should take pride that God has shown them that they are spiritually poor. The rich will die like a wild flower in the grass. The sun rises with burning heat and dries up the plants. The flower falls off, and its beauty is gone. In the same way the rich will die while they are still taking care of business.

**Psalm 101:2-4 NCV**   I will be careful to live an innocent life. When will you come to me? I will live an innocent life in my house. I will not look at anything wicked. I hate those who turn against you; they will not be found near me. Let those who want to do wrong stay away from me; I will have nothing to do with evil.

**Psalm 139:23-24 ESV**   Search me, O God, and know my heart! Try me and know my thoughts! And see if there be any grievous way in me, and lead me in the way everlasting!

**Proverbs 14:27 NCV**   Respect for the LORD gives life. It is like a fountain that can save people from death.

**Matthew 5:27-28 HCSB**   You have heard that it was said, Do not commit adultery. But I tell you, everyone who looks at a woman to lust for her has already committed adultery with her in his heart.

**Matthew 26:41 ESV**   Watch and pray that you may not enter into temptation. The spirit indeed is willing, but the flesh is weak.

**Romans 14:12-13 NASB**   Each one of us will give an account of himself to God. Therefore let us not judge one another anymore, but rather determine this—not to put an obstacle or a stumbling block in a brother's way.

**Philippians 4:8 GNT**   Fill your minds with those things that are good and that deserve praise: things that are true, noble, right, pure, lovely, and honorable.

**2 Timothy 1:14 CEV**   You have been trusted with a wonderful treasure. Guard it with the help of the Holy Spirit, who lives within you.

**Titus 1:16 NIV**   They claim to know God, but by their actions they deny him.

**1 Peter 5:8 NIV**   Be self-controlled and alert. Your enemy the devil prowls around like a roaring lion looking for someone to devour.

**Judges 5:3 MSG**  To God, yes to God, I'll sing, Make music to God.

**Psalm 19:14 HCSB**  May the words of my mouth and the meditation of my heart be acceptable to You, LORD, my rock and my Redeemer.

**Psalm 27:5-6 ESV**  He will hide me in his shelter in the day of trouble; he will conceal me under the cover of his tent; he will lift me high upon a rock. And now my head shall be lifted up above my enemies all around me, and I will offer in his tent sacrifices with shouts of joy; I will sing and make melody to the LORD.

**Psalm 33:1-3 CEV**  You are the LORD's people. Obey him and celebrate! He deserves your praise. Praise the LORD with harps! Use harps with ten strings to make music for him. Sing a new song. Shout! Play beautiful music.

**Psalm 107:22 HCSB**  Let them offer sacrifices of thanksgiving and announce His works with shouts of joy.

**Psalm 119:54-55 NLT**  Your decrees have been the theme of my songs wherever I have lived. I reflect at night on who you are, O LORD; therefore, I obey your instructions.

**Psalm 150:3-6 NKJV**  Praise Him with the sound of the trumpet; Praise Him with the lute and harp! Praise Him with the timbrel and dance; Praise Him with stringed instruments and flutes! Praise Him with loud cymbals; Praise Him with clashing cymbals! Let everything that has breath praise the LORD. Praise the LORD!

**Ephesians 5:19-20 AMP**  Speak out to one another in psalms and hymns and spiritual songs, offering praise with voices [and instruments] and making melody with all your heart to the Lord, At all times and for everything giving thanks in the name of our Lord Jesus Christ to God the Father.

**Colossians 3:2-3 NIV**  Set your minds on things above, not on earthly things. For you died, and your life is now hidden with Christ in God.

**Proverbs 1:8-9 NCV**   Listen to your father's teaching and do not forget your mother's advice. Their teaching will be like flowers in your hair or a necklace around your neck.

**John 17:15-18 NIV**   My prayer is not that you take them out of the world but that you protect them from the evil one. They are not of the world, even as I am not of it. Sanctify them by the truth; your word is truth. As you sent me into the world, I have sent them into the world.

**2 Corinthians 1:12 NIV**   Now this is our boast: Our conscience testifies that we have conducted ourselves in the world, and especially in our relations with you, in the holiness and sincerity that are from God. We have done so not according to worldly wisdom but according to God's grace.

**Ephesians 4:27 NCV**   Do not give the devil a way to defeat you.

**Ephesians 4:29-30 CEV**   Stop all your dirty talk. Say the right thing at the right time and help others by what you say. Don't make God's Spirit sad. The Spirit makes you sure that someday you will be free from your sins.

**Ephesians 5:11-15 GNT**   Have nothing to do with the worthless things that people do, things that belong to the darkness. Instead, bring them out to the light (It is really too shameful even to talk about the things they do in secret.) And when all things are brought out to the light, then their true nature is clearly revealed; for anything that is clearly revealed becomes light. . . . So be careful how you live.

**Hebrews 10:24 NLT**   Let us think of ways to motivate one another to acts of love and good works.

**James 5:16 NASB**   Confess your sins to one another, and pray for one another so that you may be healed. The effective prayer of a righteous man can accomplish much.

**NEW BEGINNINGS**

**Psalm 37:23-24 NLT**   The LORD directs the steps of the godly. He delights in every detail of their lives. Though they stumble, they will never fall, for the LORD holds them by the hand.

**Psalm 40:2-4 NIV**   He lifted me out of the slimy pit, out of the mud and mire; he set my feet on a rock and gave me a firm place to stand. He put a new song in my mouth, a hymn of praise to our God. Many will see and fear and put their trust in the LORD. Blessed is the man who makes the LORD his trust.

**Psalm 51:10 ESV**   Create in me a clean heart, O God, and renew a right spirit within me.

**Ezekiel 36:26 TNIV**   I will give you a new heart and put a new spirit in you; I will remove from you your heart of stone and give you a heart of flesh.

**Titus 3:3-5 NIV**   At one time we too were foolish, disobedient, deceived and enslaved by all kinds of passions and pleasures. We lived in malice and envy, being hated and hating one another. But when the kindness and love of God our Savior appeared, he saved us.

**1 Peter 4:4-5 NLT**   Of course, your former friends are very surprised when you no longer join them in the wicked things they do, and they say evil things about you. But just remember that they will have to face God, who will judge everyone, both the living and the dead.

**2 Peter 1:3-4 TNIV**   His divine power has given us everything we need for a godly life through our knowledge of him who called us by his own glory and goodness. Through these he has given us his very great and precious promises, so that through them you may participate in the divine nature, having escaped the corruption in the world caused by evil desires.

**Deuteronomy 30:11-14 CEV**  You know God's laws, and it isn't impossible to obey them. His commands aren't in heaven, so you can't excuse yourselves by saying, "How can we obey the LORD's commands? They are in heaven, and no one can go up to get them, then bring them down and explain them to us." And you can't say, "How can we obey the LORD's commands? They are across the sea, and someone must go across, then bring them back and explain them to us." No, these commands are nearby and you know them by heart. All you have to do is obey!

**Psalm 18:20-22 NIV**  The LORD has dealt with me according to my righteousness; according to the cleanness of my hands he has rewarded me. For I have kept the ways of the LORD; I have not done evil by turning from my God. All his laws are before me; I have not turned away from his decrees.

**Psalm 119:4-8 BBE**  You have put your orders into our hearts, so that we might keep them with care. If only my ways were ordered so that I might keep your rules! Then I would not be put to shame, as long as I have respect for all your teaching. I will give you praise with an upright heart in learning your right decisions. I will keep your rules: O give me not up completely.

**Proverbs 8:32-33 NIV**  Now then, my sons, listen to me; blessed are those who keep my ways. Listen to my instruction and be wise; do not ignore it.

**2 Corinthians 10:5 NLT**  We destroy every proud obstacle that keeps people from knowing God. We capture their rebellious thoughts and teach them to obey Christ.

# OCCULT

**Leviticus 19:26–28 ESV**   You shall not interpret omens or tell fortunes. You shall not round off the hair on your temples or mar the edges of your beard. You shall not make any cuts on your body for the dead or tattoo yourselves: I am the LORD.

**Leviticus 19:31 TNIV**   Do not turn to mediums or seek out spiritists, for you will be defiled by them. I am the LORD your God.

**2 Kings 21:6 MSG**   He practiced black magic and fortunetelling. He held séances and consulted spirits from the underworld. Much evil—in GOD's judgment, a career in evil. And GOD was angry.

**1 Chronicles 10:13 ESV**   Saul died for his breach of faith. He broke faith with the LORD in that he did not keep the command of the LORD, and also consulted a medium, seeking guidance.

**Luke 10:17–19 TNIV**   The seventy-two returned with joy and said, "Lord, even the demons submit to us in your name." He replied, "I saw Satan fall like lightning from heaven. I have given you authority to trample on snakes and scorpions and to overcome all the power of the enemy; nothing will harm you."

**1 Timothy 4:1–5 NKJV**   Now the Spirit expressly says that in latter times some will depart from the faith, giving heed to deceiving spirits and doctrines of demons, speaking lies in hypocrisy, having their own conscience seared with a hot iron, forbidding to marry, and commanding to abstain from foods which God created to be received with thanksgiving by those who believe and know the truth. For every creature of God is good, and nothing is to be refused if it is received with thanksgiving; for it is sanctified by the word of God and prayer.

**Psalm 34:17-20 GNT**  The righteous call to the Lord, and he listens; he rescues them from all their troubles. The Lord is near to those who are discouraged; he saves those who have lost all hope. Good people suffer many troubles, but the Lord saves them from them all; the Lord preserves them completely; not one of their bones is broken.

**Psalm 56:13 NRSV**  You have delivered my soul from death, and my feet from falling, so that I may walk before God in the light of life.

**Psalm 62:5-6 NKJV**  My soul, wait silently for God alone, for my expectation is from Him. He only is my rock and my salvation; He is my defense; I shall not be moved.

**Jeremiah 15:20-21 NIV**  "I will make you a wall to this people, a fortified wall of bronze; they will fight against you but will not overcome you, for I am with you to rescue and save you," declares the LORD. "I will save you from the hands of the wicked and redeem you from the grasp of the cruel."

**John 16:32-33 NIV**  "I am not alone, for my Father is with me. I have told you these things, so that in me you may have peace. In this world you will have trouble. But take heart! I have overcome the world."

**Romans 12:21 NRSV**  Do not be overcome by evil, but overcome evil with good.

**1 John 4:4 NCV**  My dear children, you belong to God and have defeated them; because God's Spirit, who is in you, is greater than the devil, who is in the world.

**1 John 5:4-5 NASB**  Whatever is born of God overcomes the world; and this is the victory that has overcome the world—our faith. Who is the one who overcomes the world, but he who believes that Jesus is the Son of God?

**Proverbs 6:20-23 HCSB**   My son, keep your father's command, and don't reject your mother's teaching. Always bind them to your heart; tie them around your neck. When you walk here and there, they will guide you; when you lie down, they will watch over you; when you wake up, they will talk to you. For a commandment is a lamp, teaching is a light, and corrective instructions are the way to life.

**Proverbs 15:5 NLT**   Only a fool despises a parent's discipline; whoever learns from correction is wise.

**Proverbs 15:20 NLT**   Sensible children bring joy to their father; foolish children despise their mother.

**Proverbs 18:15 MSG**   Wise men and women are always learning, always listening for fresh insights.

**Romans 1:28-31 ESV**   Since they did not see fit to acknowledge God, God gave them up to a debased mind to do what ought not to be done. They were filled with all manner of unrighteousness. . . . They are gossips, slanderers, haters of God, insolent, haughty, boastful, inventors of evil, disobedient to parents, foolish, faithless, heartless, ruthless.

**Romans 14:19 CEV**   We should try to live at peace and help each other have a strong faith.

**Ephesians 6:2-3 AMP**   Honor (esteem and value as precious) your father and your mother—this is the first commandment with a promise—that all may be well with you and that you may live long on the earth.

**1 Thessalonians 2:11-12 NIV**   You know that we dealt with each of you as a father deals with his own children, encouraging, comforting and urging you to live lives worthy of God, who calls you into his kingdom and glory.

**1 Peter 4:8 NIV**   Above all, love each other deeply, because love covers over a multitude of sins.

**Deuteronomy 26:11 NLT**   Afterward you may go and celebrate because of all the good things the LORD your God has given to you and your household.

**Isaiah 61:10 NIV**   I delight greatly in the LORD; my soul rejoices in my God. For he has clothed me with garments of salvation and arrayed me in a robe of righteousness, as a bridegroom adorns his head like a priest, and as a bride adorns herself with her jewels.

**Luke 14:12-14 NIV**   Jesus said to his host, "When you give a luncheon or dinner, do not invite your friends, your brothers or relatives, or your rich neighbors; if you do, they may invite you back and so you will be repaid. But when you give a banquet, invite the poor, the crippled, the lame, the blind, and you will be blessed. Although they cannot repay you, you will be repaid at the resurrection of the righteous."

**Romans 13:13-14 NCV**   Let us live in a right way, like people who belong to the day. We should not have wild parties or get drunk. There should be no sexual sins of any kind, no fighting or jealousy. But clothe yourselves with the Lord Jesus Christ and forget about satisfying your sinful self.

**Ephesians 5:17-19 MSG**   Don't live carelessly, unthinkingly. Make sure you understand what the Master wants. Don't drink too much wine. That cheapens your life. Drink the Spirit of God, huge draughts of him. Sing hymns instead of drinking songs! Sing songs from your heart to Christ.

**1 Peter 4:2-4 NCV**   Strengthen yourselves so that you will live here on earth doing what God wants, not the evil things people want. In the past you wasted too much time doing what nonbelievers enjoy. You were guilty of sexual sins, evil desires, drunkenness, wild and drunken parties, and hateful idol worship. Nonbelievers think it is strange that you do not do the many wild and wasteful things they do, so they insult you.

**Psalm 25:4–5 NRSV**   Make me to know your ways, O Lord; teach me your paths. Lead me in your truth, and teach me, for you are the God of my salvation; for you I wait all day long.

**Psalm 37:7–8 GNT**   Be patient and wait for the Lord to act; don't be worried about those who prosper or those who succeed in their evil plans. Don't give in to worry or anger; it only leads to trouble.

**Proverbs 14:29 NIV**   A patient man has great understanding, but a quick-tempered man displays folly.

**Isaiah 30:18 NLT**   The LORD still waits for you to come to him so he can show you his love and compassion. For the LORD is a faithful God. Blessed are those who wait for him to help them.

**Lamentations 3:21–25 NRSV**   This I call to mind, and therefore I have hope: The steadfast love of the Lord never ceases, his mercies never come to an end; they are new every morning; great is your faithfulness. "The Lord is my portion," says my soul, "therefore I will hope in him." The Lord is good to those who wait for him, to the soul that seeks him.

**Micah 7:7 NLT**   As for me, I look to the LORD for his help. I wait confidently for God to save me, and my God will certainly hear me.

**Romans 12:12 NIV**   Be joyful in hope, patient in affliction, faithful in prayer.

**1 Corinthians 13:4 NASB**   Love is patient, love is kind and is not jealous; love does not brag and is not arrogant,

**Ephesians 4:2 GNT**   Be always humble, gentle, and patient. Show your love by being tolerant with one another.

**Psalm 119:165 NASB**  Those who love Your law have great peace, and nothing causes them to stumble.

**Proverbs 14:30 WEB**  The life of the body is a heart at peace, but envy rots the bones.

**Isaiah 54:10 NIV**  "Though the mountains be shaken and the hills be removed, yet my unfailing love for you will not be shaken nor my covenant of peace be removed," says the LORD, who has compassion on you.

**Matthew 11:28-30 NLT**  Come to me, all of you who are weary and carry heavy burdens, and I will give you rest. Take my yoke upon you. Let me teach you, because I am humble and gentle, and you will find rest for your souls. For my yoke fits perfectly, and the burden I give you is light.

**John 16:33 NIV**  I have told you these things, so that in me you may have peace. In this world you will have trouble. But take heart! I have overcome the world.

**Romans 14:19 GNT**  We must always aim at those things that bring peace and that help strengthen one another.

**Romans 15:13 NIV**  May the God of hope fill you with all joy and peace as you trust in him, so that you may overflow with hope by the power of the Holy Spirit.

**Colossians 3:15 NLT**  And let the peace that comes from Christ rule in your hearts. For as members of one body you are all called to live in peace. And always be thankful.

**2 Thessalonians 3:16 NASB**  Now may the Lord of peace Himself continually grant you peace in every circumstance. The Lord be with you all!

# PEER PRESSURE

**Exodus 23:2 GNT**   Do not follow the majority when they do wrong or when they give testimony that perverts justice.

**Deuteronomy 13:6-8 NCV**   Someone might try to lead you to serve other gods—it might be your brother, your son or daughter, the wife you love, or a close friend. The person might say, "Let's go and worship other gods." (These are gods that neither you nor your ancestors have known, gods of the people who live around you, either nearby or far away, from one end of the land to the other.) Do not give in to such people. Do not listen or feel sorry for them, and do not let them go free or protect them.

**Proverbs 3:3-4 NIV**   Let love and faithfulness never leave you; bind them around your neck, write them on the tablet of your heart. Then you will win favor and a good name in the sight of God and man.

**2 Corinthians 6:8 CEV**   Whether we were honored or dishonored or praised or cursed, we always told the truth about ourselves. But some people said we did not.

**Philippians 2:3-4 NASB**   Do nothing from selfishness or empty conceit, but with humility of mind regard one another as more important than yourselves; do not merely look out for your own personal interests, but also for the interests of others.

**1 Peter 2:11-12 MSG**   Friends, this world is not your home, so don't make yourselves cozy in it. Don't indulge your ego at the expense of your soul. Live an exemplary life among the natives so that your actions will refute their prejudices. Then they'll be won over to God's side and be there to join in the celebration when he arrives.

**1 Peter 3:15-16 CEV**   Always be ready to give an answer when someone asks you about your hope. Give a kind and respectful answer and keep your conscience clear. This way you will make people ashamed for saying bad things about your good conduct as a follower of Christ.

**Genesis 24:47–48 NIV**   I put the ring in her nose and the bracelets on her arms, and I bowed down and worshiped the LORD. I praised the LORD, the God of my master Abraham, who had led me on the right road to get the granddaughter of my master's brother for his son.

**Genesis 35:2–4 BBE**   Jacob said to all his people, Put away the strange gods which are among you, and make yourselves clean, and put on a change of clothing: And let us go up to Beth-el: and there I will make an altar to God, who gave me an answer in the day of my trouble, and was with me wherever I went. Then they gave to Jacob all the strange gods which they had, and the rings which were in their ears; and Jacob put them away under the holy tree at Shechem.

**Exodus 21:6 MSG**   His master is to bring him before God and to a door or doorpost and pierce his ear with an awl, a sign that he is a slave for life.

**Deuteronomy 14:1–2 TNIV**   You are the children of the LORD your God. Do not cut yourselves or shave the front of your heads for the dead, for you are a people holy to the LORD your God. Out of all the peoples on the face of the earth, the LORD has chosen you to be his treasured possession.

**Isaiah 53:5–6 HCSB**   He was pierced because of our transgressions, crushed because of our iniquities; punishment for our peace was on Him, and we are healed by His wounds. We all went astray like sheep; we all have turned to our own way; and the LORD has punished Him for the iniquity of us all.

**Jeremiah 4:17–18 NIV**   "They surround her like men guarding a field, because she has rebelled against me," declares the LORD. "Your own conduct and actions have brought this upon you. This is your punishment. How bitter it is! How it pierces to the heart!"

**1 Corinthians 6:13 MSG**   Since the Master honors you with a body, honor him with your body!

**Psalm 20:4 NIV**   May he give you the desire of your heart and make all your plans succeed.

**Psalm 33:11 NIV**   The plans of the LORD stand firm forever, the purposes of his heart through all generations.

**Psalm 37:37 NLT**   Look at those who are honest and good, for a wonderful future awaits those who love peace.

**Proverbs 13:4 HCSB**   The slacker craves, yet has nothing, but the diligent is fully satisfied.

**Proverbs 16:9 ESV**   The heart of man plans his way, but the LORD establishes his steps.

**Proverbs 20:18 CEV**   Be sure you have sound advice before making plans

**Proverbs 21:5 ESV**   The plans of the diligent lead surely to abundance, but everyone who is hasty comes only to poverty.

**Romans 8:29-30 NCV**   God knew them before he made the world, and he chose them to be like his Son so that Jesus would be the firstborn of many brothers and sisters. God planned for them to be like his Son; and those he planned to be like his Son, he also called; and those he called, he also made right with him; and those he made right, he also glorified.

**Hebrews 10:23 NCV**   Let us hold firmly to the hope that we have confessed, because we can trust God to do what he promised.

**Hebrews 10:36 NASB**   You have need of endurance, so that when you have done the will of God, you may receive what was promised.

**1 Samuel 16:7 NASB**   The Lord said to Samuel, "Do not look at his appearance or at the height of his stature, because I have rejected him; for God sees not as man sees, for man looks at the outward appearance, but the Lord looks at the heart."

**Proverbs 3:3-4 NLT**   Never let loyalty and kindness get away from you! Wear them like a necklace; write them deep within your heart. Then you will find favor with both God and people, and you will gain a good reputation.

**Proverbs 22:1 NCV**   Being respected is more important than having great riches. To be well thought of is better than silver or gold.

**Luke 9:25-26 NCV**   It is worthless to have the whole world if they themselves are destroyed or lost. If people are ashamed of me and my teaching, then the Son of Man will be ashamed of them when he comes in his glory and with the glory of the Father and the holy angels.

**Romans 6:13 NCV**   Do not offer the parts of your body to serve sin, as things to be used in doing evil. Instead, offer yourselves to God as people who have died and now live. Offer the parts of your body to God to be used in doing good.

**Philippians 2:3-7 NCV**   When you do things, do not let selfishness or pride be your guide. Instead, be humble and give more honor to others than to yourselves. Do not be interested only in your own life, but be interested in the lives of others. In your lives you must think and act like Christ Jesus. Christ himself was like God in everything. But he did not think that being equal with God was something to be used for his own benefit. But he gave up his place with God and made himself nothing. He was born to be a man and became like a servant.

# PORNOGRAPHY

**Psalm 119:37–38 NKJV**   Turn away my eyes from looking at worthless things, and revive me in Your way. Establish Your word to Your servant, who is devoted to fearing You.

**Proverbs 6:25–26 CEV**   Don't let yourself be attracted by the charm and lovely eyes of someone like that. A woman who sells her love can be bought for as little as the price of a meal.

**Ezekiel 20:30 NLT**   Do you plan to pollute yourselves just as your ancestors did? Do you intend to keep prostituting yourselves by worshiping vile images?

**Romans 6:19 NLT**   Previously, you let yourselves be slaves to impurity and lawlessness, which led ever deeper into sin. Now you must give yourselves to be slaves to righteous living so that you will become holy.

**Ephesians 4:19–20 ESV**   They have become callous and have given themselves up to sensuality, greedy to practice every kind of impurity. But that is not the way you learned Christ!

**Philippians 4:8 CEV**   Keep your minds on whatever is true, pure, right, holy, friendly, and proper. Don't ever stop thinking about what is truly worthwhile and worthy of praise.

**2 Peter 2:19 CEV**   They promise freedom to everyone. But they are merely slaves of filthy living, because people are slaves of whatever controls them.

**1 John 2:15–16 NCV**   If you love the world, the love of the Father is not in you. These are the ways of the world: wanting to please our sinful selves, wanting the sinful things we see, and being too proud of what we have. None of these come from the Father.

# POSSESSIONS  189

**Psalm 24:1 NIV**   The earth is the LORD's, and everything in it, the world, and all who live in it.

**Proverbs 3:9-10 NKJV**   Honor the LORD with your possessions, and with the firstfruits of all your increase; so your barns will be filled with plenty, and your vats will overflow with new wine.

**Luke 14:33 NCV**   In the same way, you must give up everything you have to be my follower.

**Acts 2:44-45 NLT**   All the believers met together constantly and shared everything they had. They sold their possessions and shared the proceeds with those in need.

**1 Timothy 6:7-9 HCSB**   We brought nothing into the world, and we can take nothing out. But if we have food and clothing, we will be content with these. But those who want to be rich fall into temptation, a trap, and many foolish and harmful desires, which plunge people into ruin and destruction.

**1 Timothy 6:17 NASB**   Instruct those who are rich in this present world not to be conceited or to fix their hope on the uncertainty of riches, but on God, who richly supplies us with all things to enjoy.

**1 Peter 2:9 ESV**   You are a chosen race, a royal priesthood, a holy nation, a people for his own possession, that you may proclaim the excellencies of him who called you out of darkness into his marvelous light.

**1 John 2:15-17 MSG**   Don't love the world's ways. Don't love the world's goods. Love of the world squeezes out love for the Father. Practically everything that goes on in the world—wanting your own way, wanting everything for yourself, wanting to appear important—has nothing to do with the Father. It just isolates you from him. The world and all its wanting, wanting, wanting is on the way out—but whoever does what God wants is set for eternity.

**Deuteronomy 5:33 TNIV**   Walk in obedience to all that the LORD your God has commanded you, so that you may live and prosper and prolong your days in the land that you will possess.

**1 Samuel 18:14 NIV**   In everything he did he had great success, because the LORD was with him.

**Psalm 40:5 NCV**   LORD my God, you have done many miracles. Your plans for us are many. If I tried to tell them all, there would be too many to count.

**Psalm 112:1-3 TNIV**   Praise the LORD. Blessed are those who fear the LORD, who find great delight in his commands. Their children will be mighty in the land; the generation of the upright will be blessed. Wealth and riches are in their houses, and their righteousness endures forever.

**Mark 9:23 NASB**   All things are possible to him who believes.

**John 11:40 ESV**   Did I not tell you that if you believed you would see the glory of God?

**Romans 8:27-28 TNIV**   The Spirit intercedes for God's people in accordance with the will of God. And we know that in all things God works for the good of those who love him, who have been called according to his purpose.

**Galatians 1:15 NCV**   God had special plans for me and set me apart for his work even before I was born. He called me through his grace.

**Ephesians 3:20 NCV**   With God's power working in us, God can do much, much more than anything we can ask or imagine.

**Philippians 4:13 NKJV**   I can do all things through Christ who strengthens me.

**Psalm 29:4–9 NCV**    The LORD's voice is powerful; the LORD's voice is majestic.... The LORD's voice makes the lightning flash. The LORD's voice shakes the desert; the LORD shakes the desert of Kadesh. The LORD's voice shakes the oaks and strips the leaves off the trees. In his temple everyone says, "Glory to God!"

**Psalm 118:16 NCV**    The power of the LORD has won the victory; with his power the LORD has done mighty things.

**Proverbs 24:5 NCV**    Wise people have great power, and those with knowledge have great strength.

**Luke 9:1 NLT**    One day Jesus called together his twelve disciples and gave them power and authority to cast out all demons and to heal all diseases.

**Acts 17:24–28 CEV**    This God made the world and everything in it. He is Lord of heaven and earth, and he doesn't live in temples built by human hands. He doesn't need help from anyone. He gives life, breath, and everything else to all people. From one person God made all nations who live on earth, and he decided when and where every nation would be. God has done all this, so that we will look for him and reach out and find him. He isn't far from any of us, and he gives us the power to live, to move, and to be who we are.

**2 Corinthians 6:7 CEV**    We have spoken the truth, and God's power has worked in us. In all our struggles we have said and done only what is right.

**Ephesians 6:12 NASB**    Our struggle is not against flesh and blood, but against the rulers, against the powers, against the world forces of this darkness, against the spiritual forces of wickedness in the heavenly places.

**1 Chronicles 16:25 ESV** Great is the LORD, and greatly to be praised, and he is to be held in awe above all gods.

**Psalm 40:3 ESV** He put a new song in my mouth, a song of praise to our God. Many will see and fear, and put their trust in the LORD.

**Psalm 43:4 TNIV** I will go to the altar of God, to God, my joy and my delight. I will praise you with the lyre, O God, my God.

**Psalm 66:16-17 AMP** Come and hear, all you who reverently and worshipfully fear God, and I will declare what He has done for me! I cried aloud to Him; He was extolled and high praise was under my tongue.

**Psalm 89:6-8 NIV** Who in the skies above can compare with the LORD? Who is like the LORD among the heavenly beings? In the council of the holy ones God is greatly feared; he is more awesome than all who surround him. O LORD God Almighty, who is like you? You are mighty, O LORD, and your faithfulness surrounds you.

**Psalm 103:1-5 HCSB** My soul, praise the LORD, and all that is within me, praise His Holy name. My soul, praise the LORD, and do not forget all His benefits. He forgives all your sin; He heals all your diseases. He redeems your life from the Pit; He crowns you with faithful love and compassion. He satisfies you with goodness; your youth is renewed like the eagle.

**Psalm 103:20-22 HCSB** Praise the LORD, all His angels of great strength, who do His word, obedient to His command. Praise the LORD, all His armies, His servants who do His will. Praise the LORD, all His works in all the places where He rules. My soul, praise the LORD!

**Hebrews 13:15 TNIV** Through Jesus, therefore, let us continually offer to God a sacrifice of praise—the fruit of lips that confess his name.

**Nehemiah 1:11 NLT**   Lord, please hear my prayer! Listen to the prayers of those of us who delight in honoring you. Please grant me success today by making the king favorable to me. Put it into his heart to be kind to me.

**Psalm 144:12 CEV**   Let's pray that our young sons will grow like strong plants and that our daughters will be as lovely as columns in the corner of a palace.

**John 17:21-24 NCV**   Father, I pray that they can be one. As you are in me and I am in you, I pray that they can also be one in us. Then the world will believe that you sent me. I have given these people the glory that you gave me so that they can be one, just as you and I are one. I will be in them and you will be in me so that they will be completely one. Then the world will know that you sent me and that you loved them just as much as you loved me. Father, I want these people that you gave me to be with me where I am. I want them to see my glory, which you gave me because you loved me before the world was made.

**Ephesians 1:17-18 CEV**   I ask the glorious Father and God of our Lord Jesus Christ to give you his Spirit. The Spirit will make you wise and let you understand what it means to know God. My prayer is that light will flood your hearts and that you will understand the hope that was given to you when God chose you. Then you will discover the glorious blessings that will be yours together with all of God's people.

**1 Thessalonians 3:13 NCV**   May your hearts be made strong so that you will be holy and without fault before our God and Father when our Lord Jesus comes with all his holy ones.

**Jude 1:2 CEV**   I pray that God will greatly bless you with kindness, peace, and love!

**2 Chronicles 7:14-15 ESV**  If my people who are called by my name humble themselves, and pray and seek my face and turn from their wicked ways, then I will hear from heaven and will forgive their sin and heal their land. Now my eyes will be open and my ears attentive to the prayer that is made in this place.

**Psalm 4:3 NCV**  You know that the LORD has chosen for himself those who are loyal to him. The LORD listens when I pray to him.

**Psalm 5:1-3 NIV**  Give ear to my words, O LORD, consider my sighing. Listen to my cry for help, my King and my God, for to you I pray. In the morning, O LORD, you hear my voice; in the morning I lay my requests before you and wait in expectation.

**Psalm 65:1-2 CEV**  Our God, you deserve praise in Zion, where we keep our promises to you. Everyone will come to you because you answer prayer.

**Psalm 66:18-20 NCV**  If I had known of any sin in my heart, the Lord would not have listened to me. But God has listened; he has heard my prayer. Praise God, who did not ignore my prayer or hold back his love from me.

**Romans 8:26 NASB**  We do not know how to pray as we should, but the Spirit Himself intercedes for us with groanings too deep for words.

**Philippians 4:5-7 HCSB**  The Lord is near. Don't worry about anything, but in everything, through prayer and petition with thanksgiving, let your requests be made known to God. And the peace of God, which surpasses every thought, will guard your hearts and your minds in Christ Jesus.

**James 5:16 NASB**  The effective prayer of a righteous man can accomplish much.

**Job 10:12 BBE** You have been kind to me, and your grace has been with me, and your care has kept my spirit safe.

**Psalm 127:3-4 NCV** Children are a gift from the LORD; babies are a reward. Children who are born to a young man are like arrows in the hand of a warrior.

**Psalm 139:13-16 NCV** You made my whole being; you formed me in my mother's body. I praise you because you made me in an amazing and wonderful way. What you have done is wonderful. I know this very well. You saw my bones being formed as I took shape in my mother's body. When I was put together there, you saw my body as it was formed. All the days planned for me were written in your book before I was one day old.

**Isaiah 49:1 NCV** Before I was born, the LORD called me to serve him. The LORD named me while I was still in my mother's womb.

**Jeremiah 1:5 AMP** Before I formed you in the womb I knew [and] approved of you [as My chosen instrument], and before you were born I separated and set you apart, consecrating you; [and] I appointed you as a prophet to the nations.

**Luke 1:44 ESV** Behold, when the sound of your greeting came to my ears, the baby in my womb leaped for joy.

**1 Thessalonians 5:16-18 NKJV** Rejoice always, pray without ceasing, in everything give thanks; for this is the will of God in Christ Jesus for you.

**3 John 1:2 NKJV** Beloved, I pray that you may prosper in all things and be in health, just as your soul prospers.

**Psalm 34:2 NKJV**   My soul shall make its boast in the Lord; the humble shall hear of it and be glad.

**Psalm 101:4-6 HCSB**   A devious heart will be far from me; I will not be involved with evil. I will destroy anyone who secretly slanders his neighbor; I cannot tolerate anyone with haughty eyes or an arrogant heart. My eyes favor the faithful of the land so that they may sit down with me. The one who follows the way of integrity may serve me.

**Proverbs 18:12-13 CEV**   Pride leads to destruction; humility leads to honor. It's stupid and embarrassing to give an answer before you listen.

**Proverbs 22:4 NIV**   Humility and the fear of the Lord bring wealth and honor and life.

**Isaiah 2:11-12 NCV**   Proud people will be made humble, and they will bow low with shame. At that time only the Lord will still be praised. The Lord All-Powerful has a certain day planned when he will punish the proud and those who brag, and they will no longer be important.

**Isaiah 13:11 NCV**   I will punish the world for its evil and wicked people for their sins. I will cause proud people to lose their pride, and I will destroy the pride of those who are cruel to others.

**Romans 12:3 TNIV**   By the grace given me I say to every one of you: Do not think of yourself more highly than you ought, but rather think of yourself with sober judgment, in accordance with the faith God has distributed to each of you.

**Romans 12:16 NCV**   Live in peace with each other. Do not be proud, but make friends with those who seem unimportant. Do not think how smart you are.

**1 Peter 5:6-7 NCV**   Be humble under God's powerful hand so he will lift you up when the right time comes. Give all your worries to him, because he cares about you.

**Numbers 23:19 NLT**   God is not a man, so he does not lie. He is not human, so he does not change his mind. Has he ever spoken and failed to act? Has he ever promised and not carried it through?

**Joshua 21:45 TNIV**   Not one of all the Lord's good promises to the house of Israel failed; every one was fulfilled.

**Psalm 1:1–3 ESV**   Blessed is the man who walks not in the counsel of the wicked, nor stands in the way of sinners, nor sits in the seat of scoffers; but his delight is in the law of the Lord, and on his law he meditates day and night. He is like a tree planted by streams of water that yields its fruit in its season, and its leaf does not wither. In all that he does, he prospers.

**Isaiah 43:1–2 ESV**   Thus says the Lord, he who created you, O Jacob, he who formed you, O Israel: "Fear not, for I have redeemed you; I have called you by name, you are mine. When you pass through the waters, I will be with you; and through the rivers, they shall not overwhelm you; when you walk through fire you shall not be burned, and the flame shall not consume you."

**John 10:9 TNIV**   I am the gate; whoever enters through me will be saved. They will come in and go out, and find pasture.

**John 15:4 NLT**   Remain in me, and I will remain in you.

**Hebrews 6:18–19 CEV**   God cannot tell lies! And so his promises and vows are two things that can never be changed. We have run to God for safety. Now his promises should greatly encourage us to take hold of the hope that is right in front of us. This hope is like a firm and steady anchor for our souls.

**1 John 5:14 NCV**   This is the boldness we have in God's presence: that if we ask God for anything that agrees with what he wants, he hears us.

# PROTECTION

**2 Samuel 22:2-4 NIV**  The LORD is my rock, my fortress and my deliverer; my God is my rock, in whom I take refuge, my shield and the horn of my salvation. He is my stronghold, my refuge and my savior— from violent men you save me. I call to the LORD, who is worthy of praise, and I am saved from my enemies.

**Psalm 4:1 CEV**  You are my God and protector. Please answer my prayer. I was in terrible distress, but you set me free. Now have pity and listen as I pray.

**Psalm 5:11 TNIV**  Let all who take refuge in you be glad; let them ever sing for joy. Spread your protection over them, that those who love your name may rejoice in you.

**Psalm 7:1 CEV**  You, LORD God, are my protector. Rescue me and keep me safe from all who chase me.

**Psalm 16:8-9 HCSB**  I keep the LORD in mind always. Because He is at my right hand, I will not be shaken. Therefore my heart is glad, and my spirit rejoices; my body also rests securely.

**Psalm 18:2 CEV**  You are my mighty rock, my fortress, my protector, the rock where I am safe, my shield, my powerful weapon, and my place of shelter.

**Psalm 59:9 AMP**  O my Strength, I will watch and give heed to You and sing praises; for God is my Defense (my Protector and High Tower).

**Psalm 68:5 AMP**  A father of the fatherless and a judge and protector of the widows is God in His holy habitation.

**Psalm 91:11 NCV**  He has put his angels in charge of you to watch over you wherever you go.

**Genesis 22:14 HCSB**   Abraham named that place The LORD Will Provide.

**1 Samuel 11:13 HCSB**   The LORD has provided deliverance.

**Psalm 95:6-7 NCV**   Come, let's worship him and bow down. Let's kneel before the LORD who made us, because he is our God and we are the people he takes care of, the sheep that he tends.

**Psalm 111:5 ESV**   He provides food for those who fear him; he remembers his covenant forever.

**Psalm 111:9 NIV**   He provided redemption for his people; he ordained his covenant forever—holy and awesome is his name.

**Psalm 119:169 MSG**   Let my cry come right into your presence, God; provide me with the insight that comes only from your Word. Give my request your personal attention, rescue me on the terms of your promise.

**Matthew 10:29-31 NCV**   Two sparrows cost only a penny, but not even one of them can die without your Father's knowing it. God even knows how many hairs are on your head. So don't be afraid. You are worth much more than many sparrows.

**Romans 11:22 ESV**   Note then the kindness and the severity of God: severity toward those who have fallen, but God's kindness to you, provided you continue in his kindness. Otherwise you too will be cut off.

**2 Peter 1:10-11 ESV**   Be all the more diligent to make your calling and election sure, for if you practice these qualities you will never fall. For in this way there will be richly provided for you an entrance into the eternal kingdom of our Lord and Savior Jesus Christ.

# PUNISHMENT

**Deuteronomy 21:18–21 NKJV**  If a man has a stubborn and rebellious son who will not obey the voice of his father or the voice of his mother, and who, when they have chastened him, will not heed them, then his father and his mother shall take hold of him and bring him out to the elders of his city, to the gate of his city. And they shall say to the elders of his city, "This son of ours is stubborn and rebellious; he will not obey our voice; he is a glutton and a drunkard." Then all the men of his city shall stone him to death with stones; so you shall put away the evil from among you, and all Israel shall hear and fear.

**Proverbs 13:24 HCSB**  The one who will not use the rod hates his son, but the one who loves him disciplines him diligently.

**Jeremiah 2:19 NCV**  "Your evil will bring punishment to you, and the wrong you have done will teach you a lesson. Think about it and understand that it is a terrible evil to turn away from the LORD your God. It is wrong not to fear me," says the Lord GOD All-Powerful.

**Jeremiah 7:26–29 NKJV**  They did not obey Me or incline their ear, but stiffened their neck. They did worse than their fathers. Therefore you shall speak all these words to them, but they will not obey you. You shall also call to them, but they will not answer you. So you shall say to them, "This is a nation that does not obey the voice of the LORD their God nor receive correction. Truth has perished and has been cut off from their mouth. Cut off your hair and cast it away, and take up a lamentation on the desolate heights; for the LORD has rejected and forsaken the generation of His wrath."

**Jeremiah 10:23–24 NIV**  I know, O LORD, that a man's life is not his own; it is not for man to direct his steps. Correct me, LORD, but only with justice—not in your anger, lest you reduce me to nothing.

**Revelation 3:19–20 NCV**  I correct and punish those whom I love. So be eager to do right, and change your hearts and lives. Here I am! I stand at the door and knock. If you hear my voice and open the door, I will come in and eat with you, and you will eat with me.

**Deuteronomy 4:29-31 CEV**   In all of your troubles, you may finally decide that you want to worship only the LORD. And if you turn back to him and obey him completely, he will again be your God. The LORD your God will have mercy—he won't destroy you or desert you. The LORD will remember his promise.

**Deuteronomy 13:4 NCV**   Serve only the LORD your God. Respect him, keep his commands, and obey him. Serve him and be loyal to him.

**Psalm 103:11-12 NLT**   His unfailing love toward those who fear him is as great as the height of the heavens above the earth. He has removed our rebellious acts as far away from us as the east is from the west.

**Proverbs 8:34-36 NCV**   Happy are those who listen to me, watching at my door every day, waiting at my open doorway. Those who find me find life, and the LORD will be pleased with them. Those who do not find me hurt themselves. Those who hate me love death.

**Proverbs 24:19-22 NIV**   Do not fret because of evil men or be envious of the wicked, for the evil man has no future hope, and the lamp of the wicked will be snuffed out. Fear the LORD and the king, my son, and do not join with the rebellious, for those two will send sudden destruction upon them, and who knows what calamities they can bring?

**Daniel 9:9-10 TNIV**   The Lord our God is merciful and forgiving, even though we have rebelled against him; we have not obeyed the LORD our God or kept the laws he gave us through his servants the prophets.

**Titus 3:1-2 CEV**   Remind your people to obey the rulers and authorities and not to be rebellious. They must always be ready to do something helpful and not say cruel things or argue. They should be gentle and kind to everyone.

# REJECTED

**Psalm 27:10 BBE**   When my father and my mother are turned away from me, then the Lord will be my support.

**Psalm 34:18 NASB**   The Lord is near to the brokenhearted and saves those who are crushed in spirit.

**Psalm 66:18-20 TNIV**   If I had cherished sin in my heart, the Lord would not have listened; but God has surely listened and has heard my prayer. Praise be to God, who has not rejected my prayer or withheld his love from me!

**Psalm 73:25-26 CEV**   In heaven I have only you, and on this earth you are all I want. My body and mind may fail, but you are my strength and my choice forever.

**Psalm 94:14 MSG**   God will never walk away from his people, never desert his precious people.

**Matthew 5:10 MSG**   You're blessed when your commitment to God provokes persecution. The persecution drives you even deeper into God's kingdom.

**Matthew 5:11-12 NASB**   Blessed are you when people insult you and persecute you, and falsely say all kinds of evil against you because of Me. Rejoice and be glad, for your reward in heaven is great; for in the same way they persecuted the prophets who were before you.

**Romans 8:37 NKJV**   In all these things we are more than conquerors through Him who loved us.

**Ephesians 4:32 CEV**   Be kind and merciful, and forgive others, just as God forgave you because of Christ.

**Hebrews 13:5-6 ESV**   I will never leave you nor forsake you. So we can confidently say, "The Lord is my helper; I will not fear; what can man do to me?"

**Matthew 5:23-24 ESV**   If you are offering your gift at the altar and there remember that your brother has something against you, leave your gift there before the altar and go. First be reconciled to your brother, and then come and offer your gift.

**Matthew 18:15-17 NCV**   If your fellow believer sins against you, go and tell him in private what he did wrong. If he listens to you, you have helped that person to be your brother or sister again. But if he refuses to listen, go to him again and take one or two other people with you. "Every case may be proved by two or three witnesses." If he refuses to listen to them, tell the church. If he refuses to listen to the church, then treat him like a person who does not believe in God or like a tax collector.

**Luke 6:35 TNIV**   Love your enemies, do good to them, and lend to them without expecting to get anything back. Then your reward will be great.

**Romans 12:10-11 NRSV**   Love one another with mutual affection; outdo one another in showing honor. Do not lag in zeal, be ardent in spirit, serve the Lord.

**Romans 13:7-8 NCV**   Pay everyone, then, what you owe. If you owe any kind of tax, pay it. Show respect and honor to them all. Do not owe people anything, except always owe love to each other, because the person who loves others has obeyed all the law.

**Galatians 6:1-2 NCV**   If someone in your group does something wrong, you who are spiritual should go to that person and gently help make him right again. But be careful, because you might be tempted to sin, too. By helping each other with your troubles, you truly obey the law of Christ.

**Hebrews 10:24 NLT**   Think of ways to encourage one another to outbursts of love and good deeds.

**Deuteronomy 8:3 ESV**   Man lives by every word that comes from the mouth of the Lord.

**2 Chronicles 14:11 TNIV**   Lord, there is no one like you to help the powerless against the mighty. Help us, Lord our God, for we rely on you, and in your name we have come against this vast army. Lord, you are our God; do not let mere mortals prevail against you.

**Psalm 59:9-10 HCSB**   I will keep watch for You, my strength, because God is my stronghold. My faithful God will come to meet me; God will let me look down on my adversaries.

**Psalm 86:11 TNIV**   Teach me your way, Lord, that I may rely on your faithfulness; give me an undivided heart, that I may fear your name.

**Psalm 146:5-8 GNT**   Happy are those who have the God of Jacob to help them and who depend on the Lord their God, the Creator of heaven, earth, and sea, and all that is in them. He always keeps his promises; he judges in favor of the oppressed and gives food to the hungry. The Lord sets prisoners free and gives sight to the blind.

**2 Corinthians 1:12 TNIV**   Now this is our boast: Our conscience testifies that we have conducted ourselves in the world, and especially in our relations with you, with integrity and godly sincerity. We have done so, relying not on worldly wisdom but on God's grace.

**Revelation 3:15-19 NCV**   I know what you do, that you are not hot or cold. I wish that you were hot or cold! But because you are lukewarm—neither hot, nor cold—I am ready to spit you out of my mouth. You say, "I am rich, and I have become wealthy and do not need anything." But you do not know that you are really miserable, pitiful, poor, blind, and naked. I advise you to buy from me gold made pure in fire so you can be truly rich. Buy from me white clothes so you can be clothed and so you can cover your shameful nakedness. Buy from me medicine to put on your eyes so you can truly see. I correct and punish those whom I love. So be eager to do right, and change your hearts and lives.

**Joel 2:12-13 TNIV**   Return to me with all your heart, with fasting and weeping and mourning. Rend your heart and not your garments. Return to the LORD your God, for he is gracious and compassionate, slow to anger and abounding in love, and he relents from sending calamity.

**Matthew 9:12-13 NCV**   When Jesus heard them, he said, "It is not the healthy people who need a doctor, but the sick. Go and learn what this means: 'I want kindness more than I want animal sacrifices.' I did not come to invite good people but to invite sinners."

**Mark 1:15 NKJV**   The time is fulfilled, and the kingdom of God is at hand. Repent, and believe in the gospel.

**Luke 15:7 NASB**   There will be more joy in heaven over one sinner who repents than over ninety-nine righteous persons who need no repentance.

**Acts 2:38 WEB**   Repent, and be baptized, everyone of you, in the name of Jesus Christ for the forgiveness of sins, and you will receive the gift of the Holy Spirit.

**Acts 8:21-23 NCV**   You cannot share with us in this work since your heart is not right before God. Change your heart! Turn away from this evil thing you have done, and pray to the Lord. Maybe he will forgive you for thinking this. I see that you are full of bitter jealousy and ruled by sin.

**2 Corinthians 7:10 NIV**   Godly sorrow brings repentance that leads to salvation and leaves no regret, but worldly sorrow brings death.

**2 Corinthians 12:21 NLT**   I will have to grieve because many of you who sinned earlier have not repented of your impurity, sexual immorality, and eagerness for lustful pleasure.

**Revelation 3:19 NKJV**   As many as I love, I rebuke and chasten. Therefore be zealous and repent.

**Leviticus 19:3 CEV**   Respect your father and your mother, honor the Sabbath, and don't make idols or images. I am the LORD your God.

**Leviticus 19:32 NIV**   Rise in the presence of the aged, show respect for the elderly and revere your God. I am the LORD.

**Proverbs 11:16 NIV**   A kindhearted woman gains respect, but ruthless men gain only wealth.

**Proverbs 15:5 BBE**   A foolish man puts no value on his father's training; but he who has respect for teaching has good sense.

**Proverbs 19:23 CEV**   Showing respect to the LORD brings true life—if you do it, you can relax without fear of danger.

**Romans 1:29–31 CEV**   They are evil, wicked, and greedy, as well as mean in every possible way. They want what others have, and they murder, argue, cheat, and are hard to get along with. They gossip, say cruel things about others, and hate God. They are proud, conceited, and boastful, always thinking up new ways to do evil. These people don't respect their parents. They are stupid, unreliable, and don't have any love or pity for others.

**Romans 12:10 HCSB**   Show family affection to one another with brotherly love. Outdo one another in showing honor.

**1 Thessalonians 4:11–12 NASB**   Make it your ambition to lead a quiet life and attend to your own business and work with your hands, just as we commanded you, so that you will behave properly toward outsiders and not be in any need.

**1 Thessalonians 5:12–13 NCV**   We ask you to appreciate those who work hard among you, who lead you in the Lord and teach you. Respect them with a very special love because of the work they do. Live in peace with each other.

**Matthew 10:42 ESV**  Whoever gives one of these little ones even a cup of cold water because he is a disciple, truly, I say to you, he will by no means lose his reward.

**Mark 16:15 TNIV**  Go into all the world and preach the gospel to all creation.

**Luke 3:10-11 TNIV**  "What should we do then?" the crowd asked. John answered, "Anyone who has two shirts should share with the one who has none, and anyone who has food should do the same."

**1 Timothy 5:8 NKJV**  If anyone does not provide for his own, and especially for those of his household, he has denied the faith and is worse than an unbeliever.

**1 Timothy 6:20 NCV**  Guard what God has trusted to you.

**Titus 3:14 TNIV**  Our people must learn to devote themselves to doing what is good, in order to provide for urgent needs and not live unproductive lives.

**James 2:15-17 NKJV**  If a brother or sister is naked and destitute of daily food, and one of you says to them, "Depart in peace, be warmed and filled," but you do not give them the things which are needed for the body, what does it profit? Thus also faith by itself, if it does not have works, is dead.

**1 John 3:16-18 ESV**  By this we know love, that he laid down his life for us, and we ought to lay down our lives for the brothers. But if anyone has the world's goods and sees his brother in need, yet closes his heart against him, how does God's love abide in him? Little children, let us not love in word or talk but in deed and in truth.

**1 John 3:22-23 NKJV**  Whatever we ask we receive from Him, because we keep His commandments and do those things that are pleasing in His sight. And this is His commandment: that we should believe on the name of His Son Jesus Christ and love one another.

**Proverbs 16:32 NRSV**  One who is slow to anger is better than the mighty, and one whose temper is controlled than one who captures a city.

**Matthew 5:38-41 NIV**  You have heard that it was said, "Eye for eye, and tooth for tooth." But I tell you, Do not resist an evil person. If someone strikes you on the right cheek, turn to him the other also. And if someone wants to sue you and take your tunic, let him have your cloak as well. If someone forces you to go one mile, go with him two miles.

**Luke 6:27-31 ESV**  I say to you who hear, Love your enemies, do good to those who hate you, bless those who curse you, pray for those who abuse you. . . . And as you wish that others would do to you, do so to them.

**Luke 6:36 HCSB**  Be merciful, just as your Father also is merciful.

**Romans 12:17-19 TNIV**  Do not repay anyone evil for evil. Be careful to do what is right in the eyes of everyone. If it is possible, as far as it depends on you, live at peace with everyone. Do not take revenge, my dear friends, but leave room for God's wrath, for it is written: "It is mine to avenge; I will repay," says the Lord.

**1 Corinthians 13:3-7 MSG**  No matter what I say, what I believe, and what I do, I'm bankrupt without love. Love never gives up. Love cares more for others than for self. Love doesn't want what it doesn't have . . . doesn't fly off the handle, doesn't keep score of the sins of others . . . puts up with anything, trusts God always, always looks for the best, never looks back, but keeps going to the end.

**2 Thessalonians 1:6-7 NASB**  It is only just for God to repay with affliction those who afflict you, and to give relief to you who are afflicted.

**1 Chronicles 29:11-14 CEV**   Your power is great, and your glory is seen everywhere in heaven and on earth. You are king of the entire world, and you rule with strength and power. You make people rich and powerful and famous. We thank you, our God, and praise you. But why should we be happy that we have given you these gifts? They belong to you, and we have only given back what is already yours.

**Ezekiel 28:4-7 CEV**   Your wisdom has certainly made you rich, because you have storehouses filled with gold and silver. You're a clever businessman and are extremely wealthy, but your wealth has led to arrogance! You compared yourself to a god, so now I, the LORD God, will make you the victim of cruel enemies. They will destroy all the possessions you've worked so hard to get.

**Luke 16:11 NIV**   If you have not been trustworthy in handling worldly wealth, who will trust you with true riches?

**1 Timothy 6:17-19 HCSB**   Instruct those who are rich in the present age not to be arrogant or to set their hope on the uncertainty of wealth, but on God, who richly provides us with all things to enjoy. Instruct them to do good, to be rich in good works, generous, willing to share, storing up for themselves a good foundation for the age to come, so that they may take hold of life that is real.

**James 1:9-11 NCV**   Believers who are poor should take pride that God has made them spiritually rich. Those who are rich should take pride that God has shown them that they are spiritually poor. The rich will die like a wild flower in the grass. The sun rises with burning heat and dries up the plants. The flower falls off, and its beauty is gone. In the same way the rich will die while they are still taking care of business.

**2 Peter 3:17 CEV**   Don't let the errors of evil people lead you down the wrong path and make you lose your balance.

**1 John 5:21 NLT**   Keep away from anything that might take God's place in your hearts.

**2 Chronicles 31:21 CEV**   He was a successful king, because he obeyed the LORD God with all his heart.

**John 14:16-17 NCV**   I will ask the Father, and he will give you another Helper to be with you forever—the Spirit of truth. The world cannot accept him, because it does not see him or know him. But you know him, because he lives with you and he will be in you.

**Romans 3:22-23 CEV**   God treats everyone alike. He accepts people only because they have faith in Jesus Christ. All of us have sinned and fallen short of God's glory.

**Romans 3:25-26 NKJV**   God had passed over the sins that were previously committed, to demonstrate at the present time His righteousness, that He might be just and the justifier of the one who has faith in Jesus.

**Romans 4:5 NCV**   People cannot do any work that will make them right with God. So they must trust in him, who makes even evil people right in his sight. Then God accepts their faith, and that makes them right with him.

**1 Corinthians 1:30 NCV**   Because of God you are in Christ Jesus, who has become for us wisdom from God. In Christ we are put right with God, and have been made holy, and have been set free from sin.

**2 Corinthians 5:21 NCV**   Christ had no sin, but God made him become sin so that in Christ we could become right with God.

**Philippians 4:5 NIV**   Let your gentleness be evident to all. The Lord is near.

**Titus 3:4-5 TNIV**   When the kindness and love of God our Savior appeared, he saved us, not because of righteous things we had done, but because of his mercy. He saved us through the washing of rebirth and renewal by the Holy Spirit.

**Proverbs 10:11 MSG**   The mouth of a good person is a deep, life-giving well, but the mouth of the wicked is a dark cave of abuse.

**Proverbs 14:29 MSG**   Slowness to anger makes for deep understanding; a quick-tempered person stockpiles stupidity.

**Proverbs 22:24–25 WEB**   Don't befriend a hot-tempered man, and don't associate with one who harbors anger: Lest you learn his ways, and ensnare your soul.

**Proverbs 29:11 BBE**   A foolish man lets out all his wrath, but a wise man keeps it back quietly.

**Matthew 7:12 NKJV**   Whatever you want men to do to you, do also to them.

**Galatians 5:19–23 NRSV**   Now the works of the flesh are obvious: fornication, impurity, licentiousness, idolatry, sorcery, enmities, strife, jealousy, anger, quarrels, dissensions, factions, envy, drunkenness, carousing, and things like these. I am warning you, as I warned you before: those who do such things will not inherit the kingdom of God. By contrast, the fruit of the Spirit is love, joy, peace, patience, kindness, generosity, faithfulness, gentleness, and self-control.

**Ephesians 4:2 NLT**   Always be humble and gentle. Be patient with each other, making allowance for each other's faults because of your love.

**Ephesians 4:29 NIV**   Do not let any unwholesome talk come out of your mouths, but only what is helpful for building others up according to their needs, that it may benefit those who listen.

**Colossians 3:8 NIV**   You must rid yourselves of all such things as these: anger, rage, malice, slander, and filthy language from your lips.

**1 Thessalonians 5:15 ESV**   See that no one repays anyone evil for evil, but always seek to do good to one another and to everyone.

**RUNAWAY**

**Genesis 31:27 NCV**   Why did you run away secretly and trick me? Why didn't you tell me? Then I could have sent you away with joy and singing and with the music of tambourines and harps.

**Psalm 25:1–2 NCV**   Lord, I give myself to you; my God, I trust you.

**Psalm 25:4–7 NCV**   Lord, tell me your ways. Show me how to live. Guide me in your truth, and teach me, my God, my Savior. I trust you all day long. Lord, remember your mercy and love that you have shown since long ago. Do not remember the sins and wrong things I did when I was young. But remember to love me always because you are good, Lord.

**Psalm 25:8–12 HCSB**   The LORD is good and upright; therefore He shows sinners the way. He leads the humble in what is right and teaches them His way. All the LORD's ways show faithful love and truth to those who keep His covenant and decrees. Because of Your name, LORD, forgive my sin, for it is great. Who is the person who fears the LORD? He will show him the way he should choose.

**Proverbs 5:21 NIV**   A man's ways are in full view of the Lord, and he examines all his paths.

**Proverbs 27:8 NCV**   A person who leaves his home is like a bird that leaves its nest.

**Joel 2:13 NKJV**   Return to the Lord your God, for He is gracious and merciful, slow to anger, and of great kindness; and He relents from doing harm.

**Micah 7:7 ESV**   As for me, I will look to the Lord; I will wait for the God of my salvation; my God will hear me.

**2 Timothy 2:22 NCV**   Run away from the evil desires of youth. Try hard to live right and to have faith, love, and peace, together with those who trust in the Lord from pure hearts.

**Psalm 10:14 TNIV**   You, God, see the trouble of the afflicted; you consider their grief and take it in hand. The victims commit themselves to you; you are the helper of the fatherless.

**Psalm 10:17 NLT**   LORD, you know the hopes of the helpless. Surely you will hear their cries and comfort them.

**Psalm 23:4 NLT**   Even when I walk through the darkest valley, I will not be afraid, for you are close beside me. Your rod and your staff protect and comfort me.

**Psalm 25:16-18 CEV**   I am lonely and troubled. Show that you care and have pity on me. My awful worries keep growing. Rescue me from sadness. See my troubles and misery and forgive my sins.

**Romans 15:13 TNIV**   May the God of hope fill you with all joy and peace as you trust in him, so that you may overflow with hope by the power of the Holy Spirit.

**James 4:8-9 NCV**   You sinners, clean sin out of your lives. You who are trying to follow God and the world at the same time, make your thinking pure. Be sad, cry, and weep! Change your laughter into crying and your joy into sadness. Humble yourself in the Lord's presence, and he will honor you.

**1 Peter 1:6-7 CEV**   On that day you will be glad, even if you have to go through many hard trials for a while. Your faith will be like gold that has been tested in a fire. And these trials will prove that your faith is worth much more than gold that can be destroyed. They will show that you will be given praise and honor and glory when Jesus Christ returns.

# SALVATION

**Psalm 27:1 NKJV**  The LORD is my light and my salvation; whom shall I fear? The LORD is the strength of my life; of whom shall I be afraid?

**Psalm 149:4 NKJV**  The LORD takes pleasure in His people; He will beautify the humble with salvation.

**Acts 4:11-12 ESV**  This Jesus is the stone that was rejected by you, the builders, which has become the cornerstone. And there is salvation in no one else, for there is no other name under heaven given among men by which we must be saved.

**2 Corinthians 6:2 WEB**  Behold, now is the day of salvation.

**2 Corinthians 7:10 NASB**  The sorrow that is according to the will of God produces a repentance without regret, leading to salvation, but the sorrow of the world produces death.

**Philippians 2:12-13 NIV**  Continue to work out your salvation with fear and trembling, for it is God who works in you to will and to act according to his good purpose.

**1 Thessalonians 5:9-10 ESV**  God has not destined us for wrath, but to obtain salvation through our Lord Jesus Christ, who died for us so that whether we are awake or asleep we might live with him.

**2 Timothy 3:14-15 NCV**  You should continue following the teachings you learned. You know they are true, because you trust those who taught you. Since you were a child you have known the Holy Scriptures which are able to make you wise. And that wisdom leads to salvation through faith in Christ Jesus.

**Hebrews 9:27-28 NIV**  Just as man is destined to die once, and after that to face judgment, so Christ was sacrificed once to take away the sins of many people; and he will appear a second time, not to bear sin, but to bring salvation to those who are waiting for him.

**Job 1:6-7 NLT**   One day the angels came to present themselves before the Lord, and Satan the Accuser came with them. "Where have you come from?" the Lord asked Satan. And Satan answered the Lord, "I have been going back and forth across the earth, watching everything that's going on."

**Ezekiel 28:14-16 NLT**   I ordained and anointed you as the mighty angelic guardian. You had access to the holy mountain of God and walked among the stones of fire. You were blameless in all you did from the day you were created until the day evil was found in you. Your great wealth filled you with violence, and you sinned. So I banished you from the mountain of God.

**2 Corinthians 11:3 NIV**   I am afraid that just as Eve was deceived by the serpent's cunning, your minds may somehow be led astray from your sincere and pure devotion to Christ.

**Ephesians 2:1-2 NLT**   Once you were dead, doomed forever because of your many sins. You used to live just like the rest of the world, full of sin, obeying Satan, the mighty prince of the power of the air. He is the spirit at work in the hearts of those who refuse to obey God.

**Ephesians 6:10-12 NRSV**   Be strong in the Lord and in the strength of his power. Put on the whole armor of God, so that you may be able to stand against the wiles of the devil. For our struggle is not against enemies of blood and flesh, but against the rulers, against the authorities, against the cosmic powers of this present darkness, against the spiritual forces of evil in the heavenly places.

**James 4:7-8 WEB**   Be subject therefore to God. But resist the devil, and he will flee from you. Draw near to God, and he will draw near to you.

**1 Peter 5:8-9 NKJV**   Be sober, be vigilant; because your adversary the devil walks about like a roaring lion, seeking whom he may devour.

# SCHOOL

**Deuteronomy 2:7 CEV**   We've had everything we needed, and the LORD has blessed us and made us successful in whatever we have done.

**Proverbs 13:20 WEB**   One who walks with wise men grows wise, but a companion of fools suffers harm.

**Isaiah 41:9-10 NKJV**   I have chosen you and have not cast you away: fear not, for I am with you; be not dismayed, for I am your God. I will strengthen you, yes, I will help you, I will uphold you with my righteous right hand.

**Matthew 25:21 NKJV**   Well done, good and faithful servant; you were faithful over a few things, I will make you ruler over many things.

**Romans 12:11-14 GNT**   Work hard and do not be lazy. Serve the Lord with a heart full of devotion. Let your hope keep you joyful, be patient in your troubles, and pray at all times. Share your belongings with your needy fellow Christians, and open your homes to strangers. Ask God to bless those who persecute you—yes, ask him to bless, not to curse.

**1 Corinthians 15:58 NCV**   Stand strong. Do not let anything change you. Always give yourselves fully to the work of the Lord, because you know that your work in the Lord is never wasted.

**Ephesians 6:7-8 NCV**   Do your work with enthusiasm. Work as if you were serving the Lord, not as if you were serving only men and women. Remember that the Lord will give a reward to everyone, slave or free, for doing good.

**2 Timothy 2:24-25 NKJV**   A servant of the Lord must not quarrel but be gentle to all, able to teach, patient, in humility correcting those who are in opposition, if God perhaps will grant them repentance.

**1 Peter 4:14 NLT**   Be happy when you are insulted for being a Christian, for then the glorious Spirit of God rests upon you.

**Leviticus 19:13-14 CEV**  Do not steal anything or cheat anyone, and don't fail to pay your workers at the end of each day. I am the LORD your God, and I command you not to make fun of the deaf or to cause a blind person to stumble.

**Psalm 39:1 NCV**  I will be careful how I act and will not sin by what I say. I will be careful what I say around wicked people.

**Proverbs 5:21-23 CEV**  The LORD sees everything, and he watches us closely. Sinners are trapped and caught by their own evil deeds. They get lost and die because of their foolishness and lack of self-control.

**Proverbs 25:28 TNIV**  Like a city whose walls are broken through is a person who lacks self-control.

**Proverbs 29:11 NASB**  A fool always loses his temper, but a wise man holds it back.

**Romans 8:12-13 NCV**  We must not be ruled by our sinful selves or live the way our sinful selves want. If you use your lives to do the wrong things your sinful selves want, you will die spiritually. But if you use the Spirit's help to stop doing the wrong things you do with your body, you will have true life.

**1 Thessalonians 4:3-4 NCV**  God wants you to be holy and to stay away from sexual sins. He wants each of you to learn to control your own body in a way that is holy and honorable.

**Titus 2:11-12 NASB**  The grace of God has appeared, bringing salvation to all men, instructing us to deny ungodliness and worldly desires and to live sensibly, righteously and godly in the present age.

**2 Peter 1:5-7 TNIV**  Make every effort to add to your faith goodness; and to goodness, knowledge; and to knowledge, self-control; and to self-control, perseverance; and to perseverance, godliness; and to godliness, mutual affection; and to mutual affection, love.

**SERVICE**

**Deuteronomy 11:13 NKJV**   Love the LORD your God and serve Him with all your heart and with all your soul.

**Deuteronomy 13:4 ESV**   You shall walk after the LORD your God and fear him and keep his commandments and obey his voice, and you shall serve him and hold fast to him.

**Joshua 22:5 CEV**   Moses taught you to love the LORD your God, to be faithful to him, and to worship and obey him with your whole heart and with all your strength.

**Matthew 6:24 ESV**   No one can serve two masters, for either he will hate the one and love the other, or he will be devoted to the one and despise the other. You cannot serve God and money.

**Romans 12:10-13 TNIV**   Be devoted to one another in love. Honor one another above yourselves. Never be lacking in zeal, but keep your spiritual fervor, serving the Lord. Be joyful in hope, patient in affliction, faithful in prayer. Share with the Lord's people who are in need. Practice hospitality.

**Galatians 5:13-14 TNIV**   You, my brothers and sisters, were called to be free. But do not use your freedom to indulge the sinful nature; rather, serve one another humbly in love. For the entire law is fulfilled in keeping this one command: "Love your neighbor as yourself."

**Galatians 5:16 CEV**   If you are guided by the Spirit, you won't obey your selfish desires.

**1 Peter 4:11 NLT**   Do you have the gift of speaking? Then speak as though God himself were speaking through you. Do you have the gift of helping others? Do it with all the strength and energy that God supplies. Then everything you do will bring glory to God through Jesus Christ. All glory and power to him forever and ever! Amen.

**Genesis 1:27-28 NIV**   God created man in his own image, in the image of God he created him; male and female he created them. God blessed them and said to them, "Be fruitful and increase in number."

**Genesis 2:24 NASB**   For this reason a man shall leave his father and his mother, and be joined to his wife; and they shall become one flesh.

**Proverbs 5:18-19 ESV**   Let your fountain be blessed, and rejoice in the wife of your youth, a lovely deer, a graceful doe. Let her breasts fill you at all times with delight; be intoxicated always in her love.

**Song of Solomon 1:15-16 NCV**   My darling, you are beautiful! Oh, you are beautiful, and your eyes are like doves. You are so handsome, my lover, and so pleasant!

**1 Corinthians 7:1-2 MSG**   Is it a good thing to have sexual relations? Certainly—but only within a certain context. It's good for a man to have a wife, and for a woman to have a husband. Sexual drives are strong, but marriage is strong enough to contain them and provide for a balanced and fulfilling sexual life in a world of sexual disorder.

**Galatians 5:19-21 NCV**   The wrong things the sinful self does are clear: being sexually unfaithful, not being pure, taking part in sexual sins. . . . I warn you now as I warned you before: Those who do these things will not inherit God's kingdom.

**Colossians 3:2-6 ESV**   Set your minds on things that are above, not on things that are on earth. For you have died, and your life is hidden with Christ in God. When Christ who is your life appears, then you also will appear with him in glory. Put to death therefore what is earthly in you: sexual immorality, impurity, passion, evil desire, and covetousness, which is idolatry.

**Hebrews 13:4 NIV**   Marriage should be honored by all, and the marriage bed kept pure, for God will judge the adulterer and all the sexually immoral.

# SEXUAL PURITY

**Proverbs 6:23-25 CEV**   The Law of the Lord is a lamp, and its teachings shine brightly. Correction and self-control will lead you through life. They will protect you from the flattering words of someone else's wife. Don't let yourself be attracted by the charm and lovely eyes of someone like that.

**1 Corinthians 6:9 NASB**   Do you not know that the unrighteous will not inherit the kingdom of God? Do not be deceived; neither fornicators, nor idolaters, nor adulterers, nor effeminate, nor homosexuals . . . will inherit the kingdom of God.

**1 Corinthians 6:13 NIV**   The body is not meant for sexual immorality, but for the Lord, and the Lord for the body.

**1 Corinthians 6:18-20 ESV**   Flee from sexual immorality. Every other sin a person commits is outside the body, but the sexually immoral person sins against his own body. Or do you not know that your body is a temple of the Holy Spirit within you, whom you have from God? You are not your own, for you were bought with a price. So glorify God in your body.

**1 Corinthians 7:2-3 TNIV**   Since sexual immorality is occurring, each man should have sexual relations with his own wife, and each woman with her own husband. The husband should fulfill his marital duty to his wife, and likewise the wife to her husband.

**1 Corinthians 10:13 ESV**   No temptation has overtaken you that is not common to man. God is faithful, and he will not let you be tempted beyond your ability, but with the temptation he will also provide the way of escape, that you may be able to endure it.

**Galatians 6:8 TNIV**   Those who sow to please their sinful nature, from that nature will reap destruction; those who sow to please the Spirit, from the Spirit will reap eternal life.

**Deuteronomy 15:10 CEV**   You should be happy to give the poor what they need, because then the LORD will make you successful in everything you do.

**Proverbs 3:27–28 NASB**   Do not withhold good from those to whom it is due, when it is in your power to do it. Do not say to your neighbor, "Go, and come back, and tomorrow I will give it," when you have it with you.

**Proverbs 11:25 NKJV**   The generous soul will be made rich, and he who waters will also be watered himself.

**Matthew 6:2–4 AMP**   Whenever you give to the poor, do not blow a trumpet before you, as the hypocrites in the synagogues and in the streets like to do, that they may be recognized and honored and praised by men. Truly I tell you, they have their reward in full already. But when you give to charity, do not let your left hand know what your right hand is doing, so that your deeds of charity may be in secret; and your Father Who sees in secret will reward you openly.

**Acts 20:35 NIV**   In everything I did, I showed you that by this kind of hard work we must help the weak, remembering the words the Lord Jesus himself said: "It is more blessed to give than to receive."

**Romans 12:13 NCV**   Share with God's people who need help. Bring strangers in need into your homes.

**Ephesians 1:3 NIV**   Praise be to the God and Father of our Lord Jesus Christ, who has blessed us in the heavenly realms with every spiritual blessing in Christ.

**Philippians 1:27 ESV**   Only let your conduct be worthy of the gospel of Christ, so that whether I come and see you or am absent, I may hear of your affairs, that you stand fast in one spirit, with one mind striving side by side for the faith of the gospel.

**SHOOTINGS**

**Deuteronomy 31:6 TNIV**   Be strong and courageous. Do not be afraid or terrified because of them, for the LORD your God goes with you; he will never leave you nor forsake you.

**2 Chronicles 7:14 AMP**   If my people, who are called by My name, shall humble themselves, pray, seek, crave, and require of necessity My face and turn from their wicked ways, then will I hear from heaven, forgive their sin, and heal their land.

**Psalm 5:12 NASB**   It is You who blesses the righteous man, O LORD, You surround him with favor as with a shield.

**Psalm 12:5 NLT**   The LORD replies, "I have seen violence done to the helpless, and I have heard the groans of the poor. Now I will rise up to rescue them, as they have longed for me to do."

**Psalm 29:11 AMP**   The Lord will give [unyielding and impenetrable] strength to His people; the Lord will bless His people with peace.

**Psalm 34:15 ESV**   The eyes of the LORD are toward the righteous and his ears toward their cry.

**Proverbs 19:3 BBE**   By his foolish behaviour a man's ways are turned upside down, and his heart is bitter against the Lord.

**Colossians 4:12 TNIV**   He is always wrestling in prayer for you, that you may stand firm in all the will of God, mature and fully assured.

**2 Thessalonians 3:16 NIV**   Now may the Lord of peace himself give you peace at all times and in every way. The Lord be with all of you.

**1 Peter 3:12 HCSB**   The eyes of the Lord are on the righteous and His ears are open to their request. But the face of the Lord is against those who do evil.

**Psalm 145:18-19 NKJV**   The LORD is near to all who call upon Him, to all who call upon Him in truth. He will fulfill the desire of those who fear Him; He also will hear their cry and save them.

**Isaiah 42:1 WEB**   Behold, my servant, whom I uphold; my chosen, in whom my soul delights: I have put my Spirit on him.

**Luke 12:7 NLT**   The very hairs on your head are all numbered. So don't be afraid; you are more valuable to God than a whole flock of sparrows.

**Romans 8:26-29 ESV**   The Spirit helps us in our weakness. For we do not know what to pray for as we ought, but the Spirit himself intercedes for us with groanings too deep for words. And he who searches hearts knows what is the mind of the Spirit, because the Spirit intercedes for the saints according to the will of God. And we know that for those who love God all things work together for good, for those who are called according to his purpose. For those whom he foreknew he also predestined to be conformed to the image of his Son.

**1 Corinthians 6:20 NKJV**   You were bought at a price; therefore glorify God in your body and in your spirit, which are God's.

**Ephesians 1:16-19 TNIV**   I have not stopped giving thanks for you, remembering you in my prayers. I keep asking that the God of our Lord Jesus Christ, the glorious Father, may give you the Spirit of wisdom and revelation, so that you may know him better. I pray that the eyes of your heart may be enlightened in order that you may know the hope to which he has called you, the riches of his glorious inheritance in his people, and his incomparably great power for us who believe.

**1 Thessalonians 1:4-5 NCV**   God loves you, and we know he has chosen you, because the Good News we brought to you came not only with words, but with power, with the Holy Spirit, and with sure knowledge that it is true.

**Psalm 25:8-11 NCV**   The Lord is good and right; he points sinners to the right way. He shows those who are humble how to do right, and he teaches them his ways. All the Lord's ways are loving and true for those who follow the demands of his agreement. For the sake of your name, Lord, forgive my many sins.

**Malachi 3:5 NCV**   The Lord All-Powerful says, "Then I will come to you and judge you. I will be quick to testify against those who take part in evil magic, adultery, and lying under oath, those who cheat workers of their pay and who cheat widows and orphans, those who are unfair to foreigners, and those who do not respect me."

**Mark 7:20-23 TNIV**   What comes out of you is what defiles you. For from within, out of your hearts, come evil thoughts, sexual immorality, theft, murder, adultery, greed, malice, deceit, lewdness, envy, slander, arrogance and folly. All these evils come from inside and defile you.

**Romans 5:20-21 CEV**   The Law came, so that the full power of sin could be seen. Yet where sin was powerful, God's kindness was even more powerful. Sin ruled by means of death. But God's kindness now rules, and God has accepted us because of Jesus Christ our Lord. This means that we will have eternal life.

**1 Corinthians 6:9-11 ESV**   Do you not know that the unrighteous will not inherit the kingdom of God? Do not be deceived: neither the sexually immoral, nor idolaters, nor adulterers, nor men who practice homosexuality, nor thieves, nor the greedy, nor drunkards, nor revilers, nor swindlers will inherit the kingdom of God. And such were some of you. But you were washed, you were sanctified, you were justified in the name of the Lord Jesus Christ and by the Spirit of our God.

**1 John 3:8 ESV**   Whoever makes a practice of sinning is of the devil, for the devil has been sinning from the beginning. The reason the Son of God appeared was to destroy the works of the devil.

**Genesis 2:18 HCSB**   Then the LORD God said, "It is not good for the man to be alone. I will make a helper who is like him."

**Deuteronomy 31:8 NRSV**   It is the Lord who goes before you. He will be with you; he will not fail you or forsake you.

**Psalm 37:4–5 GNT**   Seek your happiness in the Lord, and he will give you your heart's desire. Give yourself to the Lord; trust in him, and he will help you.

**Proverbs 18:24 NIV**   A man of many companions may come to ruin, but there is a friend who sticks closer than a brother.

**Hosea 2:19–20 NCV**   I will make you my promised bride forever. I will be good and fair; I will show you my love and mercy. I will be true to you as my promised bride, and you will know the LORD.

**Matthew 19:12 NCV**   There are different reasons why some men cannot marry. Some men were born without the ability to become fathers. Others were made that way later in life by other people. And some men have given up marriage because of the kingdom of heaven. But the person who can marry should accept this teaching about marriage.

**1 Corinthians 7:28–35 NIV**   Those who marry will face many troubles in this life, and I want to spare you this. . . . I would like you to be free from concern. An unmarried man is concerned about the Lord's affairs—how he can please the Lord. But a married man is concerned about the affairs of this world—how he can please his wife—and his interests are divided. An unmarried woman or virgin is concerned about the Lord's affairs: Her aim is to be devoted to the Lord in both body and spirit. But a married woman is concerned about the affairs of this world—how she can please her husband. I am saying this for your own good, not to restrict you, but that you may live in a right way in undivided devotion to the Lord.

**Psalm 25:6-8 NIV**   Remember, O Lord, your great mercy and love, for they are from of old. Remember not the sins of my youth and my rebellious ways; according to your love remember me, for you are good, O Lord. Good and upright is the Lord; therefore he instructs sinners in his ways.

**Psalm 32:5 TNIV**   I acknowledged my sin to you and did not cover up my iniquity. I said, "I will confess my transgressions to the Lord." And you forgave the guilt of my sin.

**Proverbs 28:13 NCV**   If you hide your sins, you will not succeed. If you confess and reject them, you will receive mercy.

**Jeremiah 8:12 NCV**   They should be ashamed of the terrible way they act, but they are not ashamed at all. They don't even know how to blush about their sins. So they will fall, along with everyone else. They will be thrown to the ground when I punish them, says the Lord.

**Ezekiel 18:30-31 NIV**   Repent! Turn away from all your offenses; then sin will not be your downfall. Rid yourselves of all the offenses you have committed, and get a new heart and a new spirit.

**Luke 17:3-4 NASB**   Be on your guard! If your brother sins, rebuke him; and if he repents, forgive him. And if he sins against you seven times a day, and returns to you seven times, saying, "I repent," forgive him.

**Romans 2:4 NLT**   Don't you see how wonderfully kind, tolerant, and patient God is with you? Does this mean nothing to you? Can't you see that his kindness is intended to turn you from your sin?

**Romans 6:13-14 TNIV**   Do not offer any part of yourself to sin as an instrument of wickedness, but rather offer yourselves to God as those who have been brought from death to life; and offer every part of yourself to him as an instrument of righteousness. For sin shall no longer be your master, because you are not under the law, but under grace.

**Romans 6:17-18 ESV**   Thanks be to God, that you who were once slaves of sin have become obedient from the heart to the standard of teaching to which you were committed, and, having been set free from sin, have become slaves of righteousness.

**Hebrews 4:15-16 NCV**   Our high priest is able to understand our weaknesses. He was tempted in every way that we are, but he did not sin. Let us, then, feel very sure that we can come before God's throne where there is grace. There we can receive mercy and grace to help us when we need it.

**James 4:8 NCV**   Come near to God, and God will come near to you. You sinners, clean sin out of your lives. You who are trying to follow God and the world at the same time, make your thinking pure.

**James 5:15-16 TNIV**   The prayer offered in faith will make them well; the Lord will raise them up. If they have sinned, they will be forgiven. Therefore confess your sins to each other and pray for each other so that you may be healed. The prayer of a righteous person is powerful and effective.

**1 John 1:9-10 NCV**   If we confess our sins, he will forgive our sins, because we can trust God to do what is right. He will cleanse us from all the wrongs we have done. If we say we have not sinned, we make God a liar, and we do not accept God's teaching.

**1 John 5:18-19 ESV**   We know that everyone who has been born of God does not keep on sinning, but he who was born of God protects him, and the evil one does not touch him. We know that we are from God, and the whole world lies in the power of the evil one.

**Psalm 4:8 GNT**   When I lie down, I go to sleep in peace; you alone, O Lord, keep me perfectly safe.

**Psalm 127:2 NLT**   It is useless for you to work so hard from early morning until late at night, anxiously working for food to eat; for God gives rest to his loved ones.

**Proverbs 3:21-24 WEB**   Keep sound wisdom and discretion: So they will be life to your soul, and grace for your neck. Then you shall walk in your way securely. Your foot won't stumble. When you lie down, you will not be afraid. Yes, you will lie down, and your sleep will be sweet.

**Proverbs 4:14-16 NASB**   Do not enter the path of the wicked and do not proceed in the way of evil men. Avoid it, do not pass by it; turn away from it and pass on. For they cannot sleep unless they do evil; and they are robbed of sleep unless they make someone stumble.

**Isaiah 26:3 NLT**   You will keep in perfect peace all who trust in you, whose thoughts are fixed on you!

**Luke 22:46 NCV**   Jesus said to them, "Why are you sleeping? Get up and pray for strength against temptation."

**2 Corinthians 6:4-8 NCV**   In every way we show we are servants of God: in accepting many hard things, in troubles, in difficulties, and in great problems. We are beaten and thrown into prison. We meet those who become upset with us and start riots. We work hard, and sometimes we get no sleep or food. We show we are servants of God by our pure lives, our understanding, patience, and kindness, by the Holy Spirit, by true love, by speaking the truth, and by God's power.

**2 Thessalonians 3:13 NLT**   As for the rest of you, dear brothers and sisters, never get tired of doing good.

**Genesis 33:10 NLT**   What a relief to see your friendly smile. It is like seeing the face of God!

**Numbers 6:24–26 MSG**   GOD bless you and keep you, GOD smile on you and gift you, GOD look you full in the face and make you prosper.

**Job 8:21 HCSB**   He will yet fill your mouth with laughter and your lips with a shout of joy.

**Job 29:24 NIV**   When I smiled at them, they scarcely believed it; the light of my face was precious to them.

**Psalm 34:4–6 MSG**   GOD met me more than halfway, he freed me from my anxious fears. Look at him; give him your warmest smile. Never hide your feelings from him. When I was desperate, I called out, and GOD got me out of a tight spot.

**Psalm 80:19 CEV**   LORD God All-Powerful, make us strong again! Smile on us and save us.

**Psalm 120:1 MSG**   Deliver me from the liars, God! They smile so sweetly but lie through their teeth.

**Proverbs 15:13 NCV**   Happiness makes a person smile, but sadness can break a person's spirit.

**Proverbs 15:30 TNIV**   Light in a messenger's eyes brings joy to the heart, and good news gives health to the bones.

**Proverbs 31:25 NASB**   Strength and dignity are her clothing, And she smiles at the future.

**Ephesians 6:7 MSG**   Work with a smile on your face, always keeping in mind that no matter who happens to be giving the orders, you're really serving God.

**Proverbs 1:10 NCV**   If sinners try to lead you into sin, do not follow them.

**Mark 14:38 NIV**   Watch and pray so that you will not fall into temptation. The spirit is willing, but the body is weak.

**1 Corinthians 6:12 BBE**   I am free to do all things; but not all things are wise. I am free to do all things; but I will not let myself come under the power of any.

**1 Corinthians 6:19-20 TNIV**   Do you not know that your bodies are temples of the Holy Spirit, who is in you, whom you have received from God? You are not your own; you were bought at a price. Therefore honor God with your bodies.

**1 Corinthians 10:13 NCV**   The only temptation that has come to you is that which everyone has. But you can trust God, who will not permit you to be tempted more than you can stand. But when you are tempted, he will also give you a way to escape so that you will be able to stand it.

**1 Corinthians 10:31 NRSV**   Do everything for the glory of God.

**2 Thessalonians 1:11 NCV**   We always pray for you, asking our God to help you live the kind of life he called you to live. We pray that with his power God will help you do the good things you want and perform the works that come from your faith.

**2 Timothy 2:22 NCV**   Run away from the evil desires of youth. Try hard to live right and to have faith, love, and peace, together with those who trust in the Lord from pure hearts.

**1 Peter 1:13 NCV**   Prepare your minds for service and have self-control. All your hope should be for the gift of grace that will be yours when Jesus Christ is shown to you.

**2 Samuel 22:29-33 NASB**  You are my lamp, O Lord; and the Lord illumines my darkness. For by You I can run upon a troop; by my God I can leap over a wall. As for God, His way is blameless; the word of the Lord is tested; He is a shield to all who take refuge in Him. For who is God, besides the Lord? And who is a rock, besides our God? God is my strong fortress.

**Psalm 5:11-12 NCV**  Protect those who love you and who are happy because of you. Lord, you bless those who do what is right; you protect them like a soldier's shield.

**Psalm 25:1-7 NCV**  Lord, I give myself to you; my God, I trust you. Do not let me be disgraced; do not let my enemies laugh at me. No one who trusts you will be disgraced, but those who sin without excuse will be disgraced. Lord, tell me your ways. Show me how to live. Guide me in your truth, and teach me, my God, my Savior. I trust you all day long. Lord, remember your mercy and love that you have shown since long ago. Do not remember the sins and wrong things I did when I was young. But remember to love me always because you are good, Lord.

**Psalm 33:18-19 TNIV**  But the eyes of the Lord are on those who fear him, on those whose hope is in his unfailing love, to deliver them from death and keep them alive in famine.

**Romans 15:13 NIV**  May the God of hope fill you with all joy and peace as you trust in him, so that you may overflow with hope by the power of the Holy Spirit.

**Ephesians 1:16 NIV**  I have not stopped giving thanks for you, remembering you in my prayers.

**2 Timothy 2:3-4 NIV**  Endure hardship with us like a good soldier of Christ Jesus. No one serving as a soldier gets involved in civilian affairs—he wants to please his commanding officer.

# SOUL

**Deuteronomy 6:5 NKJV**   You shall love the LORD your God with all your heart, with all your soul, and with all your strength.

**Psalm 16:9-11 MSG**   I'm happy from the inside out, and from the outside in, I'm firmly formed. You canceled my ticket to hell—that's not my destination! Now you've got my feet on the life path, all radiant from the shining of your face. Ever since you took my hand, I'm on the right way.

**Psalm 42:5-6 NIV**   Why are you downcast, O my soul? Why so disturbed within me? Put your hope in God, for I will yet praise him, my Savior and my God.

**Psalm 51:10-12 NKJV**   Create in me a clean heart, O God, and renew a steadfast spirit within me. Do not cast me away from Your presence, and do not take Your Holy Spirit from me. Restore to me the joy of Your salvation, and uphold me by Your generous Spirit.

**Psalm 62:5 NKJV**   My soul, wait silently for God alone, for my expectation is from Him.

**Psalm 103:1-2 NRSV**   Bless the Lord, O my soul, and all that is within me, bless his holy name. Bless the Lord, O my soul, and do not forget all his benefits.

**Jeremiah 31:25 MSG**   I'll refresh tired bodies; I'll restore tired souls.

**Lamentations 3:22-25 NRSV**   The steadfast love of the Lord never ceases, his mercies never come to an end; they are new every morning; great is your faithfulness. "The Lord is my portion," says my soul, "therefore I will hope in him." The Lord is good to those who wait for him, to the soul that seeks him.

**Hebrews 4:12-13 NIV**   The word of God is living and active. Sharper than any double-edged sword, it penetrates even to dividing soul and spirit, joints and marrow; it judges the thoughts and attitudes of the heart.

**Luke 6:38 CEV**   If you give to others, you will be given a full amount in return. It will be packed down, shaken together, and spilling over into your lap. The way you treat others is the way you will be treated.

**Romans 12:11-12 CEV**   Never give up. Eagerly follow the Holy Spirit and serve the Lord. Let your hope make you glad. Be patient in time of trouble and never stop praying.

**2 Corinthians 6:6-8 NCV**   We use our right living to defend ourselves against everything. Some people honor us, but others blame us. Some people say evil things about us, but others say good things. Some people say we are liars, but we speak the truth.

**Philippians 3:14 TNIV**   I press on toward the goal to win the prize for which God has called me heavenward in Christ Jesus.

**1 Timothy 6:11-14 CEV**   Try your best to please God and to be like him. Be faithful, loving, dependable, and gentle. Fight a good fight for the faith and claim eternal life. God offered it to you when you clearly told about your faith, while so many people listened. Now I ask you to make a promise. . . . Promise to obey completely and fully all that you have been told until our Lord Jesus Christ returns.

**Hebrews 10:24-25 CEV**   We should keep on encouraging each other to be thoughtful and to do helpful things. Some people have gotten out of the habit of meeting for worship, but we must not do that. We should keep on encouraging each other, especially since you know that the day of the Lord's coming is getting closer.

**Hebrews 12:1-2 CEV**   Such a large crowd of witnesses is all around us! So we must get rid of everything that slows us down, especially the sin that just won't let go. And we must be determined to run the race that is ahead of us. We must keep our eyes on Jesus.

**Nehemiah 8:10 MSG**   The joy of God is your strength!

**Psalm 18:31-35 NIV**   Who is God besides the LORD? And who is the Rock except our God? It is God who arms me with strength and makes my way perfect. He makes my feet like the feet of a deer; he enables me to stand on the heights. He trains my hands for battle; my arms can bend a bow of bronze. You give me your shield of victory, and your right hand sustains me; you stoop down to make me great.

**Psalm 27:13-14 NKJV**   I would have lost heart, unless I had believed that I would see the goodness of the LORD in the land of the living. Wait on the LORD; be of good courage, and He shall strengthen your heart.

**Psalm 73:26 WEB**   My flesh and my heart may fail, but God is the strength of my heart and my portion forever.

**Isaiah 30:15 HCSB**   You will be delivered by returning and resting; your strength will lie in quiet confidence.

**2 Corinthians 12:9-10 CEV**   [The Lord] replied, "My kindness is all you need. My power is strongest when you are weak." So if Christ keeps giving me his power, I will gladly brag about how weak I am. Yes, I am glad to be weak or insulted or mistreated or to have troubles and sufferings, if it is for Christ. Because when I am weak, I am strong.

**Ephesians 3:14-20 NCV**   I bow in prayer before the Father from whom every family in heaven and on earth gets its true name. I ask the Father in his great glory to give you the power to be strong inwardly through his Spirit. I pray that Christ will live in your hearts by faith and that your life will be strong in love and be built on love. And I pray that you and all God's holy people will have the power to understand the greatness of Christ's love—how wide and how long and how high and how deep that love is. Christ's love is greater than anyone can ever know, but I pray that you will be able to know that love. Then you can be filled with the fullness of God. With God's power working in us, God can do much, much more than anything we can ask or imagine.

**Psalm 32:3-5 MSG**  When I kept it all inside, my bones turned to powder, my words became daylong groans. The pressure never let up; all the juices of my life dried up. Then I let it all out; I said, "I'll make a clean breast of my failures to GOD." Suddenly the pressure was gone—my guilt dissolved, my sin disappeared.

**Isaiah 26:3-4 BBE**  The man whose heart is unmoved you will keep in peace, because his hope is in you. Let your hope be in the Lord for ever: for the Lord Jah is an unchanging Rock.

**Isaiah 59:1 HCSB**  Indeed, the LORD's hand is not too short to save, and His ear is not too deaf to hear.

**2 Corinthians 1:8-11 TNIV**  We were under great pressure, far beyond our ability to endure, so that we despaired of life itself. Indeed, we felt we had received the sentence of death. But this happened that we might not rely on ourselves but on God, who raises the dead. He has delivered us from such a deadly peril, and he will deliver us again. On him we have set our hope that he will continue to deliver us, as you help us by your prayers.

**Philippians 4:6-7 NASB**  Be anxious for nothing, but in everything by prayer and supplication with thanksgiving let your requests be made known to God. And the peace of God, which surpasses all comprehension, will guard your hearts and your minds.

**James 1:2-5 MSG**  Consider it a sheer gift, friends, when tests and challenges come at you from all sides. You know that under pressure, your faith-life is forced into the open and shows its true colors. So don't try to get out of anything prematurely. Let it do its work so you become mature and well-developed, not deficient in any way. If you don't know what you're doing, pray to the Father. He loves to help.

**1 Peter 5:7 TNIV**  Cast all your anxiety on him because he cares for you.

**Proverbs 12:24 NKJV**   The hand of the diligent will rule, but the lazy man will be put to forced labor.

**Proverbs 16:3 MSG**   Put God in charge of your work, then what you've planned will take place.

**Jeremiah 29:11-14 NRSV**   Surely I know the plans I have for you, says the Lord, plans for your welfare and not for harm, to give you a future with hope. Then when you call upon me and come and pray to me, I will hear you. When you search for me, you will find me; if you seek me with all your heart, I will let you find me.

**Matthew 13:52 CEV**   Every student of the Scriptures who becomes a disciple in the kingdom of heaven is like someone who brings out new and old treasures from the storeroom.

**2 Timothy 2:15 NCV**   Make every effort to give yourself to God as the kind of person he will approve. Be a worker who is not ashamed and who uses the true teaching in the right way.

**2 Timothy 2:24-26 MSG**   God's servant must not be argumentative, but a gentle listener and a teacher who keeps cool, working firmly but patiently with those who refuse to obey. You never know how or when God might sober them up with a change of heart and a turning to the truth, enabling them to escape the Devil's trap, where they are caught and held captive, forced to run his errands.

**1 Peter 5:6-8 TNIV**   Humble yourselves, therefore, under God's mighty hand, that he may lift you up in due time. Cast all your anxiety on him because he cares for you. Be alert and of sober mind. Your enemy the devil prowls around like a roaring lion looking for someone to devour.

**2 Peter 3:14 NKJV**   Be diligent to be found by Him in peace, without spot and blameless.

**Genesis 39:3-4 NIV**   When his master saw that the Lord was with him and that the Lord gave him success in everything he did, Joseph found favor in his eyes.

**Deuteronomy 5:16 CEV**   Respect your father and mother, and you will live a long and successful life in the land I am giving you.

**Deuteronomy 8:17-18 CEV**   When you become successful, don't say, "I'm rich, and I've earned it all myself." Instead, remember that the LORD your God gives you the strength to make a living. That's how he keeps the promise he made to your ancestors.

**Joshua 1:8 NKJV**   This Book of the Law shall not depart from your mouth, but you shall meditate in it day and night, that you may observe to do according to all that is written in it. For then you will make your way prosperous, and then you will have good success.

**2 Chronicles 26:5 NLT**   As long as the king sought guidance from the Lord, God gave him success.

**Psalm 90:17 NLT**   May the Lord our God show us his approval and make our efforts successful. Yes, make our efforts successful!

**Proverbs 16:3 CEV**   Share your plans with the LORD, and you will succeed.

**Proverbs 28:13 GNT**   You will never succeed in life if you try to hide your sins. Confess them and give them up; then God will show mercy to you.

**1 Thessalonians 5:16-18 TNIV**   Rejoice always, pray continually, give thanks in all circumstances; for this is God's will for you in Christ Jesus.

**Psalm 32:6-7 BBE**  For this cause let every saint make his prayer to you at a time when you are near: then the overflowing of the great waters will not overtake him. You are my safe and secret place; you will keep me from trouble; you will put songs of salvation on the lips of those who are round me.

**Psalm 145:18-19 NRSV**  The Lord is near to all who call on him, to all who call on him in truth. He fulfills the desire of all who fear him; he also hears their cry, and saves them.

**Romans 8:16-18 NCV**  We are God's children. If we are God's children, we will receive blessings from God together with Christ. But we must suffer as Christ suffered so that we will have glory as Christ has glory. The sufferings we have now are nothing compared to the great glory that will be shown to us.

**1 Thessalonians 1:6 NCV**  You suffered much, but still you accepted the teaching with the joy that comes from the Holy Spirit.

**1 Peter 2:20-21 MSG**  If you're treated badly for good behavior and continue in spite of it to be a good servant, that is what counts with God. This is the kind of life you've been invited into, the kind of life Christ lived. He suffered everything that came his way so you would know that it could be done, and also know how to do it, step-by-step.

**1 Peter 5:8-10 NCV**  Control yourselves and be careful! The devil, your enemy, goes around like a roaring lion looking for someone to eat. Refuse to give in to him, by standing strong in your faith. You know that your Christian family all over the world is having the same kinds of suffering. And after you suffer for a short time, God, who gives all grace, will make everything right. He will make you strong and support you and keep you from falling. He called you to share in his glory in Christ, a glory that will continue forever.

**Psalm 107:19-20 CEV**   You were in serious trouble, but you prayed to the LORD, and he rescued you. By the power of his own word, he healed you and saved you from destruction.

**Psalm 118:16-21 NCV**   "The power of the LORD has won the victory; with his power the LORD has done mighty things." I will not die, but live, and I will tell what the LORD has done. The LORD has taught me a hard lesson, but he did not let me die. . . . LORD, I thank you for answering me. You have saved me.

**Psalm 143:7 CEV**   Please hurry, LORD, and answer my prayer. I feel hopeless. Don't turn away and leave me here to die.

**Matthew 4:5-7 MSG**   For the second test the Devil took him to the Holy City. He sat him on top of the Temple and said, "Since you are God's Son, jump." The Devil goaded him by quoting Psalm 91: "He has placed you in the care of angels. They will catch you so that you won't so much as stub your toe on a stone." Jesus countered with another citation from Deuteronomy: "Don't you dare test the Lord your God."

**John 14:1 TNIV**   Do not let your hearts be troubled. Trust in God; trust also in me.

**Philippians 1:22-26 MSG**   As long as I'm alive in this body, there is good work for me to do. . . . I am sure that it's better for me to stick it out here. So I plan to be around awhile, companion to you as your growth and joy in this life of trusting God continues. You can start looking forward to a great reunion when I come visit you again. We'll be praising Christ, enjoying each other.

**James 4:7-10 MSG**   So let God work his will in you. Yell a loud no to the Devil and watch him scamper. Say a quiet yes to God and he'll be there in no time. . . . Get down on your knees before the Master; it's the only way you'll get on your feet.

# TALENTS

**Exodus 28:3 ESV**   You shall speak to all the skillful, whom I have filled with a spirit of skill.

**Exodus 31:3–5 NKJV**   I have filled him with the Spirit of God, in wisdom, in understanding, in knowledge, and in all manner of workmanship, to design artistic works, to work in gold, in silver, in bronze, in cutting jewels for setting, in carving wood.

**Deuteronomy 8:18 NASB**   You shall remember the LORD your God, for it is He who is giving you power to make wealth.

**1 Chronicles 22:15–16 ESV**   You have an abundance of workmen: stonecutters, masons, carpenters, and all kinds of craftsmen without number, skilled in working gold, silver, bronze, and iron. Arise and work! The LORD be with you!

**Romans 11:29 NKJV**   For the gifts and the calling of God are irrevocable.

**Romans 12:6 AMP**   Having gifts (faculties, talents, qualities) that differ according to the grace given us, let us use them.

**1 Corinthians 12:8–11 ESV**   To one is given through the Spirit the utterance of wisdom, and to another the utterance of knowledge according to the same Spirit, to another faith by the same Spirit, to another gifts of healing by the one Spirit, to another the working of miracles, to another prophecy, to another the ability to distinguish between spirits, to another various kinds of tongues, to another the interpretation of tongues. All these are empowered by one and the same Spirit, who apportions to each one individually as he wills.

**1 Peter 4:10 NASB**   As each one has received a special gift, employ it in serving one another as good stewards of the manifold grace of God.

**Leviticus 19:16 GNT**  Do not spread lies about anyone, and when someone is on trial for his life, speak out if your testimony can help him. I am the Lord.

**Psalm 19:14 NKJV**  Let the words of my mouth and the meditation of my heart be acceptable in Your sight, O LORD, my strength and my Redeemer.

**Proverbs 8:6–8 BBE**  Give ear, for my words are true, and my lips are open to give out what is upright. For good faith goes out of my mouth, and false lips are disgusting to me. All the words of my mouth are righteousness; there is nothing false or twisted in them.

**Proverbs 12:22 NLT**  The LORD hates those who don't keep their word, but he delights in those who do.

**Proverbs 15:1–2 NCV**  A gentle answer will calm a person's anger, but an unkind answer will cause more anger. Wise people use knowledge when they speak, but fools pour out foolishness.

**Proverbs 15:4 GNT**  Kind words bring life, but cruel words crush your spirit.

**Proverbs 21:23 NCV**  Those who are careful about what they say keep themselves out of trouble.

**Matthew 12:34–35 NKJV**  Out of the abundance of the heart the mouth speaks. A good man out of the good treasure of his heart brings forth good things, and an evil man out of the evil treasure brings forth evil things.

**2 Timothy 2:16–17 ESV**  Avoid irreverent babble, for it will lead people into more and more ungodliness, and their talk will spread like gangrene.

**TATTOO**

**Leviticus 19:28 NKJV**   You shall not make any cuttings in your flesh for the dead, nor tattoo any marks on you: I am the LORD.

**Proverbs 1:8-9 MSG**   Pay close attention, friend, to what your father tells you; never forget what you learned at your mother's knee. Wear their counsel like flowers in your hair, like rings on your fingers.

**Romans 12:1-2 WEB**   I beg you, brothers, by the mercies of God, to present your bodies a living sacrifice, holy, acceptable to God, which is your spiritual service. Don't be fashioned according to this world, but be transformed by the renewing of your mind, so that you may prove what is the good and acceptable and perfect will of God.

**1 Corinthians 6:17-18 BBE**   He who is united to the Lord is one spirit. Keep away from the desires of the flesh.

**1 Corinthians 6:19-20 TNIV**   Do you not know that your bodies are temples of the Holy Spirit, who is in you, whom you have received from God? You are not your own; you were bought at a price. Therefore honor God with your bodies.

**Ephesians 2:10 NLT**   We are God's masterpiece.

**1 Timothy 2:9-10 TNIV**   I also want the women to dress modestly, with decency and propriety, adorning themselves, not with elaborate hairstyles or gold or pearls or expensive clothes, but with good deeds, appropriate for women who profess to worship God.

**2 Timothy 2:22 NLT**   Run from anything that stimulates youthful lusts. Follow anything that makes you want to do right. Pursue faith and love and peace, and enjoy the companionship of those who call on the Lord with pure hearts.

**James 1:25 GNT**   If you look closely into the perfect law that sets people free, and keep on paying attention to it and do not simply listen and then forget it, but put it into practice—you will be blessed by God in what you do.

**Psalm 149:3 WEB**  Let them praise his name in the dance! Let them sing praises to him with tambourine and harp!

**Daniel 1:17 TNIV**  To these four young men God gave knowledge and understanding of all kinds of literature and learning. And Daniel could understand visions and dreams of all kinds.

**Mark 8:36 TNIV**  What good is it for you to gain the whole world, yet forfeit your soul?

**Romans 12:14–16 CEV**  Ask God to bless everyone who mistreats you. Ask him to bless them and not to curse them. When others are happy, be happy with them, and when they are sad, be sad. Be friendly with everyone. Don't be proud and feel that you are smarter than others. Make friends with ordinary people.

**1 Timothy 4:12 MSG**  Get the word out. Teach all these things. And don't let anyone put you down because you're young. Teach believers with your life: by word, by demeanor, by love, by faith, by integrity. Stay at your post reading Scripture, giving counsel, teaching.

**Hebrews 12:5–6 GNT**  Have you forgotten the encouraging words which God speaks to you as his children? "My child, pay attention when the Lord corrects you, and do not be discouraged when he rebukes you. Because the Lord corrects everyone he loves, and punishes everyone he accepts as a child."

**2 Peter 1:5–8 TNIV**  Make every effort to add to your faith goodness; and to goodness, knowledge; and to knowledge, self-control; and to self-control, perseverance; and to perseverance, godliness; and to godliness, mutual affection; and to mutual affection; love. For if you possess these qualities in increasing measure, they will keep you from being ineffective and unproductive in your knowledge of our Lord Jesus Christ.

**TEMPTED**

**Psalm 25:4–5 NRSV**  Make me to know your ways, O Lord; teach me your paths. Lead me in your truth, and teach me, for you are the God of my salvation; for you I wait all day long.

**Matthew 4:1–4 CEV**  The Holy Spirit led Jesus into the desert, so that the devil could test him. After Jesus had gone without eating for forty days and nights, he was very hungry. Then the devil came to him and said, "If you are God's Son, tell these stones to turn into bread." Jesus answered, "The Scriptures say: 'No one can live only on food. People need every word that God has spoken.'"

**1 Corinthians 10:12–14 NKJV**  Let him who thinks he stands take heed lest he fall. No temptation has overtaken you except such as is common to man; but God is faithful, who will not allow you to be tempted beyond what you are able, but with the temptation will also make the way of escape, that you may be able to bear it. Therefore, my beloved, flee from idolatry.

**Galatians 6:1–2 NIV**  If someone is caught in a sin, you who are spiritual should restore him gently. But watch yourself, or you also may be tempted. Carry each other's burdens, and in this way you will fulfill the law of Christ.

**Hebrews 2:18 HCSB**  Since He Himself was tested and has suffered, He is able to help those who are tested.

**Hebrews 4:14–15 BBE**  Let us be strong in our faith. For we have not a high priest who is not able to be touched by the feelings of our feeble flesh; but we have one who has been tested in all points as we ourselves are tested, but without sin.

**James 1:12–14 WEB**  Blessed is the man who endures temptation, for when he has been approved, he will receive the crown of life, which the Lord promised to those who love him. Let no man say when he is tempted, "I am tempted by God," for God can't be tempted with evil, and he himself tempts no one. But each one is tempted, when he is drawn away by his own lust, and enticed.

**Exodus 23:1-2 MSG** Don't pass on malicious gossip. Don't link up with a wicked person and give corrupt testimony. Don't go along with the crowd in doing evil and don't fudge your testimony in a case just to please the crowd.

**Psalm 19:7 NASB** The law of the LORD is perfect, restoring the soul; The testimony of the LORD is sure, making wise the simple.

**Psalm 96:3-5 NIV** Declare his glory among the nations, his marvelous deeds among all peoples. For great is the LORD and most worthy of praise; he is to be feared above all gods. For all the gods of the nations are idols, but the LORD made the heavens.

**Matthew 19:18 TNIV** Jesus replied, "You shall not murder, you shall not commit adultery, you shall not steal, you shall not give false testimony."

**Mark 14:55-56 NASB** Now the chief priests and the whole Council kept trying to obtain testimony against Jesus to put Him to death, and they were not finding any. For many were giving false testimony against Him, but their testimony was not consistent.

**1 John 5:10-12 ESV** Whoever believes in the Son of God has the testimony in himself. Whoever does not believe God has made him a liar, because he has not believed in the testimony that God has borne concerning his Son. And this is the testimony, that God gave us eternal life, and this life is in his Son. Whoever has the Son has life; whoever does not have the Son of God does not have life.

**Revelation 12:11 NASB** And they overcame him because of the blood of the Lamb and because of the word of their testimony, and they did not love their life even when faced with death.

**Deuteronomy 8:10 NASB** When you have eaten and are satisfied, you shall bless the LORD your God for the good land which He has given you.

**Ezra 3:11 NIV** With praise and thanksgiving they sang to the LORD: "He is good; his love to Israel endures forever." And all the people gave a great shout of praise to the LORD, because the foundation of the house of the LORD was laid.

**Psalm 18:1–3 NIV** I love you, O LORD, my strength. The LORD is my rock, my fortress and my deliverer; my God is my rock, in whom I take refuge. He is my shield and the horn of my salvation, my stronghold. I call to the LORD, who is worthy of praise, and I am saved from my enemies.

**Psalm 100:4 NKJV** Enter into His gates with thanksgiving, and into His courts with praise. Be thankful to Him, and bless His name.

**Psalm 105:1 NASB** Oh give thanks to the LORD, call upon His name; make known His deeds among the peoples.

**Psalm 118:1 ESV** Oh give thanks to the LORD, for he is good; for his steadfast love endures forever!

**Ephesians 1:3 GNT** Let us give thanks to the God and Father of our Lord Jesus Christ! For in our union with Christ he has blessed us by giving us every spiritual blessing in the heavenly world.

**Philippians 4:6 ESV** Do not be anxious about anything, but in everything by prayer and supplication with thanksgiving let your requests be made known to God.

**1 Thessalonians 5:17–18 ESV** Pray without ceasing, give thanks in all circumstances; for this is the will of God in Christ Jesus for you.

**Acts 8:21–23 GNT**   You have no part or share in our work, because your heart is not right in God's sight. Repent, then, of this evil plan of yours, and pray to the Lord that he will forgive you for thinking such a thing as this. For I see that you are full of bitter envy and are a prisoner of sin.

**Romans 2:15 BBE**   Because the work of the law is seen in their hearts, their sense of right and wrong giving witness to it, while their minds are at one time judging them and at another giving them approval.

**Romans 12:2 WEB**   Don't be fashioned according to this world, but be transformed by the renewing of your mind, so that you may prove what is the good and acceptable and perfect will of God.

**2 Corinthians 4:2 MSG**   We don't twist God's Word to suit ourselves. Rather, we keep everything we do and say out in the open, the whole truth on display, so that those who want to can see and judge for themselves in the presence of God.

**Philippians 2:1–3 NCV**   Does your life in Christ give you strength? Does his love comfort you? Do we share together in the spirit? Do you have mercy and kindness? If so, make me very happy by having the same thoughts, sharing the same love, and having one mind and purpose. When you do things, do not let selfishness or pride be your guide. Instead, be humble and give more honor to others than to yourselves.

**Colossians 3:15 NCV**   Let the peace that Christ gives control your thinking.

**2 Timothy 3:8 HCSB**   These also resist the truth, men who are corrupt in mind, worthless in regard to the faith.

**James 4:17 NCV**   Anyone who knows the right thing to do, but does not do it, is sinning.

**Psalm 90:12 HCSB**   Teach us to number our days carefully so that we may develop wisdom in our hearts.

**Proverbs 5:21 NLT**   The LORD sees clearly what a man does, examining every path he takes.

**Ecclesiastes 3:6 NCV**   There is a time to look for something and a time to stop looking for it. There is a time to keep things and a time to throw things away.

**Ecclesiastes 3:10-11 NCV**   I saw the hard work God has given people to do. God has given them a desire to know the future. He does everything just right and on time, but people can never completely understand what he is doing.

**Mark 6:31 NIV**   Because so many people were coming and going that they did not even have a chance to eat, he said to them, "Come with me by yourselves to a quiet place and get some rest."

**Acts 1:7-8 GNT**   The times and occasions are set by my Father's own authority, and it is not for you to know when they will be. But when the Holy Spirit comes upon you, you will be filled with power.

**Romans 13:12-14 CEV**   Night is almost over, and day will soon appear. We must stop behaving as people do in the dark and be ready to live in the light. So behave properly, as people do in the day. Don't go to wild parties or get drunk or be vulgar or indecent. Don't quarrel or be jealous. Let the Lord Jesus Christ be as near to you as the clothes you wear. Then you won't try to satisfy your selfish desires.

**Ephesians 5:15-16 NCV**   So be very careful how you live. Do not live like those who are not wise, but live wisely. Use every chance you have for doing good, because these are evil times.

**1 Peter 4:2-3 NCV**   Strengthen yourselves so that you will live here on earth doing what God wants, not the evil things people want. In the past you wasted too much time doing what nonbelievers do.

**Psalm 6:6-9 ESV**   I am weary with my moaning; every night I flood my bed with tears; I drench my couch with my weeping. My eye wastes away because of grief; it grows weak because of all my foes. Depart from me, all you workers of evil, for the Lord has heard the sound of my weeping. The Lord has heard my plea; the Lord accepts my prayer.

**Isaiah 40:28-29 CEV**   The LORD is the eternal God, Creator of the earth. He never gets weary or tired; his wisdom cannot be measured. The LORD gives strength to those who are weary.

**Isaiah 40:30-31 NIV**   Even youths grow tired and weary, and young men stumble and fall; but those who hope in the Lord will renew their strength. They will soar on wings like eagles; they will run and not grow weary, they will walk and not be faint.

**Matthew 11:28-30 MSG**   Are you tired? Worn out? Burned out on religion? Come to me. Get away with me and you'll recover your life. I'll show you how to take a real rest. Walk with me and work with me—watch how I do it. Learn the unforced rhythms of grace. I won't lay anything heavy or ill-fitting on you. Keep company with me and you'll learn to live freely and lightly.

**Hebrews 3:12-14 CEV**   My friends, watch out! Don't let evil thoughts or doubts make any of you turn from the living God. You must encourage one another each day. And you must keep on while there is still a time that can be called "today." If you don't, then sin may fool some of you and make you stubborn. We were sure about Christ when we first became his people. So let's hold tightly to our faith until the end.

**Hebrews 12:12-13 NCV**   You have become weak, so make yourselves strong again. Keep on the right path, so the weak will not stumble but rather be strengthened.

# TRAGEDY

**Psalm 18:2 MSG**  I love you, God—you make me strong. God is bedrock under my feet, the castle in which I live, my rescuing knight. My God—the high crag where I run for dear life, hiding behind the boulders, safe in the granite hideout.

**Psalm 23:4 NKJV**  Yea, though I walk through the valley of the shadow of death, I will fear no evil; for You are with me; Your rod and Your staff, they comfort me.

**Psalm 46:1 MSG**  God is a safe place to hide, ready to help when we need him.

**Psalm 56:8 NLT**  You keep track of all my sorrows. You have collected all my tears in your bottle. You have recorded each one in your book.

**Psalm 147:3 NCV**  He heals the brokenhearted and bandages their wounds.

**Isaiah 26:3 ESV**  You keep him in perfect peace whose mind is stayed on you, because he trusts in you.

**Lamentations 3:21–24 TNIV**  Yet this I call to mind and therefore I have hope: Because of the Lord's great love we are not consumed, for his compassions never fail. They are new every morning; great is your faithfulness. I say to myself, "The Lord is my portion; therefore I will wait for him."

**Matthew 11:28 WEB**  Come to me, all you who labor and are heavily burdened, and I will give you rest.

**James 5:13 ESV**  Is anyone among you suffering? Let him pray.

**1 John 4:4 CEV**  You belong to God, and you have defeated these enemies. God's Spirit is in you and is more powerful than the one that is in the world.

**Psalm 34:4-7 GNT**   I prayed to the Lord, and he answered me; he freed me from all my fears. The oppressed look to him and are glad; they will never be disappointed. The helpless call to him, and he answers; he saves them from all their troubles. His angel guards those who honor the Lord and rescues them from danger.

**Psalm 46:1 NCV**   God is our protection and our strength. He always helps in times of trouble.

**Psalm 55:22 NASB**   Cast your burden upon the LORD and He will sustain you; He will never allow the righteous to be shaken.

**Romans 5:3-5 NCV**   We also have joy with our troubles, because we know that these troubles produce patience. And patience produces character, and character produces hope. And this hope will never disappoint us, because God has poured out his love to fill our hearts. He gave us his love through the Holy Spirit, whom God has given to us.

**James 1:2-3 NIV**   Consider it pure joy, my brothers, whenever you face trials of many kinds, because you know that the testing of your faith develops perseverance.

**1 Peter 1:6-7 ESV**   In this you rejoice, though now for a little while, if necessary, you have been grieved by various trials, so that the tested genuineness of your faith—more precious than gold that perishes though it is tested by fire—may be found to result in praise and glory and honor at the revelation of Jesus Christ.

**1 Peter 4:12-13 NIV**   Do not be surprised at the painful trial you are suffering, as though something strange were happening to you. But rejoice that you participate in the sufferings of Christ, so that you may be overjoyed when his glory is revealed.

**Psalm 9:9 BBE**   The Lord will be a high tower for those who are crushed down, a high tower in times of trouble.

**Psalm 22:24 NCV**   He does not ignore those in trouble. He doesn't hide from them but listens when they call out to him.

**Psalm 107:19-20 NKJV**   They cried out to the LORD in their trouble; and He saved them out of their distresses. He sent His word and healed them, and delivered them from their destructions.

**Psalm 142:1-3 HCSB**   I cry aloud to the LORD; I plead aloud to the LORD for mercy. I pour out my complaint before Him; I reveal my trouble to Him. Although my spirit is weak within me, You know my way. Along this path I travel they have hidden a trap for me.

**Proverbs 28:14 NIV**   Blessed is the man who always fears the LORD, but he who hardens his heart falls into trouble.

**2 Corinthians 1:3-4 CEV**   Praise God, the Father of our Lord Jesus Christ! The Father is a merciful God, who always gives us comfort. He comforts us when we are in trouble, so that we can share that same comfort with others in trouble.

**Philippians 4:13-14 NKJV**   I can do all things through Christ who strengthens me. Nevertheless you have done well that you shared in my distress.

**James 1:2-3 GNT**   Consider yourselves fortunate when all kinds of trials come your way, for you know that when your faith succeeds in facing such trials, the result is the ability to endure.

**2 Peter 3:18 CEV**   Let the wonderful kindness and the understanding that come from our Lord and Savior Jesus Christ help you to keep on growing. Praise Jesus now and forever! Amen.

**Job 31:24-28 HCSB**   If I placed my confidence in gold or called fine gold my trust, if I have rejoiced because my wealth is great or because my own hand has acquired so much, if I have gazed at the sun when it was shining or at the moon moving in splendor, so that my heart was secretly enticed and I threw them a kiss, this would also be a crime deserving punishment, for I would have denied God above.

**Psalm 9:9-10 GNT**   The Lord is a refuge for the oppressed, a place of safety in times of trouble. Those who know you, Lord, will trust you; you do not abandon anyone who comes to you.

**Psalm 18:2-3 AMP**   The Lord is my Rock, my Fortress, and my Deliverer; my God, my keen and firm Strength in Whom I will trust and take refuge, my Shield, and the Horn of my salvation, my High Tower. I will call upon the Lord, Who is to be praised; so shall I be saved from my enemies.

**Psalm 32:10 CEV**   All kinds of troubles will strike the wicked, but your kindness shields those who trust you, LORD.

**Psalm 69:16-18 CEV**   Answer me, LORD! You are kind and good. Pay attention to me! You are truly merciful. Don't turn away from me. I am your servant, and I am in trouble. Please hurry and help! Come and save me from my enemies.

**Proverbs 30:5 NKJV**   Every word of God is pure; He is a shield to those who put their trust in Him.

**Isaiah 12:2 GNT**   God is my savior; I will trust him and not be afraid. The Lord gives me power and strength; he is my savior.

**Jeremiah 17:7-8 ESV**   Blessed is the man who trusts in the LORD, whose trust is the LORD. He is like a tree planted by water, that sends out its roots by the stream, and does not fear when heat comes, for its leaves remain green, and is not anxious in the year of drought, for it does not cease to bear fruit.

**Numbers 23:19 NCV**   God is not a human being, and he will not lie. He is not a human, and he does not change his mind. What he says he will do, he does. What he promises, he makes come true.

**Jeremiah 33:3 NASB**   Call to Me and I will answer you, and I will tell you great and mighty things, which you do not know.

**John 1:17 CEV**   Jesus Christ brought us undeserved kindness and truth.

**John 8:32 NASB**   You will know the truth, and the truth will make you free.

**John 11:25-26 ESV**   Jesus said to her, "I am the resurrection and the life. Whoever believes in me, though he die, yet shall he live, and everyone who lives and believes in me shall never die. Do you believe this?"

**John 14:6 TNIV**   Jesus answered, "I am the way and the truth and the life. No one comes to the Father except through me."

**John 17:17 WEB**   Sanctify them in your truth. Your word is truth.

**Romans 1:18-19 HCSB**   God's wrath is revealed from heaven against all godlessness and unrighteousness of people who by their unrighteousness suppress the truth, since what can be known about God is evident among them, because God has shown it to them.

**Romans 1:24-25 GNT**   God has given those people over to do the filthy things their hearts desire, and they do shameful things with each other. They exchange the truth about God for a lie; they worship and serve what God has created instead of the Creator himself, who is to be praised forever! Amen.

**Ephesians 4:15 GNT**   Instead, by speaking the truth in a spirit of love, we must grow up in every way to Christ, who is the head.

**Proverbs 3:7 NASB**   Do not be wise in your own eyes; fear the LORD and turn away from evil.

**Proverbs 3:11-12 CEV**   My child, don't turn away or become bitter when the LORD corrects you. The LORD corrects everyone he loves.

**Jeremiah 2:19 NCV**   "Your evil will bring punishment to you, and the wrong you have done will teach you a lesson. Think about it and understand that it is a terrible evil to turn away from the LORD your God. It is wrong not to fear me," says the Lord GOD All-Powerful.

**Ezekiel 18:30-31 GNT**   Turn away from all the evil you are doing, and don't let your sin destroy you. Give up all the evil you have been doing, and get yourselves new minds and hearts.

**Acts 14:15 NCV**   We are bringing you the Good News and are telling you to turn away from these worthless things and turn to the living God.

**1 Thessalonians 5:18-19 CEV**   Whatever happens, keep thanking God because of Jesus Christ. This is what God wants you to do. Don't turn away God's Spirit.

**2 Timothy 3:2-5 NKJV**   For men will be lovers of themselves, lovers of money, boasters, proud, blasphemers, disobedient to parents, unthankful, unholy, unloving, unforgiving, slanderers, without self-control, brutal, despisers of good, traitors, headstrong, haughty, lovers of pleasure rather than lovers of God, having a form of godliness but denying its power. And from such people turn away!

**Hebrews 6:4-6 CEV**   What about those who turn away after they have received the good message of God and the powers of the future world? There is no way to bring them back. What they are doing is the same as nailing the Son of God to a cross and insulting him in public!

**Psalm 119:27-28 GNT** Help me to understand your laws, and I will meditate on your wonderful teachings. I am overcome by sorrow; strengthen me, as you have promised.

**Psalm 119:34-37 WEB** Give me understanding, and I will keep your law. Yes, I will obey it with my whole heart. Direct me in the path of your commandments, for I delight in them. Turn my heart toward your statutes, not toward selfish gain. Turn my eyes away from looking at worthless things. Revive me in your ways.

**Psalm 139:2-4 NKJV** You know my sitting down and my rising up; You understand my thought afar off. You comprehend my path and my lying down, and are acquainted with all my ways. For there is not a word on my tongue, but behold, O Lord, You know it altogether.

**Proverbs 2:6-12 HCSB** The LORD gives wisdom; from His mouth come knowledge and understanding. He stores up success for the upright; He is a shield for those who live with integrity so that He may guard the paths of justice and protect the way of His loyal followers. Then you will understand righteousness, justice, and integrity—every good path. For wisdom will enter your mind, and knowledge will delight your heart. Discretion will watch over you, and understanding will guard you, rescuing you from the way of evil—from the one who says perverse things.

**Proverbs 28:5 WEB** Evil men don't understand justice; but those who seek Yahweh understand it fully.

**1 Corinthians 2:10 NLT** We know these things because God has revealed them to us by his Spirit, and his Spirit searches out everything and shows us even God's deep secrets.

**1 Corinthians 2:11-12 ESV** No one comprehends the thoughts of God except the Spirit of God. Now we have received not the spirit of the world, but the Spirit who is from God, that we might understand the things freely given us by God.

**Psalm 133:1 NKJV**  Behold, how good and how pleasant it is For brethren to dwell together in unity!

**Romans 12:16 ESV**  Live in harmony with one another. Do not be haughty, but associate with the lowly.

**Romans 15:5-6 TNIV**  May the God who gives endurance and encouragement give you the same attitude of mind toward each other that Christ Jesus had, so that with one mind and one voice you may glorify the God and Father of our Lord Jesus Christ.

**1 Corinthians 1:10 AMP**  I urge and entreat you, brethren, by the name of our Lord Jesus Christ, that all of you be in perfect harmony and full agreement in what you say, and that there be no dissensions or factions or divisions among you, but that you be perfectly united in your common understanding and in your opinions and judgments.

**Ephesians 4:11-13 CEV**  Christ chose some of us to be apostles, prophets, missionaries, pastors, and teachers, so that his people would learn to serve and his body would grow strong. This will continue until we are united by our faith and by our understanding of the Son of God. Then we will be mature, just as Christ is, and we will be completely like him.

**Philippians 2:1-2 NASB**  If there is any encouragement in Christ, if there is any consolation of love, if there is any fellowship of the Spirit, if any affection and compassion, make my joy complete by being of the same mind, maintaining the same love, united in spirit, intent on one purpose.

**Colossians 2:2 NLT**  Be encouraged and knit together by strong ties of love.

**Colossians 3:14-15 NASB**  Beyond all these things put on love, which is the perfect bond of unity. Let the peace of Christ rule in your hearts, to which indeed you were called in one body; and be thankful.

**Psalm 9:17-20 NCV**   Wicked people will go to the grave, and so will all those who forget GOD. But those who have troubles will not be forgotten. The hopes of the poor will never die. LORD, rise up and judge the nations. Don't let people think they are strong. Teach them to fear you, LORD. The nations must learn that they are only human.

**Psalm 18:18-20 NCV**   They attacked me at my time of trouble, but the LORD supported me. He took me to a safe place. Because he delights in me, he saved me. The LORD spared me because I did what was right. Because I have not done evil, he has rewarded me.

**Psalm 99:8 HCSB**   LORD our God, You answered them. You were a God who forgave them, but punished their misdeeds.

**Proverbs 4:16-17 MSG**   Evil people are restless unless they're making trouble; They can't get a good night's sleep unless they've made life miserable for somebody. Perversity is their food and drink, violence their drug of choice.

**Proverbs 19:3 GNT**   Some people ruin themselves by their own stupid actions and then blame the Lord.

**Ephesians 6:12 NIV**   Our struggle is not against flesh and blood, but against the rulers, against the authorities, against the powers of this dark world and against the spiritual forces of evil in the heavenly realms.

**Ephesians 6:16-18 NKJV**   Taking the shield of faith with which you will be able to quench all the fiery darts of the wicked one. . . . Praying always with all prayer and supplication in the Spirit, being watchful to this end with all perseverance and supplication for all the saints.

**2 Peter 3:9 WEB**   The Lord is not slow concerning his promise, as some count slowness; but is longsuffering towards us, not wishing that any should perish, but that all should come to repentance.

**Exodus 19:5 NKJV**   If you will indeed obey My voice and keep My covenant, then you shall be a special treasure to Me above all people; for all the earth is Mine.

**Psalm 16:7 NCV**   I praise the LORD because he advises me. Even at night, I feel his leading.

**Psalm 29:4–9 NASB**   The voice of the LORD is powerful, the voice of the LORD is majestic. The voice of the LORD breaks the cedars. . . . The voice of the LORD hews out flames of fire. The voice of the LORD shakes the wilderness. . . . The voice of the LORD makes the deer to calve and strips the forests bare; and in His temple everything says, "Glory!"

**Psalm 68:33 NCV**   He speaks with a thundering voice.

**Proverbs 30:5–6 ESV**   Every word of God proves true; he is a shield to those who take refuge in him. Do not add to his words, lest he rebuke you and you be found a liar.

**Joel 2:11 NKJV**   The LORD gives voice before His army, for His camp is very great; for strong is the One who executes His word. For the day of the LORD is great and very terrible; who can endure it?

**Matthew 17:5 NASB**   While he was still speaking, a bright cloud overshadowed them, and behold, a voice out of the cloud said, "This is My beloved Son, with whom I am well-pleased; listen to Him!"

**John 8:47 CEV**   Anyone who belongs to God will listen to his message. But you refuse to listen, because you don't belong to God.

**John 10:3–5 ESV**   The sheep hear his voice, and he calls his own sheep by name and leads them out. When he has brought out all his own, he goes before them, and the sheep follow him, for they know his voice. A stranger they will not follow, but they will flee from him, for they do not know the voice of strangers.

**Psalm 16:8 GNT**   I am always aware of the Lord's presence; he is near, and nothing can shake me.

**Psalm 55:16-19 GNT**   I call to the Lord God for help, and he will save me. Morning, noon, and night my complaints and groans go up to him, and he will hear my voice. He will bring me safely back from the battles that I fight against so many enemies. God, who has ruled from eternity, will hear me and defeat them; for they refuse to change, and they do not fear him.

**Ecclesiastes 3:1-8 ESV**   For everything there is a season, and a time for every matter under heaven: a time to be born, and a time to die . . . a time to kill, and a time to heal; a time to break down, and a time to build up; a time to weep, and a time to laugh; a time to mourn, and a time to dance . . . a time to love, and a time to hate; a time for war, and a time for peace.

**Isaiah 2:3-4 NLT**   The LORD's teaching will go out from Zion; his word will go out from Jerusalem. The LORD will mediate between nations and will settle international disputes. They will hammer their swords into plowshares and their spears into pruning hooks. Nation will no longer fight against nation, nor train for war anymore.

**1 Timothy 2:1-4 GNT**   I urge that petitions, prayers, requests, and thanksgivings be offered to God for all people; for kings and all others who are in authority, that we may live a quiet and peaceful life with all reverence toward God and with proper conduct. This is good and it pleases God our Savior, who wants everyone to be saved and to come to know the truth.

**James 4:1-2 NKJV**   Where do wars and fights come from among you? Do they not come from your desires for pleasure that war in your members? You lust and do not have. You murder and covet and cannot obtain. You fight and war. Yet you do not have because you do not ask.

**2 Corinthians 10:3-6 ESV**   Though we walk in the flesh, we are not waging war according to the flesh. For the weapons of our warfare are not of the flesh but have divine power to destroy strongholds. We destroy arguments and every lofty opinion raised against the knowledge of God, and take every thought captive to obey Christ, being ready to punish every disobedience, when your obedience is complete.

**Ephesians 6:12-13 NASB**   Our struggle is not against flesh and blood, but against the rulers, against the powers, against the world forces of this darkness, against the spiritual forces of wickedness in the heavenly places. Therefore, take up the full armor of God, so that you will be able to resist in the evil day, and having done everything, to stand firm.

**Ephesians 6:16 HCSB**   In every situation take the shield of faith, and with it you will be able to extinguish the flaming arrows of the evil one.

**Ephesians 6:17-18 NKJV**   Take the helmet of salvation, and the sword of the Spirit, which is the word of God; praying always with all prayer and supplication in the Spirit, being watchful to this end with all perseverance and supplication for all the saints.

**Colossians 2:15 TNIV**   Having disarmed the powers and authorities, he made a public spectacle of them, triumphing over them by the cross.

**1 Timothy 6:12 NASB**   Fight the good fight of faith; take hold of the eternal life.

**1 John 5:4-5 ESV**   Everyone who has been born of God overcomes the world. And this is the victory that has overcome the world—our faith. Who is it that overcomes the world except the one who believes that Jesus is the Son of God?

# WARNINGS

**Deuteronomy 4:24–25 NCV**   The LORD your God is a jealous God, like a fire that burns things up. Even after you have lived in the land a long time and have had children and grandchildren, don't do evil things. Don't make any kind of idol, and don't do what the LORD your God says is evil, because that will make him angry.

**Proverbs 29:1 CEV**   If you keep being stubborn after many warnings, you will suddenly discover you have gone too far.

**Matthew 7:21 WEB**   Not everyone who says to me, "Lord, Lord," will enter into the Kingdom of Heaven; but he who does the will of my Father who is in heaven.

**Romans 16:17 BBE**   It is my desire, brothers, that you will take note of those who are causing division and trouble among you, quite against the teaching which was given to you: and keep away from them.

**1 Corinthians 10:10–11 CEV**   Don't even grumble, as some of them did and were killed by the destroying angel. These things happened to them as a warning to us.

**1 Timothy 6:20 NIV**   Guard what has been entrusted to your care. Turn away from godless chatter and the opposing ideas of what is falsely called knowledge.

**Titus 3:10 NCV**   Avoid someone who causes arguments.

**1 Peter 2:11 NKJV**   Beloved, I beg you as sojourners and pilgrims, abstain from fleshly lusts which war against the soul.

**2 Peter 3:17 GNT**   Be on your guard, then, so that you will not be led away by the errors of lawless people and fall from your safe position.

**Revelation 22:18 CEV**   Here is my warning for everyone who hears the prophecies in this book: If you add anything to them, God will make you suffer all the terrible troubles written in this book.

**Deuteronomy 8:17–18 NCV**    You might say to yourself, "I am rich because of my own power and strength," but remember the Lord your God! It is he who gives you the power to become rich, keeping the agreement he promised to your ancestors, as it is today.

**Psalm 49:10–12 NLT**    Those who are wise must finally die, just like the foolish and senseless, leaving all their wealth behind. The grave is their eternal home, where they will stay forever. They may name their estates after themselves, but their fame will not last. They will die, just like animals.

**Psalm 49:16–20 ESV**    Be not afraid when a man becomes rich, when the glory of his house increases. For when he dies he will carry nothing away; his glory will not go down after him. For though, while he lives, he counts himself blessed—and though you get praise when you do well for yourself—his soul will go to the generation of his fathers, who will never again see light. Man in his pomp yet without understanding is like the beasts that perish.

**Proverbs 13:11 NKJV**    Wealth gained by dishonesty will be diminished, but he who gathers by labor will increase.

**Proverbs 15:16 MSG**    A simple life in the Fear-of-God is better than a rich life with a ton of headaches.

**Proverbs 19:14 NCV**    Houses and wealth are inherited from parents, but a wise wife is a gift from the Lord.

**Philippians 4:19–20 CEV**    I pray that God will take care of all your needs with the wonderful blessings that come from Christ Jesus! May God our Father be praised forever and ever. Amen.

**Hebrews 13:5 ESV**    Keep your life free from love of money, and be content with what you have, for he has said, "I will never leave you nor forsake you."

**Psalm 48:14 NKJV**   This is God, our God forever and ever; He will be our guide even to death.

**Psalm 143:10 AMP**   Teach me to do Your will, for You are my God; let Your good Spirit lead me into a level country and into the land of uprightness.

**Isaiah 30:21 NASB**   Your ears will hear a word behind you, "This is the way, walk in it," whenever you turn to the right or to the left.

**Isaiah 48:17 GNT**   I am the Lord your God, the one who wants to teach you for your own good and direct you in the way you should go.

**John 16:13-14 NCV**   When the Spirit of truth comes, he will lead you into all truth. He will not speak his own words, but he will speak only what he hears, and he will tell you what is to come. The Spirit of truth will bring glory to me, because he will take what I have to say and tell it to you.

**Ephesians 5:15-17 ESV**   Look carefully then how you walk, not as unwise but as wise, making the best use of the time, because the days are evil. Therefore do not be foolish, but understand what the will of the Lord is.

**Hebrews 10:36 NASB**   For you have need of endurance, so that when you have done the will of God, you may receive what was promised.

**1 Peter 2:15 NLT**   It is God's will that your honorable lives should silence those ignorant people who make foolish accusations against you.

**1 John 2:16-17 NCV**   These are the ways of the world: wanting to please our sinful selves, wanting the sinful things we see, and being too proud of what we have. None of these come from the Father, but all of them come from the world. The world and everything that people want in it are passing away, but the person who does what God wants lives forever.

**Psalm 51:6 HCSB**   You desire integrity in the inner self, and You teach me wisdom deep within.

**Psalm 111:10 NASB**   The fear of the LORD is the beginning of wisdom.

**Proverbs 1:5-7 GNT**   These proverbs can even add to the knowledge of the wise and give guidance to the educated, so that they can understand the hidden meanings of proverbs and the problems that the wise raise. To have knowledge, you must first have reverence for the Lord. Stupid people have no respect for wisdom and refuse to learn.

**Proverbs 2:1-6 ESV**   If you receive my words and treasure up my commandments with you, making your ear attentive to wisdom and inclining your heart to understanding; yes, if you call out for insight and raise your voice for understanding, if you seek it like silver and search for it as for hidden treasures, then you will understand the fear of the LORD and find the knowledge of God. For the LORD gives wisdom; from his mouth come knowledge and understanding.

**Proverbs 3:14-17 NCV**   Wisdom is worth more than silver; it brings more profit than gold. Wisdom is more precious than rubies; nothing you could want is equal to it. With her right hand wisdom offers you a long life, and with her left hand she gives you riches and honor. Wisdom will make your life pleasant and will bring you peace.

**James 1:5 NASB**   If any of you lacks wisdom, let him ask of God, who gives to all generously and without reproach, and it will be given to him.

**James 3:17 GNT**   The wisdom from above is pure first of all; it is also peaceful, gentle, and friendly; it is full of compassion and produces a harvest of good deeds; it is free from prejudice and hypocrisy.

# WITCHCRAFT

**Deuteronomy 18:11–12 CEV** Don't try to use any kind of magic or witchcraft to tell fortunes or to cast spells or to talk with spirits of the dead. The LORD is disgusted with anyone who does these things.

**Galatians 5:19–21 CEV** People's desires make them give in to immoral ways, filthy thoughts, and shameful deeds. They worship idols, practice witchcraft, hate others, and are hard to get along with. People become jealous, angry, and selfish. They not only argue and cause trouble, but they are envious. They get drunk, carry on at wild parties, and do other evil things as well. I told you before, and I am telling you again: No one who does these things will share in the blessings of God's kingdom.

**Ephesians 6:11–12 NASB** Put on the full armor of God, so that you will be able to stand firm against the schemes of the devil. For our struggle is not against flesh and blood, but against the rulers, against the powers, against the world forces of this darkness, against the spiritual forces of wickedness in the heavenly places.

**Colossians 2:8 NASB** See to it that no one takes you captive through philosophy and empty deception, according to the tradition of men, according to the elementary principles of the world, rather than according to Christ.

**2 Thessalonians 2:9 NCV** The Man of Evil will come by the power of Satan. He will have great power, and he will do many different false miracles, signs, and wonders.

**James 4:7 WEB** Be subject therefore to God. But resist the devil, and he will flee from you.

**1 John 4:4 NKJV** You are of God, little children, and have overcome them, because He who is in you is greater than he who is in the world.

**Matthew 5:16 TNIV**   Let your light shine before others, that they may see your good deeds and glorify your Father in heaven.

**Mark 16:15-16 NKJV**   Go into all the world and preach the gospel to every creature. He who believes and is baptized will be saved; but he who does not believe will be condemned.

**2 Corinthians 6:4-8 CEV**   In everything and in every way we show that we truly are God's servants. We have always been patient, though we have had a lot of trouble, suffering, and hard times. We have been beaten, put in jail, and hurt in riots. We have worked hard and have gone without sleep or food. But we have kept ourselves pure and have been understanding, patient, and kind. The Holy Spirit has been with us, and our love has been real. We have spoken the truth, and God's power has worked in us. In all our struggles we have said and done only what is right. Whether we were honored or dishonored or praised or cursed, we always told the truth about ourselves.

**2 Timothy 1:8-9 WEB**   Don't be ashamed therefore of the testimony of our Lord, nor of me, his prisoner; but suffer hardship with the gospel according to the power of God, who saved us, and called us with a holy calling, not according to our works, but according to his own purpose and grace, which was given to us in Christ Jesus before times eternal.

**Hebrews 12:1-3 BBE**   For this reason, as we are circled by so great a cloud of witnesses, putting off every weight, and the sin into which we come so readily, let us keep on running in the way which is marked out for us, having our eyes fixed on Jesus, the guide and end of our faith, who went through the pains of the cross, not caring for the shame, because of the joy which was before him, and who has now taken his place at the right hand of God's seat of power. Give thought to him who has undergone so much of the hate of sinners against himself, so that you may not be tired and feeble of purpose.

**Deuteronomy 30:14 NKJV**   The word is very near you, in your mouth and in your heart, that you may do it.

**2 Samuel 22:31 NIV**   As for God, his way is perfect; the word of the LORD is flawless. He is a shield for all who take refuge in him.

**Psalm 19:8 TNIV**   The precepts of the LORD are right, giving joy to the heart. The commands of the LORD are radiant, giving light to the eyes.

**Psalm 107:19-21 NASB**   Then they cried out to the LORD in their trouble; He saved them out of their distresses. He sent His word and healed them, and delivered them from their destructions. Let them give thanks to the LORD for His lovingkindness, and for His wonders to the sons of men!

**Psalm 119:105 CEV**   Your word is a lamp that gives light wherever I walk.

**Psalm 119:127-131 NCV**   I love your commands more than the purest gold. I respect all your orders, so I hate lying ways. Your rules are wonderful. That is why I keep them. Learning your words gives wisdom and understanding for the foolish. I am nearly out of breath. I really want to learn your commands.

**Luke 21:33 NASB**   Heaven and earth will pass away, but My words will not pass away.

**John 1:1 NKJV**   In the beginning was the Word, and the Word was with God, and the Word was God.

**Hebrews 4:12 NASB**   For the word of God is living and active and sharper than any two-edged sword, and piercing as far as the division of soul and spirit, of both joints and marrow, and able to judge the thoughts and intentions of the heart.

**Exodus 4:10-12 NASB**   Then Moses said to the LORD, "Please, Lord, I have never been eloquent, neither recently nor in time past, nor since You have spoken to Your servant; for I am slow of speech and slow of tongue." The LORD said to him, "Who has made man's mouth? Or who makes him mute or deaf, or seeing or blind? Is it not I, the LORD? "Now then go, and I, even I, will be with your mouth, and teach you what you are to say."

**Proverbs 10:19 HCSB**   When there are many words, sin is unavoidable, but the one who controls his lips is wise.

**Proverbs 12:14 WEB**   A man shall be satisfied with good by the fruit of his mouth.

**Proverbs 16:24 NIV**   Pleasant words are a honeycomb, sweet to the soul and healing to the bones.

**Proverbs 18:4 BBE**   The words of a man's mouth are like deep waters: the fountain of wisdom is like a flowing stream.

**Ecclesiastes 9:17 GNT**   It is better to listen to the quiet words of someone wise than to the shouts of a ruler at a council of fools.

**Jeremiah 1:9 NKJV**   Then the LORD put forth His hand and touched my mouth, and the LORD said to me: "Behold, I have put My words in your mouth."

**Matthew 12:36 NIV**   But I tell you that men will have to give account on the day of judgment for every careless word they have spoken.

**2 Timothy 1:13 NKJV**   Hold fast the pattern of sound words which you have heard from me, in faith and love which are in Christ Jesus.

**Titus 3:10 MSG**   Warn a quarrelsome person once or twice, but then be done with him.

**2 Chronicles 15:7 NCV**   Don't give up, because you will get a reward for your good work.

**Psalm 112:5-7 NCV**   Those who are fair in their business will never be defeated. Good people will always be remembered. They won't be afraid of bad news; their hearts are steady because they trust the LORD.

**2 Corinthians 9:8 MSG**   God can pour on the blessings in astonishing ways so that you're ready for anything and everything, more than just ready to do what needs to be done.

**Colossians 3:23 NLT**   Work willingly at whatever you do, as though you were working for the Lord rather than for people.

**1 Thessalonians 4:11-12 CEV**   Try your best to live quietly, to mind your own business, and to work hard, just as we taught you to do. Then you will be respected by people who are not followers of the Lord, and you won't have to depend on anyone.

**1 Thessalonians 5:14 NCV**   Warn those who do not work. Encourage the people who are afraid. Help those who are weak. Be patient with everyone.

**2 Thessalonians 3:10-13 ESV**   If anyone is not willing to work, let him not eat. For we hear that some among you walk in idleness, not busy at work, but busybodies. Now such persons we command and encourage in the Lord Jesus Christ to do their work quietly and to earn their own living. As for you, brothers, do not grow weary in doing good.

**2 Timothy 2:21-22 NCV**   All who make themselves clean from evil will be used for special purposes. They will be made holy, useful to the Master, ready to do any good work. But run away from the evil desires of youth. Try hard to live right and to have faith, love, and peace, together with those who trust in the Lord from pure hearts.

**Proverbs 14:12-14 ESV**   There is a way that seems right to a man, but its end is the way to death. Even in laughter the heart may ache, and the end of joy may be grief. The backslider in heart will be filled with the fruit of his ways, and a good man will be filled with the fruit of his ways.

**Jeremiah 15:19 ESV**   Thus says the LORD: "If you return, I will restore you, and you shall stand before me. If you utter what is precious, and not what is worthless, you shall be as my mouth. They shall turn to you, but you shall not turn to them."

**Matthew 6:24 NCV**   You cannot serve both God and worldly riches.

**Mark 16:15 MSG**   Go into the world. Go everywhere and announce the Message of God's good news to one and all.

**Colossians 3:2-3 TNIV**   Set your minds on things above, not on earthly things. For you died, and your life is now hidden with Christ in God.

**Colossians 3:5-10 ESV**   Put to death therefore what is earthly in you: sexual immorality, impurity, passion, evil desire, and covetousness, which is idolatry. On account of these the wrath of God is coming. In these you too once walked, when you were living in them. But now you must put them all away: anger, wrath, malice, slander, and obscene talk from your mouth. Do not lie to one another, seeing that you have put off the old self with its practices and have put on the new self, which is being renewed in knowledge after the image of its creator.

**1 John 2:15 ESV**   Do not love the world or the things in the world. If anyone loves the world, the love of the Father is not in him.

**1 John 5:3-5 TNIV**   This is love for God: to keep his commands. And his commands are not burdensome, for everyone born of God overcomes the world. This is the victory that has overcome the world, even our faith. Who is it that overcomes the world? Only the one who believes that Jesus is the Son of God.

# WORRIED

**Proverbs 3:5-6 NKJV**  Trust in the LORD with all your heart, and lean not on your own understanding; in all your ways acknowledge Him, and He shall direct your paths.

**Psalm 42:11 HCSB**  Why am I so depressed? Why this turmoil within me? Put your hope in God, for I will still praise Him, my Savior and my God.

**Psalm 55:2-16 GNT**  Listen to me and answer me; I am worn out by my worries. I am terrified by the threats of my enemies, crushed by the oppression of the wicked. They bring trouble on me; they are angry with me and hate me. I am terrified, and the terrors of death crush me. I am gripped by fear and trembling; I am overcome with horror. . . . But I call to the Lord God for help, and he will save me.

**Psalm 55:22 GNT**  Leave your troubles with the Lord, and he will defend you; he never lets honest people be defeated.

**Matthew 6:33 NIV**  Seek first his kingdom and his righteousness, and all these things will be given to you as well.

**Luke 12:22-25 NLT**  Don't worry about everyday life—whether you have enough food to eat or clothes to wear. For life consists of far more than food and clothing. Look at the ravens. They don't need to plant or harvest or put food in barns because God feeds them. And you are far more valuable to him than any birds! Can all your worries add a single moment to your life? Of course not!

**1 Peter 5:7-9 NCV**  Give all your worries to him, because he cares about you. Control yourselves and be careful! The devil, your enemy, goes around like a roaring lion looking for someone to eat. Refuse to give in to him, by standing strong in your faith. You know that your Christian family all over the world is having the same kinds of suffering.

**Exodus 34:14 TNIV**  Do not worship any other god, for the Lord, whose name is Jealous, is a Jealous God.

**Psalm 95:6-7 ESV**  Oh come, let us worship and bow down; let us kneel before the Lord, our Maker! For he is our God, and we are the people of his pasture, and the sheep of his hand.

**Psalm 96:8-10 NIV**  Ascribe to the Lord the glory due his name; bring an offering and come into his courts. Worship the Lord in the splendor of his holiness; tremble before him, all the earth. Say among the nations, "The Lord reigns."

**Isaiah 51:15 NLT**  I am the Lord your God, who stirs up the sea, causing its waves to roar. My name is the Lord of Heaven's Armies.

**Matthew 2:11 NIV**  On coming to the house, they saw the child with his mother Mary, and they bowed down and worshiped him. Then they opened their treasures and presented him with gifts of gold and of incense and of myrrh.

**Matthew 4:10-11 TNIV**  Jesus said to him, "Away from me, Satan! For it is written: 'Worship the Lord your God, and serve him only.'" Then the devil left him, and angels came and attended him.

**John 4:23-24 NIV**  A time is coming and has now come when the true worshipers will worship the Father in spirit and truth, for they are the kind of worshipers the Father seeks. God is spirit, and his worshipers must worship in spirit and in truth.

**Romans 12:1 TNIV**  I urge you, brothers and sisters, in view of God's mercy, to offer your bodies as a living sacrifice, holy and pleasing to God—this is true worship.

**Revelation 14:7 NIV**  He said in a loud voice, "Fear God and give him glory, because the hour of his judgment has come. Worship him who made the heavens, the earth, the sea and the springs of water."

# WRONGDOING

**Job 11:13-15 NCV**  You must give your whole heart to him and hold out your hands to him for help. Put away the sin that is in your hand; let no evil remain in your tent. Then you can lift up your face without shame, and you can stand strong without fear.

**Psalm 51:10-12 NRSV**  Create in me a clean heart, O God, and put a new and right spirit within me. Do not cast me away from your presence, and do not take your holy spirit from me. Restore to me the joy of your salvation, and sustain in me a willing spirit.

**Ezekiel 18:30-31 NIV**  Repent! Turn away from all your offenses; then sin will not be your downfall. Rid yourselves of all the offenses you have committed, and get a new heart and a new spirit.

**Romans 12:17 NCV**  If someone does wrong to you, do not pay him back by doing wrong to him. Try to do what everyone thinks is right.

**2 Corinthians 5:10 TNIV**  For we must all appear before the judgment seat of Christ, that everyone may receive what is due them for the things done while in the body, whether good or bad.

**Galatians 5:19-21 NCV**  The wrong things the sinful self does are clear: being sexually unfaithful, not being pure, taking part in sexual sins, worshiping gods, doing witchcraft, hating, making trouble, being jealous, being angry, being selfish, making people angry with each other, causing divisions among people, feeling envy, being drunk, having wild and wasteful parties, and doing other things like these. I warn you now as I warned you before: Those who do these things will not inherit God's kingdom.

**Titus 1:15-16 GNT**  Everything is pure to those who are themselves pure; but nothing is pure to those who are defiled and unbelieving, for their minds and consciences have been defiled. They claim that they know God, but their actions deny it. They are hateful and disobedient, not fit to do anything good.

**Psalm 22:30-31 GNT**   Future generations will serve him; they will speak of the Lord to the coming generation. People not yet born will be told: "The Lord saved his people."

**Psalm 94:12 MSG**   How blessed the man you train, GOD, the woman you instruct in your Word.

**Psalm 112:5-7 NCV**   It is good to be merciful and generous. Those who are fair in their business will never be defeated. Good people will always be remembered. They won't be afraid of bad news; their hearts are steady because they trust the LORD.

**Ecclesiastes 11:9 MSG**   You who are young, make the most of your youth. Relish your youthful vigor. Follow the impulses of your heart. If something looks good to you, pursue it. But know also that not just anything goes; you have to answer to God for every last bit of it.

**Ecclesiastes 12:1 NKJV**   Remember now your Creator in the days of your youth, before the difficult days come.

**1 Corinthians 13:11 NCV**   When I was a child, I talked like a child, I thought like a child, I reasoned like a child. When I became a man, I stopped those childish ways.

**Galatians 6:4 WEB**   But let each man test his own work, and then he will take pride in himself and not in his neighbor.

**2 Timothy 2:22 NLT**   Run from anything that stimulates youthful lusts.

**1 Peter 4:1-3 NCV**   Since Christ suffered while he was in his body, strengthen yourselves with the same way of thinking Christ had. The person who has suffered in the body is finished with sin. Strengthen yourselves so that you will live here on earth doing what God wants, not the evil things people want. In the past you wasted too much time doing what nonbelievers enjoy.

# Bible Versions

# IN APPRECIATION:

To the team at Howard Books for your diligence
Rick Graham for counting every verse
Rachel, Kim, George, Katelynn, Janice, and Maureen
for topic ideas and your prayers
Michelle, Judy, Lynne, Jennifer, and Sandy
for your prayers and continual support
To all prayer warriors who continue to pray for
A Passion to Pray Ministries
And to our Lord Jesus who allows us
wonderful and unique ways to serve Him.
To Christ be the glory,
Merry and Tiffany


With special thanks to my editor, Philis Boultinghouse:
My mother's heart joins yours in praying and believing that this book
will influence teens to choose His ways, His Heart, His Life!
Always looking forward,
Merry

Let us hold firmly to the faith we profess.
Hebrews 4:14 TNIV

# *Another Great Scripture Resource*

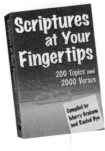

**Are you struggling with grief?**
**Searching for God's comforting mercy**
   **and grace?**
**Trying to learn how to raise your children**
   **in the Lord's way?**

Wouldn't you like to have the most significant verses from the Bible on those topics
right at your fingertips? ***Well, now you do!***

---